EVALUATION IN
ENVIRONMENTAL PI

MW00681051

EVALUATION IN ENVIRONMENTAL PLANNING
Assessing Environmental, Social, Economic, and Political Trade-offs

Donald M. McAllister

The MIT Press
Cambridge, Massachusetts, and London, England

Fourth printing, 1988
First MIT Press paperback edition, February 1982

Copyright © 1980 by
The Massachusetts Institute of Technology

All rights reserved. No part of this book may be reproduced in any form
or by any means, electronic or mechanical, including photocopying, recording, or by any information storage and retrieval system, without permission in writing from the publisher.

This book was set in IBM Composer Press Roman by To the Lighthouse
Press, printed and bound by Halliday Lithograph Corporation, in the United
States of America.

Library of Congress Cataloging in Publication Data

McAllister, Donald M
    Evaluation in environmental planning.
    Bibliography: p.
    Includes index.
    1. Environmental policy—Evaluation. I. Title.
HC79.E5M315   301.31'07'23   79–20006
ISBN 0-262-13146-3 (hard)
ISBN 0-262-63087-7 (paper)

Truth is our element of life, yet if a man fasten his attention on a single aspect of truth and apply himself to that alone for a long time, the truth becomes distorted and not itself but falsehood. . . .

Is it any better if the student, to avoid this offence and to liberalize himself, aims to make a mechanical whole of history, or science, or philosophy, by a numerical addition of all the facts that fall within his vision? The world refuses to be analyzed by addition and subtraction.

Ralph Waldo Emerson
"Intellect," *First Essays*

PREFACE

After teaching a graduate course on evaluation in environmental planning for several years at UCLA's School of Architecture and Urban Planning, I felt that a book on the subject might be useful. Evaluation is a central function of planning and a variety of methodologies have been developed over the years that seem to vie for the planner's attention. However, no single method is generally superior; each has its limits. Yet among the books, monographs, and articles on the topic, widely scattered across the disciplines, each tends to describe and advocate a single method. By collecting together in one volume information on a variety of methods, their strengths and weaknesses can be better understood. Furthermore, common weaknesses can be spotted that help identify directions for improvement.

The common strength of existing methodologies is at the same time the source of a major weakness. The evaluation of plans should be systematic and scientifically sound. Toward this goal the methods deserve substantial commendation for advancing the field in both thought and practice. But in focusing attention on technical rigor, the methods have placed evaluation on too narrow a base, ignoring important broader considerations.

Part I of this book attempts a beginning, at least, to redress the problem of narrowness by including chapters on human values, democratic philosophy, and environmental values. The discussions of these subjects, going well beyond the immediate bounds of evaluation, focus attention on those aspects I feel are most relevant to our topic. Some readers will be well versed in these subjects and therefore may prefer simply to skim the chapters or read the concluding sections. The selective nature of these chapters and the implications that are derived for the conduct of evaluations are necessarily personal. Other people surveying the same subjects might emphasize other aspects and reach different conclusions. To readers new to the field of evaluation, the relevance of these chapters may not be fully apparent on first reading, but review should substantiate their usefulness.

The intended audience for this book is broad, including citizens actively engaged in planning issues as well as the academic and professional communities. I have made a special effort to minimize the use of technical jargon so that readers do not have to be mathematicians and economists to understand the material.

Following the tradition in the evaluation literature, a fundamental premise here is that public planning is not simply an instrument of preferential politics for serving only the interests of the select group in power. It assumes that the planning function seeks to give due consideration to all interests in designing and evaluating plans. Of course neither view is an adequate description of reality. Most planning contains some mixture of the two. To the degree that a particular planning effort seeks to be representative and systematic, the underlying philosophy and approaches presented here should be applicable.

Although there are many similarities and overlaps in the approaches to evaluation among different planning fields, this book does not attempt a general overview. It focuses attention on before-the-fact (or "ex-ante") evaluations of plans. Therefore many of the issues it examines are quite different from those addressed in the growing literature on evaluative research, which is primarily concerned with after-the-fact (or "ex-post") evaluations of social action programs. Moreover, it is directed at plans that have important environmental implications, in which evaluations must deal with the thorny problems of trading off environmental factors against economic and other considerations. Some of the issues in preparing environmental impact statements and similar documents are not addressed here, because they are receiving due attention elsewhere.

No new evaluation method is proposed in this volume, nor are detailed directions offered on "how to do it" in practice. Instead, the conclusions might be seen as containing suggested guidelines for conducting evaluations. This approach springs from the view that plan assessment is more an art than a science, an art requiring planners to design each evaluation process to fit the characteristics and requirements of the particular situation. Accordingly, excellent evaluations will result from the exercise of sound personal judgment more than from following a rigid set of standardized procedures. Planners should have a solid understanding of the strengths and weaknesses of various evaluation methods, and use them as a mechanic uses his tool kit, selecting that set of techniques most suitable to the problem at hand.

In developing my thinking on the topic and preparing this manuscript, I owe many thanks. First I wish to extend my thanks to the students who have taken my evaluation course for the many provocative ideas that have come out of our discussions.

Lawrence Susskind at MIT and Dennis Ducsik at Clark University made penetrating critiques of the manuscript as reviewers for MIT Press, which helped me greatly in making improvements.

For their valuable comments on various drafts, I owe a special debt to my colleagues in the Urban Planning Program at UCLA, including W. David Conn, John Friedmann, J. Eugene Grigsby, Peter Marris, Harvey Perloff, and Donald Shoup. To Martin Wachs I owe a heavy debt for his invaluable comments on the first draft.

Ets Otomo typed the many drafts of this manuscript in her usual proficient and pleasant manner for which I am very grateful.

Finally, I want to thank Martin Wachs and Harvey Perloff for enabling me to reorganize my teaching responsibilities the past two years so that I could have large blocks of uninterrupted writing time.

Of course the help of these people should not be interpreted as a general agreement with the ideas presented in this book. Important differences of opinion were expressed, but naturally the choice of positions taken here was mine and I am solely responsible for whatever shortcomings remain.

I
INTRODUCTION AND BACKGROUND CONSIDERATIONS

1
INTRODUCTION

Local governments each week make thousands of decisions affecting the quality of the natural environment and the use of rapidly depleting natural resources. Should a wildlife habitat be developed as a residential neighborhood? Should a rapid transit system be built at great expense in order to improve a congested city's transportation services and cut auto-related air pollution and energy consumption? Should a polluting manufacturer be permitted to locate in an area plagued with chronic unemployment? Should a community adopt a slow-growth policy to protect its rural character and public finance position, while restricting the freedom of people who would like to move to the area? Decisions on such issues are significant to local residents, and all local decisions, taken together, have major implications for our future living environment.

State governments and the federal government, too, make many decisions having far-reaching environmental implications. Should severe safety controls be adopted for establishing and operating nuclear power plants, controls so strict that all plans for new plants could be sidelined? Should a new land-use control be adopted that protects all prime agricultural land from being converted to urban uses? Should a statewide plan be adopted that regulates development in the coastal zone at substantial expense and reduction in private property rights in order to protect and preserve the unique environmental resources of the coast for the enjoyment of all people? Should a wild river be dammed to provide additional water and electricity to a growing metropolitan population hundreds of miles away? Clearly the wisdom of our decisions on these and similar issues will profoundly affect our future welfare.

The wisdom of our decisions will be determined by the care and methods we use to evaluate our alternatives. Evaluation—obtaining, organizing and weighing information on the consequences, or impacts, of alternatives—is the subject of this book. More specifically the focus is on concepts and systematic methods for evaluating public actions having important consequences for our natural environment: air, water, land, and life. The interest in these actions is not limited, however, to their environmental impacts; the full spectrum of environmental, social, economic, and political consequences must be considered in reaching wise decisions.

All types of public actions having environmental repercussions are relevant to the discussion. Projects entailing major construction are perhaps the most common source of environmental impacts and are the most frequent subject of systematic evaluation methods. But many programs and policies have major implications for the quality of the environment and the use of rapidly dwindling natural resources. All should be subjected to systematic scrutiny.

1.1 EVALUATION IN PRACTICE

Evaluations of public actions today range the spectrum from nonexistent or haphazard to systematic and technically competent. A disappointingly small proportion of the decisions by local governments is made on the basis of systematic evaluations of the alternatives. Evaluations are often ad hoc, quick, and impressionistic. A sense of urgency tends to prevail over a sense of caution, usually fostered by a growing backlog of issues that decision-makers must address. The situation at the state level, in general, is only slightly better.

A much greater proportion of decisions at the federal level, having important environmental consequences, is preceded by systematic evaluations. This is due in large part to the adoption of certain legislative requirements. For example, the Flood Control Act of 1936 required that an evaluation be made of the benefits and costs of each proposed water project, eventually leading to the development and standardized use of cost-benefit analysis. The National Environmental Policy Act of 1969 required that environmental impact statements be prepared for all federal actions expected to significantly affect the environment. Although the impact statement is not a formal evaluation like cost-benefit analysis, it is a useful source of evaluative information.

In general, there has been a strong trend in the United States, beginning in the 1950s, toward a more thorough assessment of public actions. In recent decades several evaluation methodologies have been developed, cost-benefit analysis being the most notable, that help clarify and summarize for decision-makers the complex considerations of proposed actions. Some of these methods have become elaborate technical procedures that themselves are difficult to understand for all but the trained analyst.

The technical style of evaluation that is prevalent in many fields today contrasts sharply with the various styles of discussion and debate that predominated in earlier decades. The wisdom contained in the U.S. Constitution continues to amaze us, yet the many complex and interrelated decisions that were made during the Constitutional Convention were made without the aid of modern analytical tools. The men who framed this political masterpiece were well read in philosophy, extremely knowledgeable in the history of political systems, and rich with first-hand experience in governing people during the colonial and confederate periods. With this background they debated each issue and decided by majority rule. The style of this period can be characterized as utilizing broad, integrated, shared knowledge, implemented by the process of discussion, debate, and compromise. By contrast the technical style that many advocate today can be characterized as utilizing deep, fractionated, unshared knowledge, implemented by written reports.

Clearly many of the problems faced today are quite different from those experienced in past decades and centuries. Many of our problems are more complex, requiring careful analysis by trained technical experts. Increasing specialization and the "knowledge explosion" seem to have put the average decision-maker and the average adult out of touch with the evolving body of scientific knowledge. These factors, and others, have contributed to the changing style of evaluation. Whether they have necessitated the change, however, is a different matter. There is no question that systematic evaluations are desirable, but there is evidence of growing discontent over the highly technical approach taken by most of the currently used methods.

1.2 THE ROLE OF EVALUATION IN PLANNING

Evaluation pervades the planning process, which in a highly simplified form can be characterized as encompassing the following five steps: (1) identify the problem to be addressed, (2) design alternative solutions to the problem, (3) evaluate the alternatives, (4) decide on the action to be taken through the appropriate political process and implement it, and (5) monitor the results.

Although evaluation is the explicit function of step 3, it also plays an important role in three other steps. Identifying the problem to be addressed (step 1) involves important value judgments, because it determines the particular interests that will be served by planning. The number of societal problems is huge by comparison to the limited number that available resources permit us to act upon. By some screening procedure we must scan the list of possibilities and select the few that are most important and amenable to solution. Although a formal evaluation is seldom conducted in this step, evaluation clearly is involved.

Designing alternatives (step 2) also involves major value-laden decisions:

deciding to explore some alternative solutions and not others, deciding to develop only one plan or several alternatives, selecting certain design elements in preference to others, pursuing large-scale solutions versus small-scale versions. Sometimes the most important planning decisions are made in this step. Evaluation also plays an important role in monitoring the results (step 5). In this step measurements and judgments must be made regarding the degree of success of an action and the occurrence of unwanted side effects, so that corrective feedback can be supplied when necessary to improve results.

The main focus of this book is assessments in steps 2 and 3, which I will refer to as "in-design" and "post-design" evaluation. However, the general principles and many of the tools discussed here also have applications in the other steps.

1.3 THE TWO PHASES OF EVALUATION: ANALYSIS AND SYNTHESIS

Evaluating a proposed action can be divided into two phases: analysis, in which the whole is divided into parts, and synthesis, in which the parts are formed into a whole. These are portrayed graphically in figure 1.1. In more specific terms the analysis phase defines and estimates the various impacts of the action. This is necessary in order to gain a detailed understanding of the many consequences of an action, but at the same time it poses a dilemma of achieving coherence from the many diverse parts. The synthesis phase attempts to solve this dilemma by bringing together the impacts into an integrated view so that a judgment can be formed on whether the action should or should not be supported.

Analysis tends to be objective, whereas synthesis is subjective. Estimating impacts is objective, because the correctness of the results, in principle, can be verified and agreed upon by all rational people.[1] Forming an integrated view is subjective, because in the process one must assess the relative importance of the impacts to the whole. The preference, which follows, of accepting or rejecting the action is a value judgment; its correctness cannot be verified. People will reach different conclusions from the same set of facts about impacts because their values differ.

Impacts can be quite diverse. A general classification of impacts is according to environmental, social, economic, or political characteristics. Examples of environmental impacts are air pollution, water pollution, wildlife,

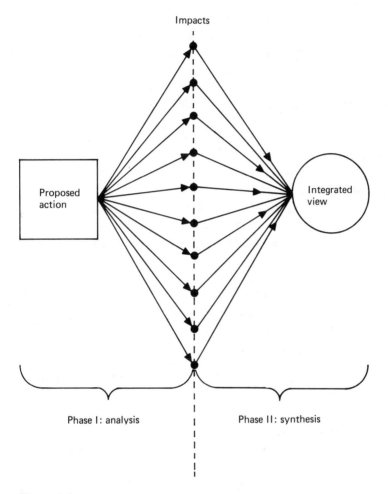

Figure 1.1
The two phases of evaluation

noise, soil erosion, landscape aesthetics, outdoor recreation resources, and the like. Social impacts include health, education, unemployment, disability, crime, discrimination, community cohesion, and many others. Economic impacts are those that can be measured directly in monetary units, such as income, taxes, property values, and the prices of goods and services. Political impacts include public access to decision-makers, the concentration of power, opportunities for citizen participation and inequalities in election and selection processes.

To accurately estimate impacts often requires the skills of technical experts in many different fields familiar with the systems in which the impacts occur and through which they are transmitted. Chemists, meteorologists, geologists, ecologists, and landscape designers are needed to estimate environmental impacts; psychologists, sociologists, anthropologists, and medical scientists, for social impacts; economists, engineers, and accountants, for economic impacts; and political scientists and public administrators, for political impacts. Thus the kinds of knowledge that are necessary for estimating impacts are diverse and quite technical. It is not the purpose of this book to discuss the technical aspects of impact estimation; no single book could contain the knowledge necessary for this task. However, the issues of scientific versus judgmental estimation and expert versus citizen roles are addressed.

The synthesis of impacts to form an opinion can be accomplished in either of two ways: informally, by personal review of the impacts, taking as much time as required for them to create a distinct impression in the mind; or formally, by applying a rating procedure that calculates a composite score of impacts. The informal approach can be characterized as judgmental and holistic; the formal as mathematical and additive.

The informal approach can be time consuming and frustrating. The impacts of alternatives are numerous and diverse, some are desirable and others undesirable; some can affect an individual directly while others only indirectly (by affecting other people in society); some occur immediately and others in the distant future; some can be predicted with certainty, but others are uncertain. All of these factors should be weighed in reaching a conclusion. Rarely is one alternative clearly superior. Each well-designed alternative typically has disadvantages as well as advantages.

Decision-makers, such as elected representatives and appointed officials, face the special difficulty of not knowing for sure which action is in the public interest. Although they can apply their own values in arriving at a personal opinion, they are usually expected to take positions in terms of the people's values, which are never fully known to them because of limited time and resources.

Most evaluation methodologies attempt to overcome these difficulties by taking the formal approach. Utilizing some form of rating system, they calculate a grand index or score, supposedly indicating how the welfare of society (or the quality of life) would be affected by an action. In effect, they convert all impacts into commensurate units so they can be added and compared. To illustrate how one works, take the simple case in which a single proposal is to be evaluated for acceptance or rejection. The various impacts of the action are estimated, then each is assigned a rating; the more important the impact, the higher the rating. If the sum of the ratings for desirable impacts exceeds that for undesirable impacts, this indicates that the action would improve the social welfare and should be supported; otherwise not.[3]

Some evaluation methodologies have established complex technical procedures for quantifying social welfare ratings that make the results appear very scientific and objective, but they are not. It makes no difference how sophisticated are the procedures for deriving them, ratings by definition constitute value judgments. Different methods are used for calculating ratings and for determining the types of impacts to which they apply. Each has its weaknesses. And because there are differences in approaches, each method can lead to a different conclusion regarding the "best" action.

Cost-benefit analysis was the first evaluation method used extensively that included a systematic rating procedure. It was originally developed to evaluate federal water projects, and in the past twenty years it has been used widely to evaluate all types of public actions. Its rating procedure, although complex, follows the simple principle of placing a monetary value on each impact. The monetary ratings then can be totaled to determine whether the benefits (which are the ratings for desirable impacts) exceed the costs (the ratings for undesirable impacts).

Recognition that cost-benefit analysis has a number of weaknesses has led recently to the development of several other evaluation methods. Typically, the new methods seek to overcome these weaknesses by reference to technical tools and procedures, particularly mathematics and statistics. But these attempts miss a crucial point: that designing or selecting an evaluation method, itself, requires an evaluation, necessitating the use of values to reach conclusions. The appropriate values cannot be found in the scientific realm of technical tools; they must be drawn from other, broader sources.

1.4 EVALUATION ISSUES

The questions in the following paragraphs identify some of the key issues addressed in this book.

How should the impact categories be selected? The number of potential impacts of an action is often more than can be addressed in an evaluation. The choice determines which impacts will be included in the analysis and which will be excluded.

Does the scientific organization of knowledge, from which the technical experts draw in estimating impacts, serve as an adequate guide for defining and describing impacts?

How should intangible impacts—those not capable of quantification—be described along with quantified impacts in evaluation reports. Sometimes more attention is given to numerical than to nonnumerical information in decision making. Is there a way to overcome this bias?

Are economic values sufficient, as some claim they are, for weighing the advantages and disadvantages of a contemplated public action, or are they inadequate as proclaimed by others? If economic values are not adequate, are other approaches for quantifying values suitable to planning and decision-making processes?

How should the incidence of impacts (or equity) be treated in evaluations? Impacts are rarely distributed uniformly among the populous. Typically, some people are affected favorably while others unfavorably. Can the distributional effects be ignored as many economists have suggested?

How should time be treated in evaluations? Impacts occur in different time periods; some are felt immediately, whereas others don't appear until the distant future. Is the economic approach of discounting future impacts to their "present value" adequate, or is some other approach preferable?

Can land-use plans be prepared solely on the basis of scientific information, drawn from ecology and the other environmental sciences?

What role should technical experts play in the evaluation process? What role should citizens and decision-makers play?

Who should synthesize the impacts? If some of the impacts are defined in technical ways that only certain experts can understand, does this mean that the expert must be relied upon to do the synthesizing? Or is there some way to translate technical impacts into terms that make sense to decision-makers and the average citizen?

Are the mathematical formulas proffered by various methodologies for calculating the social welfare acceptable evaluation tools?

How can technically oriented evaluation procedures be reconciled with demands for greater governmental sensitivity to citizens' wishes and with requirements for citizen participation in planning?

A common theme running through my answers to these questions is that while technically oriented evaluation methods have contributed a great deal to advancing the interest of systematically assessing public actions, they have gone well beyond the objective capability of science to improve the wisdom of public decisions. Needed is a new view, quite different than the views advanced by these methods, of the role of technical procedures and technical experts, emphasizing the importance of impact estimation, disclaiming any capability to calculate a grand index of social welfare, and leaving the subjective realm of human values and impact synthesis to organized processes of personal review, citizen participation, discussion, and debate.

2
HUMAN VALUES

2.1 INTRODUCTION

A person might gather through study and personal experience all the available facts about the world around him, but without values he would be able to make only the simplest decisions. Tolstoy in his religious autobiography recounts the major personal crisis in his life: after questioning for many years his purposes in life, he finally rejected them. He began searching for answers to such fundamental questions as, what is my life for? Why should I write? So what if I am a famous author? Why should I educate my children?

The questions were not waiting, and I had to answer them at once; if I did not answer them, I could not live.
I felt that what I was standing on had given way, that I had no foundation to stand on, that that which I lived by no longer existed, and that I had nothing to live by.
My life came to a standstill.[1]

Considering the central role of values in governing human action, it is surprising that the educational process does not devote more attention to them. What are human values? Where do they come from? What functions do they serve? How are they related to facts and beliefs? How are they formed, and under what conditions are they changed? Although there are a diversity of opinions and no definitive answers to these and similar questions, the literature offers many valuable insights. This chapter reviews some of the fundamental concepts on human values and derives some implications for conducting evaluations of public actions. Naturally, a brief account of such a large and complex subject cannot give anything more than a sampling of the literature.

People think and act on the basis of their view of the world, which is determined by their values as well as by their knowledge of facts and their beliefs. In addition to the fundamental notion of purpose in life, human values broadly conceived include preferences, prizing, interests, desires, likes and dislikes, loves and hates, goals, responsibilities, moral obligations, rights and wrongs, goods and bads, and many others. Psychologists and political scientists study attitudes, economists analyze preferences, sociologists investigate norms and sanctions, anthropologists observe folkways and mores, and philosophers construct theories of value, attempting to embrace all (or many) of these concepts, which in the broad sense are values.

Human values serve as guides for personal decision making, attaching significance and importance to objects and events, directing choices toward things considered desirable or good and away from things considered undesirable or bad. Seldom is only a single value involved in a decision; most require selecting and weighing several values simultaneously. Although impulses for compatibility and harmony affect the development of value systems, conflicts among values are virtually inevitable in any personal decision involving limited time, energy, or resources; even the most harmonious values can come into competition with each other when time or resources are allocated.

Values not only help guide personal actions they also play a key role in directing the thought process. Indeed, this could be considered the more important function, since most actions spring from thoughts. The mind is directed at the things of greatest interest. Categories of thought are formed to serve them, and new information is tested against them and categorized accordingly. The learning process is directed at understanding them: their special qualities, their variety of forms, where they come from, what they are affected by, the implications they have for other things. Personal perceptions of the world are filtered by one's interests. People can't possibly grasp everything that the eyes and ears are mechanically capable of detecting. Values serve to select out those items which will receive attention and to screen out the rest.

In describing a scene, reporting a trip, or studying history, a selection process is at work, consciously or subconsciously. As I am writing this chapter I am forced to select from the large literature the few thoughts that can be compressed into these pages. My purpose is to report those aspects I believe are most useful to the subject of plan evaluation. But other values of which I am not conscious are also likely to be affecting my choices.

Among the many values individuals hold, one of the main distinctions is between personal and social values. Although there is no clear dividing line, personal values are those that serve principally the individual, whereas social values serve primarily society at large. Personal values tend to govern decisions in which other people are not seriously affected, such as in choosing food, clothing, friends, education, and leisure activities. Social values come into the picture when an action is believed to seriously affect the welfare of others. Obligations and responsibilities, rights and wrongs, shoulds and shouldn'ts are taught and enforced in a variety of ways to guide individual behavior away from social conflict and towards social harmony. The tension between personal and social values, of course, gives rise to many of our social, economic, political, and public policy issues. The conflicts between the interests of the individual and the interests of society are constantly challenging us and, no doubt, always will.

2.2 FACTS VS. VALUES: MEANS VS. ENDS

Some authors have claimed that values are entirely independent of facts, whereas, at the other extreme, the position has been taken that values are governed by facts and therefore are susceptible to scientific explanation. The old sayings, "beauty is in the eye of the beholder," and "one man's meat is another man's poison," suggest that values are subjective—formed within each person and not capable of verification by others. Preferences based upon the sense responses of sight, sound, and smell seem purely subjective. Even beyond the senses, on an issue as fundamental as the life of a human being, we find widespread disagreement in the context of capital punishment.

Yet despite the subjective component of values it would not be impertinent, in reaction to a statement that something is good, to ask: "good for what?" Sensual criteria, which seem beyond objective verification, are only a few among the many upon which values are grounded. Food is selected partly for its taste, but, depending upon the person, other factors are also applied, such as health, controlling body weight, preparation time, cost, protecting animals from slaughter, and energy conservation. Thus something as basic to human life as food is not considered strictly as an end in itself but also a means to other ends. Values that attach to means, called "instrumental values," are susceptible to scientific inquiry. In principle at least, systematic analysis can be used to determine the cause-effect linkages between the means and the ends they are thought to promote. The more effective is a means for promoting a desired end, the higher should be its instrumental value. It can be concluded then that values are not independent of facts and, more specifically, that facts can play a key role in shaping the validity of instrumental values.

The information available for establishing cause-effect linkages is not uniform in type or quality; science, personal knowledge, and beliefs all have a part to play. The power of science is strongest in describing physical and chemical relationships, but comparatively weak in predicting human behavior. Much of our knowledge about the effects of actions on people is gained through personal experience, and even though it is not systematically obtained and analyzed, in many situations it is more useful than what science has to offer.[2] In cases where both scientific knowledge and personal knowledge are weak, we are forced to rely on beliefs.

The rational view sees instrumental values as being determined by the most accurate knowledge on the linkages between means and ends, and by the subjective strength of the values attaching to ends, called "terminal values." In practice, of course, people are seldom aware of the best information and use what is most readily available. Perhaps more important is that, once formed, instrumental values tend to be perpetuated by the forces of custom and habit.

The subjective nature of instrumental values can be reduced by the application of facts, but it cannot be eliminated because terminal values are also a determining factor. This is seen most clearly when alternative means are compared on the basis of multiple ends. Seldom is one means the most effective in promoting all of the ends. Different means are usually favored by different ends, and the relative importance or significance of the ends must be weighed in reaching a decision. For example, if taste, weight control, and cost were the governing criteria for an individual in forming his food preferences, he would have to judge the relative importance of these (as well as the effect of the food items on them) in making his selections.

The dichotomy between means and ends is useful for addressing the issue of facts versus values, but it is a gross simplification. The links between means and ends do not form a simple set of lines, but a complex web of interrelations in which means affect other means, means affect many ends, ends affect means, and ends affect other ends. Sometimes an end is the consequence of a special combination of means, and the effect cannot be apportioned among the causes. Perhaps the most serious complication is the fact that some objects and events are, simultaneously, means *and* ends. A prime example of this is work, which for many people is the central purpose in life, as well as being the means to financial security, material comfort, and so forth.

Another oversimplification is the view that there is only one class of ends. "Ultimate ends" should be distinguished from "visible ends." The ultimate ends of human action are our ideals. We might be conscious of them, but they seldom serve as direct guides because they are too far beyond the reach of any actions we might plan for the present. Long term and worldwide peace, truth, beauty, happiness, and harmony are examples. The goals of contemplated actions are more limited. They are visible, reachable, and more predictable. They serve as better guides for judging how well we are doing on a near term basis. They are not fixed, only tentative, and are changed as new conditions warrant. Ultimate ends are like the final destination of a ship on a lengthy voyage. The visible ends are bounded by them but must be determined by more immediate considerations: sailing around bodies of land, stopping at ports for provisions, steering to compensate for winds and currents, skirting storms or maneuvering through them, occasionally having to deal with emergencies that push the ultimate destination completely out of the mind. Considered in sequence, the visible ends that govern behavior in one period become the means for reaching the ends in the next.

The terminology, here, can be applied to the task of evaluating public actions. In evaluation, a variety of alternative means for solving a problem (or a set of problems) are assessed. Each means is a plan of action that has numerous components; each, through various cause-effect linkages, can have many consequences, not only for the intended ends but for unintended means and ends as well. The plans are compared on the basis of the types and magnitudes of impacts they are expected to have on visible ends, and the terminal values attached to them. Examples of visible ends include human life, health, job opportunities, income (as an indicator of financial security and material comfort), equity, self-respect, sense of accomplishment, recreation opportunities, landscape aesthetics, and sense of community.

2.3 ON THE SOURCE OF HUMAN VALUES

What is the root source of values? Instrumental values are formed out of an interest in serving terminal values, but where do terminal values come from?

It is generally agreed that these values arise from the interaction of man and his environment, but there are many different theories. One school of thought emphasizes the nature of man; another emphasizes the character of the social environment.

Many believe that the biological and psychological nature of man results in impulses that generate motivating behavior toward certain ends. Man seems to share with other forms of life the impulse to survive. Growing out of this, perhaps, is an impulse to outlive one's life in some way. Impulses for enjoyment, for development of one's human potentials, and for harmony are also possibilities. The same general idea is also expressed in terms of basic needs that man seeks to meet. Several different lists of human needs have been proposed. One that is frequently cited today is the "hierarchy of needs" advanced by Abraham Maslow.[3]

Maslow identified five categories of needs that, according to his studies, operate in all people and cultures. They are (1) physiological, (2) safety, (3) belongingness, (4) esteem, and (5) self-actualization. Physiological needs cover the most basic life-supporting elements, such as homeostasis, warmth, food, and water. Safety needs are concerned with protection from extreme occurrences such as war, disease, natural catastrophe, and crime. Belongingness includes the need for love and affection. Esteem has two parts: self-esteem and esteem from others. The highest order need, self-actualization, is the need to be self-fulfilled and altruistic.

The theory proposes that the five needs are organized in a hierarchy, from physiological at the bottom to self-actualization at the top. The hierarchical principle suggests that a certain category of need will not play an important role in personal behavior until all the needs below it are satisfied. So, for example, if safety needs are not met, the need for love will not be a strong motivating factor.

Another school of thought on the source of values emphasizes the role of the social and natural environment. Man's environment gives rise to certain opportunities, threats, and challenges to which he responds. Values are formed and reformed through trial and error; the value-seeking behavior in one period generates results, some intended and others not, which extend reflective thought and produce refinements in values in the next period. The actions proceeding from values sometimes result in new unsought opportunities for reaching new destinations, and the challenges, mistakes, and adaptations proceed onward in a continuous stream. This school of thought emphasizes the role of reflective thought in shaping values, creating "desirable" ends rather than impulsive "desires." Also, it suggests that ends have value only insofar as there are means to reach them. Finally, it emphasizes that the values governing behavior are not focused on ideals but on "ends-in-view," which are constantly being modified in the changing field of action.[4]

The social environment is also seen to be the stage on which social values are formed and evolve. As individuals interact in a social context, the conflicts and outright threats generated by the clash of personal values, and the opportunities that are seen from the possibilities for cooperative behavior lead to new values, new actions and new conditions that modify each other over time. Since man can only be human when raised in a social setting, as evidenced by the cases of feral children and other isolates, it can be argued that social values produced in this interactive environment are as fundamental as personal values.

There is a certain complementarity between the two schools of thought contrasted here, because they are directed at somewhat different levels of detail. The first emphasizes understanding broad categories of values, within which wide ranges of specific values can be encompassed. The second school attempts to develop a more detailed understanding of how the specific values governing behavior are established.

2.4 VALUE FORMATION

The formation of personal and social values in the individual derives from a complex of sources and forces. The views of parents, friends, teachers, religious figures, scientists, and political leaders are prominent; ideas presented on television, in movies, in newspapers and magazines, and in books are also influential, and the conflicting attitudes between these sources must be faced. Pressures for consistency oppose those for growth. Pressures for conformity work against those for nonconformity. The impulse for spontaneity is countered by the call for reflective thought. And the relative painlessness of value formation, when one is surrounded by uniformity in attitudes, comes at the loss of freedom and individuality supported by variety.

Amidst the diversity of opposing factors, research indicates that the external pressure for conformity is matched by an internal force for harmony. The quest for harmony is revealed by the theories of balance, congruity, and cognitive dissonance, and the empirical evidence that supports them.[5]

The theory of balance says that people tend to seek balance in their attitudes toward people and objects.[6] For example, if a close friend shares with one an intense like for some object, a state of balance is said to exist. On the other hand, if the friend voices a dislike for an object that one likes, "unbalance" is said to exist, and there will be a tendency for the person to adjust his attitude, either toward the friend, the object, or both, to achieve a state of balance. Unbalance would also exist if a disliked person voices a like for an object that one also likes.

The principle of "congruity" treats in a similar manner the consistency of attitudes toward people and value positions.[7] To illustrate, if a highly respected person asserts a view on a political issue that one shares, "congruity" is said to exist. But if the respected person voices a contrary political view, then incongruity exists, and there will be a tendency for the person receiving the statement to modify or perhaps change his attitudes. For example, he could decide that the one issuing the statement no longer deserves his respect; alternatively he could change his view about the political issue; or he might modify his view about both, reducing the degree of incongruity. The principle also predicts that people are more receptive to statements by highly respected people than by others. It is interesting to note, though, that attitude changes toward value positions resulting from statements by liked or respected people tend to dissipate over time, apparently because, as time passes, one tends to disassociate the value statement and the person.

A large amount of evidence exists to support the theory of cognitive dissonance which suggests that dissonance will exist if compensation does not match the deed.[8] A great deal of research on the theory deals with liked or disliked objects or actions that are tied to a penalty or a reward. Consonance is said to exist if, for example, one receives a large reward for engaging in a very distasteful act. On the other hand, if one receives a small reward for a very distasteful act, then dissonance is said to exist, which the person will attempt to reduce. If the reward can't be adjusted, the person will tend to change his attitude toward the act. For example, children paid a small sum to eat a disliked vegetable tend, afterward, to improve their attitude toward the vegetable. Adults paid to make a public presentation voicing views they personally disagree with tend to adjust their opinions toward favoring the publicly stated view.

Dissonance also results from decisions in which the rejected as well as the selected alternative has both advantages and disadvantages, a characteristic very common to public decision situations. There is a tendency for people to adjust their attitudes following such a decision—increasing their preference for the chosen alternative and decreasing their preference for the rejected one. People will even seek out information that supports these adjustments. A related finding is the tendency for irrevocable decisions to cause less dissonance than revocable ones. Apparently people are more likely to convince themselves of the wisdom of a decision that cannot be changed than one that can.

The theories of balance, congruity, and cognitive dissonance all suggest that people make both internal and external adjustments to avoid major discordance in values. People make internal adjustments by altering their likes, attitudes, and beliefs. Externally, they select friends and adjust friendships. They select the information to which they are exposed, tending to avoid information that conflicts with their values and choosing information that supports them. Sometimes in avoiding discordance people act irrationally, as when the smoker dismisses the evidence linking cancer with cigarettes. The selections of educational programs, occupations, group memberships, communities, and neighborhoods are also guided by the desires for harmony and the avoidance of discordance. Thus in many ways people protect themselves from situations that could raise doubts about their acquired values, particularly those that are central to their value system because changes in these would cause the greatest degree of discordance.

The tendency to protect acquired values can also be explained by Peter Marris's concept of the conservation impulse.[9] Accordingly, people are deeply conservative and feel threatened when their view of the world, including basic assumptions and purposes, is challenged. To give any credence to conflicting views disorients people, for it calls into question their guides for personal decision making. Consequently, potentially disruptive views are avoided and ignored.

The impulses for harmony and conservatism represent forces for uniformity and stability that are apparent in most cultures. The adoption of religions, moral philosophies, laws, and social pressures extended them while seeking social harmony and attempting to protect society from internal threats to its survival.

Perhaps the most stable cultures have been found among isolated "primitive" societies situated in equable environments. These appeal to our utopian instinct, but their disadvantages, too, must be counted. Like biological organisms, cultures that become too rigid and specialized are vulnerable to changes in external conditions. Societies that did not have the flexibility to deal with emergent threats from other societies or from the natural environment did not survive. Old customs that were contradicted by new knowledge or changing conditions were either discarded or buried. The most common threat, of course, was from competing cultures, but more than one civilization is believed to have fallen because it misused its natural environment.[10] The tolerance for nonconformity is thought to be an essential element to cultural adaptability; new ideas are at first held by only a few before they become accepted by the majority. Toynbee concluded that past civilizations challenged by their social and natural environment were more successful than those that were not, because they became accustomed to facing adversity.[11]

Today the desire for change is an integral value in many societies, and strangely there is a certain conservative impulse to protect it rather than replace it with conservation values. The scale of modern cities is well beyond the unifying power of small town sanctions, and urban man lives in a pluralistic society where anyone with unusual views can find a group of like-minded compatriots.

Value changes in society today are relatively rapid by comparison to previous centuries. Though painfully slow for seekers of change, they are destructively fast for the disoriented. Both terminal and instrumental values are changing for a variety of reasons that can generally be understood in terms of the previous discussion on sources of values.

Broad shifts in the emphasis of terminal values might be explained in terms of the Maslow hierarchy. As the basic needs of more and more people are being met, there is a corresponding shift toward meeting higher level needs. Those who climb out of poverty become among the most conspicuous in displaying their material possessions for social esteem. And many who had the benefit of financial security and material comfort from an early age develop a strong interest in doing public service.

The changing importance of certain visible ends, however, is more closely related to changes in social and environmental conditions. This is most evident in the arena of public issues. Each new advance in social justice brings demands from other groups for equal treatment. The call for smaller families to control population, and the boredom of educated women with the chores of keeping house, add new impetus to the demands for women's rights. When high unemployment or inflation occurs, it takes top priority in government programming. The rising levels of pollution and destruction of the natural environment raised interest in environmental pollution. And awareness that the reserves of certain critical natural resources are being rapidly depleted has revived the conservation movement.

Changes in instrumental values are, of course, closely tied to the shifts in terminal values. When an end becomes important, the best means to achieve it also becomes important. Although this is the most obvious reason, it is not the only one. Science and technology are also contributors. Science advances our knowledge of means-ends relationships. Favored means are shown by new information to be ineffective or to be causes of unwanted side effects, and thereby lose favor. Unfavored means are found to be more effective and gain favor. Technological advances alter causal linkages. Ineffective means are transformed into effective ones. And totally new means are created to solve problems, while the old means are discarded.

2.5 VALUE CONFLICTS IN PUBLIC ACTION

A pervasive aspect of public decision making is the conflicts in values that arise among the affected members of society. The distinction made in welfare economics between private and collective (or "public") goods provides a useful insight into these conflicts. "Private" goods (and services) are those that are divisible in the sense that the benefits can be limited to the possessor of the good. The fact that a private good is divisible means that it is possible to produce different versions of the same type of good to meet the diversity of values. Thus clothes, cars, furniture, and other private goods are produced in a variety of sizes, shapes, designs, colors, and functions to meet the particular values of different people.

"Collective" goods (and services), on the other hand, are not divisible, which means that their benefits (as well as disbenefits) cannot be limited to a single possessor but instead extend to many people. Examples are national defense, police protection, public education, landscape aesthetics, clean air, quiet, land-use planning, and many others. There are different degrees of collectiveness in public goods. The effects of some extend only to a limited number of people. For example, the visual benefits of an undeveloped hillside extend only to those within view of it. At the other extreme, the effects of collective goods like foreign policy extend to everyone in the nation.

Because a collective good is indivisible, its characteristics cannot be modified to fit the values of each recipient. Thus the decision process for establishing the characteristics of a collective good can create serious conflicts among the affected people. For example, some members of most communities would like to have large land areas reserved for open space, whereas others oppose this because it limits growth and requires some people to give up their private property. Some metropolitan residents oppose the construction of new freeways because of the increased air pollution, noise, development, and community disruption they create; others favor more freeways because of the increased access they provide and the economic development they tend to foster.

Economic theory tells us that private goods will be produced by private enterprise, but collective goods in most cases will not. Thus collective goods frequently are the object of public action, and in these cases, interpersonal value conflicts are virtually inevitable. Like the married couple whose values conflict over the choice of a home, compromise is often necessary to an acceptable decision. Three hundred acres of open space can be reserved rather than six hundred, and one freeway can be built rather than two. Although compromise cannot eliminate conflict, it can reduce it to a tolerable level.

Another means of reducing conflict is to "vote with the feet." A person who dislikes the decisions of his local or state government may decide to move to another locality or state that is pursuing goals more compatible with his own. Obviously, this can be a personally disruptive and costly method of reducing conflict, but it is not an unimportant option.

2.6 IMPLICATIONS FOR CONDUCTING EVALUATIONS

A few general implications for conducting evaluations can be drawn from this discussion. First, evaluations of proposed public actions should be made on the basis of their consequences for ends, not means disconnected to ends. The importance of means can be properly judged only in light of the best available information linking them to ends. An example of a violation of this basic principle in evaluation reports is in reporting pollution impacts without indicating their implications for people. Air pollution, for example, is reported in terms of technical measures such as concentrations of carbon monoxide, particulate matter, sulfer oxides, and photochemical oxidants, which have meaning to the experts who regularly work with them but not to others. How could a nonexpert compare the importance, say, of particulates to unemployment? He couldn't, because the pollution indicator is not an end in itself. The interest in controlling air pollution arises from its connection with certain visible ends, such as human health, aesthetics, property protection, food production, and recreation opportunities.

It should be the responsibility of evaluators to estimate and report the implications of pollution impacts, and other means, for the ends with which they are linked. This will enable the many nontechnical participants in the public decision-making process to make informed judgments rather than to grope in the dark. Sometimes the best information on cause-effect linkages does not have the stamp of scientific validation, but this is no reason to ignore it. The best information, even if it is only an educated guess, is better than nothing at all, provided the uncertainty of the estimates is indicated.

Another implication is that evaluators should not assume that their values are a good indicator of the values held by the people whom their work is intended to serve. Like everyone else, their values developed around a core of special interests. The selection of friends, courses of study, their occupation, associations, reading material, leisure activities, and so forth, were guided with the interest in reinforcing their values and avoiding conflicts. Like everyone else, there are values they agree with and values they don't agree with. And there are values so divergent from their own that they appear unintelligible and ignorant, because they don't have the basis for understanding them.

The selection of categories and measures for representing impacts seems like a simple act, but it is a major step in evaluating plans. It focuses the attention of the formal impact estimation process on the limited set of consequences presumed to be the most significant. Evaluators must not assume that the impact categories that make the most sense to them are the ones that will be the most meaningful to the users of the information. Their judgments in the matter should be tested against the views of their clients.

Finally, it is important to observe that technical experts, including evaluators, have no special claims in judging terminal values. It is true that they are in an advantageous position to judge the instrumental values falling within the locus of their specialization. But once their knowledge of means-ends linkages is communicated, and attention is focused on weighing the relative importance of ends, there is no reason to believe that their value judgments are superior to the average educated citizen.

If anyone might be considered an expert on human values, it would be the people who study widely the history of societies and civilizations with a special eye to understanding the factors that contribute to their survival and welfare. Whether or not these experts should be given a special role in public decision making cannot be determined on the basis of their expertise alone, and ultimately must be decided through the political process.

In sum, evaluators should not assume that their values are a good indicator of what their client's values are or ought to be. Impact categories and measures should be selected so as to make the most sense to the users of the information. And impacts should be reported in the form of ends, and not left as disconnected means. These might be considered partial guidelines for conducting evaluations, as well as criteria for selecting an evaluation method. They will be applied in later chapters where several methods are examined.

2.7 BIBLIOGRAPHY ON HUMAN VALUES

Albert, Ethel. "Values and Value Systems," in the *International Encyclopedia of the Social Sciences,* vol. 16. New York: The Macmillan Company and Free Press, 1968.

Baier, K., and N. Rescher (eds.). *Values and the Future.* New York: Free Press, 1969.

Benedict, Ruth. *Patterns of Culture.* New York: Houghton Mifflin, 1934.

Boulding, Kenneth E. *The Image.* Ann Arbor, Mich.: University of Michigan Press, 1956.

Carter, Vernon Gill, and Tom Dale. *Soil and Civilization.* Norman, Okla.: University of Oklahoma Press, 1955.

Dewey, John, and James H. Tufts. *Ethics*. New York: Holt, 1932.

Dewey, John, "Theory of Valuation," in *International Encyclopedia of Unified Science*. Chicago: University of Chicago Press, 1939.

Festinger, F. A. *A Theory of Cognitive Dissonance*. New York: Harper, 1957.

Heider, F., "Attitudes and Cognitive Organization," *Journal of Psychology*, vol. 21 (January 1946), pp. 197-212.

Kluckhohn, Florence, and Fred Strodtbeck. *Variations in Value Orientation*. Evanston, Ill.: Row, Peterson, 1961.

Laszlo, Ervin, and James B. Wilbur (eds.). *Human Values and Natural Science*. New York: Gordon and Breach, 1970.

Lepley, Ray. (ed.). *Value: A Cooperative Inquiry*. New York: Columbia University Press, 1949.

Marris, Peter. *Loss and Change*. Garden City, N.Y.: Anchor/Doubleday, 1975.

Maslow, A. H. *Motivation and Personality*. New York: Harper and Row, 1954.

Osgood, C. E., and P. H. Tannenbaum, "The Principle of Congruity in the Prediction of Attitude Change," *Psychological Review*, vol. 62 (January 1955), pp. 42-55.

Pepper, Stephen C. *The Sources of Value*. Berkeley and Los Angeles, Calif.: University of California Press, 1958.

Perry, R. B. *General Theory of Value*. New York: Longman's Green, 1926.

Rokeach, Milton. *The Nature of Human Values*. New York: Free Press, 1973.

Toynbee, Arnold J. *A Study of History*, 12 volumes. New York: Oxford University Press, 1935-1961.

Zajonc, Robert B. "The Concepts of Balance, Congruity, and Dissonance," *Public Opinion Quarterly*, vol. 24 (Summer, 1960), pp. 280-296.

3
PHILOSOPHY OF DEMOCRACY

3.1 INTRODUCTION

A premise upon which the thinking in this book is based is that evaluation methods and processes, as components of the political system in which they are used, should be compatible with the values of that system. Thus the subject of this chapter, philosophy of democracy, is considered an essential background to the assessment and design of evaluation procedures used in democratic societies.

Most of the great philosophers through the ages devoted some of their attention to issues of political organization and many made important observations on democratic forms of government. There are many disagreements among these great thinkers on the desirability of democracy—some fundamental, others due to differences in human conditions in the times and places they wrote, still others due to differences in the definition of "democracy." Yet each of these philosophers had important insights into the strengths and weaknesses of democracy that deserve to be included as part of the philosophical literature on democracy.

The purpose of this chapter is not to present a comprehensive survey of the literature but to provide an overview of the essential elements of it that bear importantly on the conduct of evaluations. The discussion draws mostly from Aristotle's *Politics* (approximately 430 B.C.); Hobbes' *Leviathan* (1651); Locke's *The Second Treatise of Government* (approximately 1688); Montesquieu's *The Spirit of the Laws* (1748); Rousseau's *The Social Contract* (1762); Hamilton, Jay, and Madison's *The Federalist* (1788); and Tocqueville's *Democracy in America* (1835). Each was selected for a specific reason. Aristotle's *Politics,* based on a massive analysis of political organizations in 156 independent Greek States, provided the first systematic comparison of political systems, and laid the foundation for all subsequent work on this subject. The works of Hobbes, Locke, Montesquieu, and Rousseau greatly influenced the thinking of the framers of the United States Constitution. *The Federalist* contains profound theories and arguments supporting the form of the Constitution. Tocqueville's *Democracy in America* is a brilliant analysis of democracy at work in early American times. The chapter is concluded with a set of derivative criteria for the conduct of evaluations based on democratic principles.

The discussion contains some basic definitions and distinctions that are elementary to most readers. These are included in the interest of being complete.

3.2 DEFINITION OF DEMOCRACY

From Plato forward, a common distinction among governmental types is whether rule is by one, the few, or the many. According to this distinction democracy is rule by the many, whereas monarchy is by one and oligarchy by the few. Most political thinkers have held to this manner of defining democracy, but Aristotle did not like it. He preferred to think of democracy as rule by the poor masses rather than the wealthy, which in his day was an empirical fact in all democratic states.

Pure democracy in Aristotle's time was a political system in which the citizens of the state literally ruled themselves, each being given an equal opportunity to hold every political office, either by rotation or drawing lots. However, pure democracy was rare, as was pure monarchy and pure oligarchy. As Aristotle pointed out, a large number of political systems can be created by mixing the various features of the three basic types. Thus among the Greek States, and throughout the world today, most political systems are mixed rather than pure forms.

In the strict sense the United States is not governed by a democracy because it is not ruled by the many but rather by the few (that is, relative to the total population). However, because the "rulers," or more appropriately, the "decisions-makers," are either elected representatives of the many or their appointees, who theoretically must serve the will of the people to remain in office, the government is considered essentially a democracy, and more precisely a representative democracy.

3.3 THE BASIC GOAL OF GOOD GOVERNMENT

Aristotle said, and it is generally agreed, that a good government seeks to advance the good of the people. In his words:

A natural impulse is . . . one reason why men desire to live a social life even when they stand in no need of mutual succour; but they are also drawn together by a common interest, in proportion as each attains a share in the good life. The good life is the chief end, both for the community as a whole and for each of us individually. . . .

... when the one, or the few, or the many, rule with a view to the common interest, the constitutions under which they do so must necessarily be right constitutions. On the other hand the constitutions directed to the personal interests of the one, or the few, or the [poor] masses, must necessarily be perversions. ... [because they are not] directed to the advantage of the whole body of citizens.[1]

What Aristotle referred to as the "good life" of all citizens, others have called the "public interest," the "common good," the "social welfare" and the "public welfare." Whatever term is used, and I will use "public welfare" in this chapter, it is the definition that is important, for it can have a major effect on the selection of the political system. The definition of "public welfare" has two components: the welfare of the individual and the manner in which individual welfares are combined to arrive at the public welfare. Some political philosophers have ventured to describe individual welfare, but these descriptions fall short of a clear definition. For example, Aristotle said that there are three constituent elements of individual welfare: external goods (such as wealth, property, power, and reputation), internal goods (principally good health) and goods of the soul (including fortitude, temperance, justice, and wisdom).[2] He argued that, although all three are important, goods of the soul are the most important to individual welfare, because they lend support to the other two (whereas external goods do not reciprocate), and because there are no limits to their utility, whereas there are finite limits to the utility of the other two. Thus he states that: "felicity ... belongs more to those who have cultivated their character and mind to the uppermost, and kept acquisition of external goods within moderate limits, than it does to those who have managed to acquire more external goods than they can possibly use, and are lacking in the goods of the soul."[3]

Hobbes emphasized in his writings the importance of personal safety, and Locke emphasized property. A twentieth century conception of personal welfare springing from modern humanistic philosophy places the greatest importance on self-development and the realization of one's potential.[4]

Although there is no uniformly agreed upon conception of individual welfare, probably the dominant view among democratic thinkers is that the determinants vary greatly from person to person, and therefore each adult is the best guide to his own welfare. The logical extension of this view is that the welfare of each adult is best advanced under conditions of liberty, with the obvious provision that each person's liberty not infringe upon that of others.

The public welfare is some combination of individual welfares, but what combination? Aristotle's formula was defined by his concept of "proportional equality" in which the importance of each citizen to the common interest is proportional to his personal characteristics such as wisdom, virtue, wealth, and good descent.

3.4 EQUALITY IN DEMOCRACY

The concept of proportional equality is a substantial contrast with the democratic fomulation of "absolute equality," in which each person's welfare is judged equally important in determining the public welfare, irrespective of personal differences in income, wealth, and so forth. An important basis for this formulation is the view that each person has equal rights.

The notion of basic human rights was advanced by many of the classical philosophers, several of whom attempted to derive them from first principles, including Locke and Rousseau. Such an analysis typically involves a description of the "original state of nature" that existed before man joined into a political compact, and the terms of the compact or "social contract" in which man gave up certain rights in order to reap the benefits of political union. Locke's version of this process greatly influenced the thinking of the founders of democracy in the United States. The following description, although rather lengthy, is the bare bones of his analysis, stripped of virtually all supporting arguments:

To understand political power right, and derive it from its original, we must consider what state men are naturally in, and that is, a state of perfect freedom to order their actions, and dispose of their possessions, and person as they think fit, within the bounds of the law of nature, without asking leave, or depending upon the will of any other man. . . .

But though this is a state of liberty, yet it is not a state of license, though man in that state have an uncontrollable liberty, to dispose of his person or possession. . . . The state of nature has a law of nature to govern it, which obliges everyone: and reason, which is that law, teaches all mankind, who will but consult it, that being equal and independent, no one ought to harm another in his life, health, liberty or possessions. For man being all the workmanship of one omnipotent, and infinitely wise maker; all the servants of one Sovereign Master, sent into the world by his order and about his business, they are his property, whose workmanship they are, made to last during his, not one another's pleasure. And being furnished with like faculties, sharing all in one community of nature there cannot be supposed any subordination among us, that may authorize us to destroy one another, as if we were made for one another's uses . . . Everyone as he is bound to preserve himself, and not quit his station willfully; so by like reason when his own preservation comes not in competition, ought he, as much as he can, to preserve the rest of mankind, and may not unless it be to do justice on an offender, take away, or impair the life or what tends to the preservation of the life, liberty, health, limb or goods of another. . . .

And that all men may be restrained from invading others rights, and from doing hurt to one another, and the law of nature be observed, which willeth the peace and preservation of all mankind, the execution of the law of nature is in that state, put into every man's hands, whereby everyone has a right to punish the transgressors of that law to such a degree, as may hinder to violation. . . .

Men being, as has been said, by nature, all free, equal and independent, no one can be put out of this estate, and subjected to political power of another, without his own consent. The only way whereby anyone divests himself of his natural liberty, and puts on the bonds of civil society is by agreeing with other men to joyn and unite into a community, for their comfortable, safe, and peaceable living one amongst another, in a secure enjoyment of their properties, and a greater security against any that are not of it. This any number of men may do, because it injures not the freedom of the rest; they are left as they were in the liberty of the state of nature. When any number of men have so consented to make one community or government, they are thereby presently incorporated and make one body politick, wherein the majority have a right to act and conclude the rest. . . .

If man in the state of nature be so free as has been said; if he be absolute lord of his own person and possessions, equal to the greatest and subject to nobody, why will he part with his freedom? Why will he give up this empire, and subject himself to the dominion and control of any other power? To which 'tis obvious to answer, that though in the state of nature he hath such a right, yet the enjoyment of it is very uncertain, and constantly exposed to the invasion of others. For all being kings as much as he, every man his equal, and the greater part no strict observers of equity and justice, the enjoyment of the property he has in this state is very unsafe, very unsecure. This makes him willing to quit a condition, which however free, is full of fears and continual dangers; and 'tis not without reason, that he seeks out, and is willing to joyn in society with others who are already united, or have a mind to unite for the mutual preservation of their lives, liberties and estates. . . .

. . . the first and fundamental positive law of all commonwealths, is the establishing of the legislative power. . . .

Though the legislative, whether placed in one or more . . . it be the supream power in every commonwealth; yet,

First, it is not nor can possibly be absolutely arbitrary over the lives and fortunes of the people. . . .

Second, [it] cannot assume to its self a power to rule by extempory arbitrary decrees, but is bound to dispense justice, and decide the rights of the subject by promulgated standing laws. . . .

Thirdly, [it] cannot take from any man any part of his property without his own consent. . . .

Fourthly, [it] cannot transfer the power of making laws to any other hands. . . .

Though in a constitutional commonwealth . . . there can be but one supream power, which is the legislative, to which all the rest are and must be subordinate, yet the legislative, being the judiciary power to act for certain ends, there remains still in the power of the people a supream power to remove or alter the legislative, when they find the legislative act contrary to the trust reposed in them.[5]

Rousseau's interpretation of the social contract is quite different from Locke's, but the net result in terms of the equality of human rights is not. The analyses of both suggest that each adult member of political society has equal rights.[6]

The importance of the principle of absolute equality is also supported by a consideration of governmental stability. The historical evidence on the matter clearly indicates that most cases of internal dissension and revolution have been the result of a perception on the part of a segment of society that they had been treated unjustly. This was true as far back as Aristotle's time. In his extensive analysis of the causes of revolution and constitutional change among the Greek states, Aristotle writes that:

We must . . . assume . . . that the reason why there is a variety of different constitutions is the fact—already mentioned—that while men are all agreed on doing homage to justice, and to the principle of proportionate equality, they fail to achieve it in practice. Democracy arose in the strength of an opinion that those who were equal in any one respect were equal absolutely, and in all respects. (Men are prone to think that the fact of their all being equally free-born means that they are absolutely equal.) Oligarchy similarly arose from an opinion that those who were unequal in some respect were altogether unequal. (Those who are superior in point of wealth readily regard themselves absolutely superior.) Acting on such opinions, the democrats proceed to claim an equal share in everything, on the ground of their equality; the oligarchs proceed to press for more, on the ground that they are unequal—that is to say, more than equal. Both democracy and oligarchy are based on a sort of justice; but both fall short of absolute justice.[7] This is the reason why either side turns to sedition if it does not enjoy its share of constitutional rights which accords with the conception of justice it happens to entertain. . . . It is the passion for equality which is . . . at the roots of sedition.[8]

Although sophisticated formulas for determining justice have been devised by great thinkers like Aristotle, the principle of absolute equality has the advantages of being simple, readily accessible to all minds and easy to apply. The value of simplicity was described by Tocqueville as follows:

A proposition must be plain, to be adopted by the understanding of a people. . . . The governments that are founded upon a single feeling which is easily defined are perhaps not the best, but they are unquestionably the strongest and the most durable in the world.[9]

Historical trends in the actuation of human rights also support the principle of absolute equality. By contrast to the legal definition today, during the pre-Christian era it was not uncommon for women and children as well as slaves to be the property of the male head of the household, who sometimes even had the right to take their lives without answering to a higher authority. Of course, slavery existed in all the southern states at the time the U.S. Constitution was drafted, and was not abolished until 1863. And woman suffrage was not adopted until the current century.

As Tocqueville observed in 1835:

The gradual development of the principle of equality is . . . a providential fact. It has all the chief characteristics of such a fact: it is universal, it is lasting, it consistently eludes all human interference, and all events as well as all men contribute to its progress.[10]

That this trend persists today, one need only consult the daily newspaper.

Thus the principle of absolute equality in democratic thought is supported by several important considerations: it has an interesting logical derivation, a critical stabilizing role, and a sound consistency with historical trends.

3.5 GOVERNMENT STRUCTURE FOR PROMOTING THE PUBLIC WELFARE IN A DEMOCRACY

It has been established that, in democratic thought, each adult is assumed to be the best guide to his welfare, and that all people are equally important in determining the public welfare. A logical conclusion from this is that majority rule, which constitutes the public will, is the best guide for promoting the public welfare.[11] Once stated, though, there still remain undetermined a vast number of details in the structure of a democratic government. It is readily acknowledged that the structure of a pure democracy, in which the people literally rule themselves, is highly impractical and that the use of representatives, elected preferably on a geographical basis, is necessary. As Montesquieu put it,

As in a country of liberty, every man who is supposed a free agent ought to be his own governor; the legislative power should reside in the whole body of the people. But since this is impossible in large states, and in small states is subject to many inconveniences, it is fit the people should transact by their representatives what they cannot transact by themselves.

The inhabitants of a particular town are much better acquainted with its wants and interests than with those of other places; and are better judges of the capacity of their neighbors than of that of the rest of their countrymen. The members, therefore, of the legislature should not be chosen from the general body of the nation; but it is proper that in every considerable place a representative should be elected by the inhabitants.

The great advantage of representatives is, their capacity of discussing public affairs. For this the people collectively are extremely unfit, which is one of the chief inconveniences of a democracy.[12]

The use of representatives, however, introduces the potential for the same type of problem that has plagued oligarchies over the centuries: namely, the misuse of power by the few in serving narrow interests. It has long been noted that even the best of men can be corrupted by being placed in a position of excessive power. Again, Montesquieu is a worthy authority:

Democratic and aristocratic states are not in their own nature free. Political liberty is to be found only in moderate governments; and even in these it is not always found. It is there only when there is no abuse of power. But constant experience shows us that every man invested with power is apt to abuse it, and to carry his authority as far as it will go. Is it not strange, though true, to say that virtue itself has need of limits?[13]

Montesquieu assumed that it was the very nature of man to pursue his own interests and thus he arrived at the solution that power must be opposed by power. This led him to an elaboration of the concept of the separation of powers, which had an enormous influence on the framers of the U.S. Constitution, and, for that matter, the framers of all modern democratic constitutions.

James Madison carried the concept of opposing power with power even further in his theory of checks on faction.[14] He felt that the potential violence from opposing factions was one of the most serious threats to democracy. His theory suggests that this threat was reduced in proportion to the degree that representative democracy was divided on a geographic basis and enlarged in territory, thereby dividing opposing factions into a large number of small, viable units.

A more basic, more universal ingredient for dealing with the problem of opposing interests that should not be overlooked, although it goes beyond the government structure, is the spirit of compromise.

There is a huge number of details, of course, that might be discussed on the subject of democratic governmental structure, but most are of little importance to the subject of evaluation. Related to the subject of structure, however, are a few issues of great importance: these are the role of citizen participation, the role of technical experts, and the problem of tyranny over the minority.

3.6 ROLE OF CITIZEN PARTICIPATION

There is no doubt that the quality of a democratic government depends on an informed, active citizenry. Citizens must exercise good judgment in the selection of representatives, policies, and programs; and they must help guard against the misuse of power. The level of basic education, obviously, is very important, but it is not sufficient. Citizens must be informed on political matters, and, in order to guarantee this, it requires that they be active in political affairs. They also must be active if they are to effectively guard against political abuses. Tocqueville laid great stress on the value of citizen participation in American democracy, a view that profoundly influenced the political philosophy of John Stuart Mill and others. He felt that local government was the cornerstone of democracy, because it provided the greatest opportunity of participation:

... municipal institutions constitute the strength of free nations. Town meetings are to liberty what primary schools are to science; they bring it within the people's reach, they teach men how to use and how to enjoy it.

A nation may establish a free government, but without municipal institutions it cannot have the spirit of liberty. Transient passions, the interests of an hour, or the chances of circumstances may create the external forms of independence, but the despotic tendency which has been driven into the interior of the social system will sooner or later reappear on the surface.[15]

The degree of citizen participation, of course, is importantly affected by the manner in which the government is structured and operated to encourage it. And, as Rousseau observed, participation and structure form a self-reinforcing system:

In a well-ordered city every man flies to the assemblies; under a bad government no one cares to stir a step to get there, because no one is interested in what happens there, because it is forseen that the general will will not prevail, and lastly because domestic cares are all-absorbing. Good laws lead to the making of better ones; bad ones bring about worse. As soon as any man says of the affairs of the State, "What does it matter to me?" the State may be given up for lost.[16]

3.7 CITIZEN PARTICIPATION AND THE ROLE OF TECHNICAL EXPERTS

The increasing complexity of societal problems, and the means of their solution, in modern times, has led to the increasing use of technical experts in government affairs, and it is sometimes believed that, because of this, citizens are less capable of providing valuable inputs. In this regard, it is important to distinguish between means and ends in public affairs. Technical experts play an essential role in designing means to specific ends. However, in the selection of ends, the people are the experts by the democratic definition of the public welfare. Accordingly, it should never be the role of technical experts to select the ends of public action. On the selection of means to ends, it must be recognized that most means have implications for a variety of ends. In these cases, technical experts play a valuable role in identifying the nature and magnitude of such impacts, but they should not be employed to select the means.

Thus the primary role of technical experts should be to design alternative means to specific ends and estimate their impacts. But it should be recognized that citizens, also, can play a valuable role in the design of means. The first reason is that the citizenry includes all the technical experts, and sometimes the best technical solution to a problem is advanced by an expert in the role of a citizen participant. The second reason is that the design of a solution sometimes requires achieving a compromise between strongly opposing factions, in which case citizen involvement may be crucial.

Thus it is that citizen participation can play a valuable role, and, in some senses, an essential role in the selection of the means, as well as the ends, of government activity, despite the increasing complexity of societal problems. Whether the essential information on desired ends should be supplied directly by the people or indirectly by their elected representatives is a subject of controversy and will probably continue to be, so long as there is a modicum of mistrust in public officials (which probably means forever). It is clear that, in periods when mistrust is high, the people will demand greater direct input than in periods when it is low. The many benefits of participation require that it be supplied.

3.8 TYRANNY OVER THE MINORITY

Aristotle disliked democracy because it led to the tyranny of the majority over the minority, and, particularly, because in his day this meant the tyranny by the poor and unknowledgeable masses over the wealthy and knowledgeable few, who would eventually withdraw from active political participation, leaving a very weak, sometimes anarchical government.

Madison, too, was greatly concerned with the threat of tyranny over the minority in democratic government. He observed that:

Justice is the end of government. It is the end of civil society. It has ever been and ever will be pursued until it be obtained, or until liberty be lost in the pursuit. In a society under the forms of which the stronger faction can readily unite and oppress the weaker, anarchy may as truly be said to reign as in a state of nature, where the weaker individual is not secured against the violence of the stronger; and as, in the later state, even the stronger individuals are prompted, by the uncertainty of their condition, to submit to a government which may protect the weak as well as themselves; so, in the former state, will the more powerful factions or parties be gradually induced, by a like motive, to wish for a government which will protect all parties, the weaker as well as the more powerful.[17]

Madison argued that the separation of powers, the employment of checks and balances, the territorial division of power, and the size of the republic would all contribute to the protection of weak factions against the oppressive force of the strong.

Tocqueville, observing the American scene a half century after Madison provided his penetrating analyses in *The Federalist,* was not convinced that the problem was solved. He wrote:

Governments usually perish from impotence or from tyranny. In the former case, their power escapes from them; it is wrested from their grasp in the latter. Many observers who have witnessed the anarchy of democratic states have imagined that the government of those states was naturally weak and impotent. The truth is that when war is once begun between parties, the government loses its control over society. But I do not think that a democratic power is naturally without force or resources; say, rather, that it is almost always by the abuse of its force and the misemployment of its resources that it becomes a failure. Anarchy is almost always produced by its tyranny or its mistakes, but not by its want of strength.

It is important not to confuse stability with force, or the greatness of a thing with its duration. In democratic republics the power that directs society is not stable, for it often changes hands and assumes a new direction. But whichever way it turns, its force is almost irresistible. The governments of the American republic appear to me to be as much centralized as those of the absolute monarchies of Europe, and more energetic than they are. I do not, therefore, imagine that they will perish from weakness.

If ever the free institutions of America are destroyed, that event may be attributed to the omnipotence of the majority, which may at some future time urge the minority to desperation and oblige them to have recourse to physical force.[18]

The minority in America of greatest concern to Tocqueville were the oppressed racial groups, particularly blacks and Indians about which he wrote with great insight.

It must be readily acknowledged that the suppression of minority interests is still with us today, and probably will always be a threat against which we must constantly be on guard. Clearly of greatest concern are the disadvantaged members of society: the poor, the ethnic minorities, the physically handicapped, and the elderly. As Madison suggested a just government will always reflect a concern for such minority groups in public decision making.

3.9 IMPLICATIONS FOR EVALUATION

The philosophy of democracy has important implications for the conduct of evaluations in democratic societies. The implications of the above discussion are presented in the following form of criteria that can be useful in assessing evaluation methodologies as well as specific evaluations. Evaluation methods will be assessed on these criteria in later chapters.

1. *The people's values*
Are the values that are reflected in the evaluation those of all the people, or only a portion of the people affected by the proposed action? For example, have the technical evaluators taken care to avoid using their own values on the assumption that theirs are a good indicator of what the average values are or ought to be? Have they consulted the values of the people or their elected representatives in selecting the alternatives to be evaluated and the impact categories to be employed?

2. *Principle of absolute equality*
Is the principle of absolute equality reflected in the values employed? It is important to remember that this principle states that the values of all people are equally important, irrespective of income, wealth, education, and other characteristics.

3. *Tyranny over the minority*
Does the evaluation address the issue of tyranny over the minority? That is, does it give explicit attention to the implications of the proposed action on minority groups, particularly the disadvantaged members of society?

4. *Citizen participation*
Does the evaluation incorporate citizen participation? Is the evaluation report clear and readily comprehendible so that the average citizen can understand it? Are impact categories and impact measurements selected to promote their common understanding? Are technical terms avoided when common-language counterparts are available? Are technical concepts and relationships, critical to an understanding of the evaluation, explained so that the average citizen can understand them? Is the evaluation report readily available to the public? Does the timing of the release of the

report facilitate thorough public review and contact with elected representatives before public action is to be taken? Does the evaluation facilitate the process of compromise, when appropriate? For example, are impacts reported in sufficient detail so that interest-group conflicts can be readily discerned and utilized for designing compromise solutions, when necessary?

5. *Misuse of power*

Was the evaluation conducted in a manner that avoids the misuse of power? For example, was there sufficient separation between the sponsors of the proposed action and the evaluators? Were judgmental items tested by securing the independent judgments of two or more qualified persons? In the case of evaluations of major public actions, were the evaluation tasks divided among a sufficient number of independent evaluators or was the evaluation information confirmed by independent review?

3.10 BIBLIOGRAPHY ON DEMOCRATIC PHILOSOPHY

Barker, Ernest. *The Politics of Aristotle.* London: Oxford University Press, 1958.

Hamilton, Alexander, James Madison, and John Jay. *The Federalist.* Edited by Benjamin Fletcher Wright. Cambridge, Mass: Belknap Press of Harvard University Press, 1961.

Hamilton, Edith, and Huntington Cairns. *The Collected Dialogues of Plato.* New York: Bollingen Foundation, 1961.

Hobbes, Thomas. *Leviathan.* Edited by Michael Oakeshott. New York: Collier Books, 1962.

Hudson, Jay William. *Why Democracy: A Study in the Philosophy of the State.* New York: D. Appleton-Century Company, 1936.

Locke, John. *Two Treatises of Government.* Edited by Peter Laslett. New York: New American Library, Inc., 1965.

Mill, John Stuart. *Considerations on Representative Government.* Edited by Currin V. Shields. Indianapolis, Ind.: The Bobbs-Merrill Company, Inc., 1958.

Montesquieu, Baron de. *The Spirit of the Laws.* Translated by Thomas Nugent. New York: Hafner Publishing Co., 1949.

Padover, Saul K. *To Secure These Blessings.* New York: Washington Square Press and the Ridge Press, Inc., 1962.

Rousseau, Jean Jacques. *The Social Contract.* Translated by G. D. H. Cole. New York: E. P. Dutton and Company, Inc., 1950.

Tocqueville, Alexis de. *Democracy in America,* vol. 1. Edited by Phillips Bradley. New York: Alfred A. Knopf, 1948.

4

ENVIRONMENTAL VALUES

4.1 INTRODUCTION

For an evaluation method to be useful it must be able to present the impacts it assesses in reasonably clear terms. Communication is critical. If evaluators do not describe impacts in forms that are understandable and meaningful to users of the information, what good is their work? The main purpose of this chapter is to place before us a variety of values expressing the significance of the natural environment, so that in later chapters we will be in a good position to judge the adequacy of different methods in representing environmental impacts. Also, humanistic values are briefly discussed because of the role they can play in augmenting environmental values to provide a fuller philosophy of social welfare. A few general words about how these values should be considered in evaluations conclude the chapter.

As we read the environmental literature these days, we commonly get the impression that interest in the environment is strictly a recent phenomenon, which of course it is not. Taking the United States as an example, a wide and rich variety of views toward nature had been expressed over a century ago, and by the first decade of the present century, most of the issues we confront today had been discussed. The selections on the following pages are drawn from this earlier literature because it offers revealing and insightful views that are as current today as when they were written, and because the recent literature is dominated by scientific thinking that in general is less expressive of values (though there are marvelous exceptions to this general trend).

Only a few authors are represented here.[1] I quote them at length—far more than custom typically allows—since no one can express their views as well as they.

4.2 ENVIRONMENTAL VALUES[2]

Whether or not man should generally be considered a part of nature, history discloses that the spread of so-called "civilization" has run over native man and nature with little distinction or regard. George Catlin was one of the first persons to take a deep interest in the conditions and cultures of American Indians. In 1823 at the age of 27 he terminated his law practice to pursue an art career. Within a few years he was firmly established as a portrait artist in Philadelphia, elected to the Philadelphia Academy of Art, and honored with an exhibition of his paintings at the American Academy of Fine Arts, but he was dissatisfied. He looked for a lifetime undertaking, and his search was ended when a delegation of Indians from the Far West on their way to Washington, stopped in Philadelphia. He decided: ". . . the history and customs of such a people, preserved by pictorial illustrations, are themes worthy the life-time of one man, and nothing short of the loss of my life, shall prevent me from visiting their country, and of becoming their historian."[3]

For two years he studied the conditions and painted portraits of Indians in the frontier area around St. Louis. Then beginning in 1832, and for the next seven years, he travelled extensively in the Far West (to the slopes of the Rockies), visiting every Indian tribe he could (forty-eight in all), painting portraits and landscapes, and writing about Indian manners and customs. His adventurous trips gained him rich insights into the character and conditions of the Indians. He observed:

Some writers, I have been grieved to see, have written down the character of the North American Indian, as dark, relentless, cruel and murderous in the last degree; with scarce a quality to stamp their existence of a higher order than that of the brutes. . . .

I have roamed about . . . visiting and associating with, some three or four hundred thousand of these people, under an almost infinite variety of circumstances; and from the very many and decided voluntary acts of their hospitality and kindness, I feel bound to pronounce them, by nature, a kind and hospitable people. I have been welcomed generally in their country, and treated to the best that they could give me, without any charges made for my board; they have often escorted me through their enemies' country at some hazard to their own lives, and aided me in passing mountains and rivers with my awkward baggage; and under all these circumstances of exposure, no Indian ever betrayed me, struck me a blow, or stole from me a shillings worth of my property, that I am aware of.[4]

As Catlin reported, the unfavorable views of Indians came from observations of those living along the expanding belt of the frontier:

. . . whose habits have been changed—whose pride has been cut down—whose country has been ransacked—whose wives and daughters have been shamefully abused—whose lands have been wrested from them—whose limbs have become enervated and naked by the excessive use of whiskey—whose friends and relations have been prematurely thrown into their graves—whose native pride and dignity have at last given way to the unnatural vices which civilized cupidity has engrafted upon them, to be silently nurtured and magnified by a burning sense of injury and injustice, and ready for that cruel vengence which often falls from the hand that is palsied by refined abuses, and yet unrestrained by the glorious influences of refined and moral cultivation.[5]

But these problems were not confined to the frontier. A system of whiskey and fur trading was becoming prevalent in the Far West, supported by government policy. Catlin foresaw that this would cause the extinction of the buffalo and with it the demise of the many Indian tribes whose cultures relied on the buffalo as the main source of food, clothing, and shelter. He recounts:

When I first arrived at this place, on my way up the river, which was in the month of May, in 1832, and had taken up my lodgings in the Fur Company's Fort, Mr. Laidlaw . . ., his chief clerk, Mr. Halsey, and many of their men, as well as the chiefs of the Sioux, told me, that only a few days before I arrived, (when an immense herd of buffaloes had showed themselves on the opposite side of the river, almost blackening the plains for a great distance), a party of five or six hundred Sioux Indians on horseback, forded the river about midday, and spending a few hours amongst them, recrossed the river at sun-down and came into the Fort with fourteen hundred fresh buffalo tongues, which were thrown down in a mass, and for which they required but a few gallons of whiskey, which was soon demolished, indulging them in a little, and harmless carouse.

This profligate waste of the lives of these noble and useful animals, when, from all that I could learn, not a skin or a pound of meat (except the tongues), was brought in fully supports me in the seemingly extravagant predictions that I have made as to their extinction, which I am certain is near at hand.[6]

Although buffalo tongues were considered a delicacy, not they but the fur were the main source of the problem.[7] Catlin summarized his views one day while sitting on a favorite bluff:

It is generally supposed, and familiarly said, that a man "falls" into a reverie; but I seated myself in the shade a few minutes since, resolved to force myself into one; and for this purpose I laid open a small pocket map of North America, and excluding my thoughts from every other object in the world, I soon succeeded in producing the desired illusion. This little chart, over which I bent, was seen in all its parts, as nothing but the green and vivid reality. I was lifted up upon an imaginary pair of wings, which easily raised and held me floating in the open air, from whence I could behold beneath me the Pacific and the Atlantic Ocean—the great cities of the East, and the mighty rivers. I could see the blue chain of the great lakes at the North—the Rocky Mountains, and beneath them and near their base, the vast, and almost boundless plains of grass, which were speckled with the bands of grazing buffaloes!

The world turned gently around, and I examined its surface; continent after
continent passed under my eye, and yet amidst them all, I saw not the vast
and vivid green, that is spread like a carpet over the Western wilds of my own
country. I saw not elsewhere in the world, the myriad herds of buffaloes—my
eyes scanned in vain, for they were not. And when I turned again to the wilds
of my native land, I beheld them all in motion! For the distance of several
hundreds of miles from North to South, they were wheeling about in vast
columns and herds—some were scattered, and ran with furious wildness—
some lay dead, others were pawing the earth for a hiding place—some were
sinking down and dying, gushing out their life's blood in deep-drawn sighs—
and others were contending in furious battle for the life they possessed, and
the ground they stood upon. . . .

. . . Hundreds and thousands were strewed upon the plains—they were flayed,
and their reddened carcasses left; and about them bands of wolves, and dogs,
and buzzards were seen devouring them. Contiguous, and in sight, were the
distant and feeble smokes of wigwams and villages, where the skins were
dragged, and dressed for white man's luxury! where they were sold for whiskey, and the poor Indians laid drunk, and were crying. I cast my eyes into the
towns and cities of the East, and there I beheld buffalo robes hanging at almost every door for traffic; and I saw also the curling smokes of a thousand
Stills—and I said, "Oh insatiable man, is thy avarice such! wouldst thou tear
the skin from the back of the last animal of this noble race, and rob thy
fellow man of his meat, and for it give him poison![8]

And from the creative mind of this man came the vision of a natural
preserve, an institutionalized national park:

It is a melancholy contemplation for one who has travelled as I have through
these realms, and seen this noble animal in all its pride and glory, to contem-
plate it so rapidly wasting from the world, drawing the irresistible conclusion
too, which one must do, that its species is soon to be extinguished, and with
it the peace and happiness (if not the actual existence) of the tribes of Indians
who are joint tenants with them, in the occupancy of these vast and idle
plains.

And what a splendid contemplation too, when one (who has travelled these
realms and can duly appreciate them) imagines them as they might in the
future be seen, (by some great protecting policy of government) preserved in
their pristine beauty and wildness, in a magnificent park, where the world
could see for ages to come, the native Indian in his classic attire, galloping
his wild horse, with sinewy bow, and shield and lance, amid the fleeting herds
of elks and buffaloes. What a beautiful and thrilling specimen for America to
preserve and hold up to the view of her refined citizens and the world, in
future ages! A nation's Park, containing man and beast, in all the wild and
freshness of their nature's beauty!

I would ask no other monument to my memory, nor any other enrollment of my name amongst the famous dead, than the reputation of having been the founder of such an instituion.[9]

The significance of nature to Catlin was the truth it revealed, unfettered by civilized customs and institutions. In his first letter from the wilds he wrote:

You will, no doubt, be somewhat surprised on the receipt of a Letter from me, so far strayed into the Western World; and still more startled, when I tell you that I am here in the full enthusiasm and practice of my art. That enthusiasm alone has brought me into this remote region, 3500 miles from my native soil; the last 2000 of which have furnished me with almost un-limited models, both in landscape and the human figure, exactly suited to my feelings. I am now in the full possession and enjoyments of those con-ditions, on which alone I was induced to pursue the art as a profession; and in anticipation of which alone, my admiration for the art could ever have been kindled into a pure flame. I mean the free use of nature's undisguised models, with the privilege of selecting for myself. If I am here losing the benefit of the fleeting fashions of the day, and neglecting that elegant polish, which the world say an artist should draw from a continual intercourse with the polite world; yet have I this consolation, that in this country, I am entirely divested of those dangerous steps and allurements which beset an artist in fashionable life; and have little to steal my thoughts away from the contemplation of the beautiful models that are about me. If, also, I have not here the benefit of that feeling of emulation, which is the life and spur to the arts, where artists are associates together; yet am I surrounded by living models of such elegance and beauty, that I feel an unceasing excitement of a much higher order—the certainty that I am drawing knowledge from the true source.[10]

Catlin's law background conjoined with his extensive first-hand knowledge of conditions in the West led him to penetrating observations on institutional flaws. Does might make right? Catlin answers, sarcastically:

It may be that power is right, and voracity a virtue; and that these people, and these noble animals, are righteously doomed to an issue that will not be averted. It can be easily proved—we have civilized science that can easily do it, or anything else that may be required to cover the inequities of civilized man in catering for his unholy appetites. It can be proved that the weak and ignorant have no rights—that there can be no virtue in darkness—that God's gifts have no meaning or merit until they are appropriated by civilized man— by him brought into the light, and converted to his use and luxury.[11]

About the time that Catlin decided to become the historian for American Indians, Ralph Waldo Emerson began penning ideas for his first book, *Nature,* published in 1836. The son of a pastor, Emerson, too, followed in the ministry.

But he retired himself after only three years, because he could not in good conscience continue to administer certain obligatory rituals which he believed had not been intended by Jesus. In 1832 at age 29, he embarked on a career as lecturer and author, which he followed the rest of his life.

Nature was dear to Emerson's heart and central to his philosophy. He was a trancendentalist, one of the movement's leading spokesmen, and it is useful to understand his version of this world-view in order to appreciate the significance he placed on nature. Emerson believed that the natural world and each human being are manifestations of God; that the mind of each person is an inlet to the one eternal Mind or Spirit, or God, which reveals eternal truth; and that truth is only imperfectly revealed directly to people to the degree that their minds are shackled by egoistic desires, for praise, power, wealth, and so on, which are obstacles to pure reason. In the following passage Emerson suggests that, in nature, man can transcend his self-centered being and become infused with true knowledge:

In the woods, we return to reason and faith. There I feel that nothing can befall me in life—no disgrace, no calamity (leaving me my eyes), which nature cannot repair. Standing on the bare ground—my head bathed by the blithe air and uplifted into infinite space—all mean egotism vanishes. I become a transparent eyeball; I am nothing; I see all; the currents of the Universal Being circulate through me; I am part or parcel of God.[12]

Emerson frequently referred to the circles of nature in the same sense that ecologists do today. His optimism, reflected in nearly everything he wrote, is derived partly from the view that these circles provide enormous benefits to man:

The misery of man appears like childish petulance, when we explore the steady and prodigal provision that has been made for his support and delight on this green ball which floats him through the heavens. . . .
Nature in its ministry to man, is not only the material, but is also the process and the result. All the parts incessantly work into each other's hands for the profit of man. The wind sows the seed; the sun evaporates the sea; the wind blows the vapor to the field; the ice, on the other side of the planet, condenses rain on this; the rain feeds the plant; the plant feeds the animal; and thus the endless circulations of the divine charity nourish man.[13]

Although Emerson seemed to maintain the biblical view that nature exists for man's sole use, and occasionally spoke of "taming nature," his philosophy was opposed to the destruction of nature. For example, in the following he expresses the view that the natural world is our house and our best source of truth; thus it serves as a reference point by which we may judge ourselves. As ecologists frequently remind us today, it would be utter folly to destroy our best reference point:

The world proceeds from the same spirit as the body of man. It is a remoter and inferior incarnation of God, a projection of God in the unconscious. But it differs from the body in one important respect. It is not, like that, now subjected to the human will. Its serene order is inviolable by us. It is, therefore, to us, the present expositor of the divine mind. It is a fixed point whereby we may measure our departure. As we degenerate, the contrast between us and our house is more evident.[14]

As well as a seminal philosopher, to whom many of the outstanding thinkers of subsequent generations have acknowledged their debt, Emerson was a great interpreter of nature's significance in our daily lives, as is illustrated in the following passages:

It seems as if the day was not wholly profane in which we have given heed to some natural object. The fall of snowflakes in a still air, preserving to each crystal its perfect form; the blowing of sleet over a wide sheet of water, and over the plains; the waving rye-field; the mimic waving of acres of houstonia, whose innumerable florets whiten a ripple before the eye; a reflection of trees and flowers in glassy lakes; the musical, streaming, odorous south wind, which converts all trees to wind-harps; the crackling and spurting of hemlock in the flames, or of pine logs, which yield glory to the walls and faces in the setting-room—these are the music and pictures of the most ancient religion.[15]

To the body and mind which have been cramped by noxious work or company, nature is medicinal and restores their tone. The tradesman, the attorney comes out of the din and craft of the street and sees the sky and woods, and is a man again. In their eternal calm, he finds himself.[16]

I see the spectacle of morning from the hilltop over against my house, from daybreak to sunrise, with emotions an angel might share. The long slender bars of cloud float like fishes in the sea of crimson light. From the earth, as a shore, I look out into that silent sea. I seem to partake its rapid transformations; the active enchantment reaches my dust, and I dilate and conspire with the morning wind. How does Nature deify us with a few cheap elements! Give me health and a day, and I will make the pomp of emperors ridiculous.[17]

Henry David Thoreau was a neighbor of Emerson's in that small town of literary giants, Concord, Massachusetts. Fourteen years the junior, Thoreau was clearly influenced by Emerson's ideas. He frequently contributed articles to the *Dial,* a transcendental periodical that both he and Emerson at times helped edit. No doubt he hoped eventually to be supported by his writing, but he received little remuneration for it, relying most of his adult life on irregular jobs, in his father's small pencil factory, as a handyman and later as a surveyor.

Thoreau scorned society for its triviality and materialism, for frittering away its energies on details, and for running fast to get someplace, anyplace, while running over itself in the process. Nature was not only a refuge from civilized man, it was a source to his philosophical mind of basic truth.

Thoreau's favorite pastime was walking in the wilds. He delighted in the fact that he could walk freely for miles around Concord, through woods and meadows, along streams and ponds, without seeing a solitary soul. He foresaw, though, that his freedom might not last. In February, 1851, he wrote in his journal:

I trust that the walkers of the present day are conscious of the blessings which they enjoy in the comparative freedom with which they can ramble over the country and enjoy the landscape, anticipating with compassion that future day when possibly it will be partitioned off into so-called pleasure-grounds, where only a few may enjoy the narrow and exclusive pleasure which is compatible with ownership—when walking over the surface of God's earth shall be construed to mean trespassing on some gentlemen's grounds, when fences shall be multiplied and man traps and other engines invented to confine men to the public road.[18]

Walking in the woods was not enough, though; carrying his transcendental views to their logical conclusion, he decided to live in the woods, which he did for two years. The experience, of course, formed the basis for *Walden,* first published in 1854. He explains:

I went to the woods because I wished to live deliberately, to front only the essential facts of life, and see if I could not learn what it had to teach, and not, when I came to die, discover that I had not lived. I did not wish to live what was not life, living is so dear; nor did I wish to practice resignation, unless it was quite necessary. I wanted to live deep and suck out all the marrow of life, to live so sturdily and Spartan-like as to put to rout all that was not life, to cut a broad swath and shave close, to drive life into a corner and reduce it to its lowest terms . . .[19]

His love for nature was overwhelming, lifting him high above the anthropocentric view, to see that nature exists not just for man but for itself as well:

We are wont to forget that the sun looks on our cultivated fields and on the prairies and forests without distinction. They all reflect and absorb his rays alike, and the former make but a small part of the glorious picture which he beholds in his daily course. In his view the earth is all equally cultivated like a garden. Therefore we should receive the benefit of his light and heat with a corresponding trust and magnanimity. What though I value the seed of these beans, and harvest that in the fall of the year? This broad field which I have looked at so long looks not to me as the principal cultivator, but away from me to influences more genial to it, which water and make it green. These beans have results which are not harvested by me. Do they not grow for woodchucks partly? The ear of wheat . . . should not be the only hope of the husbandman; its kernal or grain . . . is not all that it bears. How, then, can our harvest fail? Shall I not rejoice also at the abundance of the weeds whose seeds are the granary of the birds?[20]

In his youth he was an avid hunter, as are so many boys, but as his philosophy matured he laid his gun to rest. He concluded from his personal experience:

No humane being, past the thoughtless age of boyhood, will wantonly murder any creature which holds its life by the same tenure that he does.[21]

Opposed to killing animals, for food as well as sport, the following reveals his optimism that mankind would eventually adopt vegetarianism:

It may be vain to ask why the imagination will not be reconciled to flesh and fat. I am satisfied that it is not. Is it not a reproach that man is a carnivorous animal? True, he can and does live, in a great measure, by preying on other animals; but this is a miserable way,—as any one who will go to snaring rabbits, or slaughtering lambs, may learn,—and he will be regarded as a benefactor of his race who will teach man to confine himself to a more innocent and wholesome diet. Whatever my own practice may be, I have no doubt that it is a part of the destiny of the human race, in its gradual improvement, to leave off eating animals . . [22]

A cornerstone of Thoreau's philosophy was the imperative to fully integrate values and lifestyle. This call of action, perhaps his most valuable message to the present generation, applies to us all:

There are nowadays professors of philosophy, but not philosophers. Yet it is admirable to profess because it was once admirable to live. To be a philosopher is not merely to have subtle thoughts, nor even to found a school, but so to love wisdom as to live, according to its dictates, a life of simplicity, independence, magnanimity, and trust. It is to solve some of the problems of life, not only theoretically, but practically. The success of great scholars and thinkers is commonly a courtier-like success, not kingly, not manly. They make shift to live merely by conformity, practically as their fathers did, and are in no sense the progenitors of a nobler race of men. But why do men degenerate ever? What makes families run out? What is the nature of the luxury which enervates and destroys nations? Are we sure that there is none of it in our own lives? The philosopher is in advance of his own age even in the outward form of his life. He is not fed, sheltered, clothed, warmed, like his contemporaries. How can a man be a philosopher and not maintain his vital heat by better methods than other men?[23]

The wording of the concluding sentence makes the statement seem particularly relevant to the cause of energy conservation. It is interesting to note that Thoreau understood that energy is common to the four basic material necessities—food, shelter, clothing, and fuel: "... 'animal life,' is nearly synonomous with 'animal heat'; for while food may be regarded as the fuel which keeps up the fire within us,—and fuel serves only to prepare that food or to increase the warmth of our bodies by addition from without,—shelter and clothing also serve only to retain heat thus generated and absolved."[24]

Our ecological understanding of environmental problems is commonly believed to be recent in origin, but this is not true. Over a hundred years ago George Perkins Marsh wrote a book providing overwhelming evidence that, through various chains of causation, man was seriously damaging his natural environment. The book, *Man and Nature* (the first edition published in 1864), has been lauded as "the fountainhead of the conservation movement" and "the beginning of land wisdom" in the United States.[25]

Born in 1801 and raised in Vermont, Marsh followed a diverse career, as a teacher, lawyer, businessman (in lumber, construction, sheep and wool, real estate, and railroads), newspaper editor, U.S. congressman, author, and ambassador to Italy (for 21 years). Though not a scientist, his keen eye for the landscape enabled him to formulate the theme for the book by 1847.[26] But it was not until his diplomatic appointment to Europe that he was able to gather the massive evidence that gave his views full authority. More than anything else Marsh was a scholar, interested in getting at the facts. He was a rapid reader in twenty different languages, which gave him wide access to the foreign literature.

Man and Nature is at least four books in one. It was an appeal to America to learn from the mistakes of Europe in mistreating nature. Second, it established a new branch of geography. Modern geographers in Marsh's time were studying the effects of nature on man; his book examines the effects of man on nature. The book was also a statement to landowners, forecasting a tragic future if the circle of "enlightened self-interest" was not expanded to encompass environmental as well as economic considerations. Finally, *Man and Nature* was a practical book on ecology as applied to resource management problems (although these terms don't appear as such anywhere in the text). Much of the material remains relevant to the present day.

Marsh described man's relationship to nature as occasionally harmonious, but for the most part not:

... the organic and the inorganic world are ... bound together by such mutual relations and adaptations as secure, if not the absolute permanence and equilibrium of both, a long continuance of the established conditions of each at any given time and place, or at least, a very slow and gradual succession of changes of those conditions. But man is everywhere a disturbing agent. Wherever he plants his foot, the harmonies of nature are turned to discords. The proportions and accommodations which insured the stability of existing arrangements are overthrown. Indigenous vegetable and animal species are extirpated, and supplanted by others of foreign origin, spontaneous production is forbidden or restricted, and the face of the earth is either lade bare or covered with a new and reluctant growth of vegetable forms, and with alien tribes of animal life. These intentional changes and substitutions constitute, indeed, great revolutions; but vast as is their magnitude and importance, they are ... insignificant in comparison with the contingent and unsought results which have flowed from them.[27]

As we are often cautioned by ecologists today, Marsh warned:

The equation of animal and vegetable life is too complicated a problem for human intelligence to solve, and we can never know how wide a circle of disturbance we produce in the harmonies of nature when we throw the smallest pebble into the ocean of organic life.[28]

But his interest in nature was not so much a pure scientific one of being able to predict *all* the consequences of an action as a practical one of learning from past experience the *serious* consequences, and how they could be avoided or ameliorated. In his book he describes the problem of the expanding sand dunes in many parts of Europe and the Mid-East. By removing protective vegetation, man has been the main cause in many cases. Several countries were successfully dealing with the problem by re-establishing certain species of plants and trees, some of which even paid the cost of the stabilization program by their harvest. Occasionally, expansive dune areas were transformed into productive agricultural districts.

Marsh surveyed what was known about the impacts of man on plants and animals. He discussed the effects, desirable and undesirable, of transferring plants and animals to foreign environments. He even included the idea of locating and introducing natural predators as a means of controlling destructive insects accidentally transported to new areas. Hunters were reducing and sometimes exterminating mammals and birds. The Stellar's sea cow had become extinct, and in the Pacific the walrus, sea otter, and certain seals seemed destined to follow in the absence of government protection. Whales had virtually disappeared from some fishing grounds, and their numbers were greatly diminished in many others. The populations of many marine fish had been immensely reduced, and the processes of agriculture and industry were fatally destructive to fresh water species. Marsh declared that:

The restoration of the primitive abundance of salt and fresh water fish, is one of the greatest material benefits that, with our present physical resources, governments can hope to confer upon their subjects. The rivers, lakes, and sea coasts once restocked, and protected by law from exhaustion by taking fish at improper seasons, by destructive methods, and in extravagant quantities, would continue indefinitely to furnish a very large supply of most healthful food, which, unlike all domestic and agricultural products, would spontaneously renew itself and cost nothing but the taking.[29]

Marsh also reviewed a variety of water projects undertaken in European countries that had caused significant geographical modifications; projects such as dikes to prevent tidal or river inundations or to gain new land area, the draining of lakes and marshes, aqueducts, canals, and reservoirs. He discussed the intended benefits of these as well as the unintended side effects, covering many of the factors common in environmental impact statements today. He also speculated on the possible climatological and ecological effects of major projects that were in progress or had been proposed, such as the Suez Canal, a canal across Central America, changing the course of the Nile, draining the Zuider Zee, as well as others.

A major focus of Marsh's book is the issue of deforestation. He had watched the process of deforestation and its many adverse side effects in his home state, and his European travels and studies convinced him that it was a subject of overwhelming importance. Many areas in Europe revealed the devastating effects of deforestation, particularly in France and Italy, where a literature had already been established on the subject and government programs attempting to rectify the problems were underway.

Forests not only supply wood, they also protect soil and regulate the flow of groundwater, preserving perennial rivers and springs and reducing floods, soil erosion, and siltation of navigable rivers:

When the forest is gone, the great reservoir of moisture stored up in its vegetable mould is evaporated, and returns only in deluges of rain to wash away the parched dust into which the mould has been converted. The well-wooded and humid hills are turned to ridges of dry rock, which encumbers the low grounds and chokes the watercourses with its debris, and—except in countries favored with an equable distribution of rain through the seasons, and a moderate and regular inclination of surface—the whole earth, until rescued by human art from physical degradation to which it tends, becomes an assemblage of bald mountains, of barren, turfless hills, and of swampy and malarious plains. There are parts of Asia Minor, of Northern Africa, of Greece, and even of Alpine Europe, where the operation of causes set in action by man has brought the face of the earth to a desolation almost as complete as that of the moon . . .[30]

The problems in America were mild by comparison; the pattern was the same but in an earlier stage of progression. Woods were cleared to create farms. Trees were cut for lumber and fuel without replacement. Springs were drying up. Floods were becoming more frequent.

How could the deforestation be halted? There was no clear solution; Marsh dismissed simple legal prohibitions and seemed to waver between government ownership and enlightened self-interest. Authorities in France agreed that the best solution to their problem was government ownership, but as to the likely effectiveness of this solution in America, Marsh was not without reservations:

It is vain to expect that legislation can do anything effectual to arrest the progress of the evil in those countries, except so far as the state is still the proprietor of extensive forests. Woodlands which have passed into private hands will everywhere be managed; in spite of legal restrictions, upon the same economical principles as other possessions, and every proprietor will, as a general rule, fell his woods, unless he believes that it will be for his pecuniary interest to preserve them.[31]

It is a great misfortune to the American Union that State Governments have so generally disposed of their original domain to private citizens. It is true that public property is not sufficiently respected in the United States; and it is also true that, within the memory of almost every man of mature age, timber was of so little value in that country, that the owners of private woodlands submitted, almost without complaint, to what would be regarded elsewhere as very aggravated trespasses upon them. Under such circumstances, it is difficult to protect the forest, whether it belong to the state or to individuals. . . .

For the prevention of the evils upon which I have so long dwelt, the American people must look to the diffusion of general intelligence on this subject, and to enlightened self interest, for which they are remarkable, not to the action of their local or general legislatures.[32]

But preserving forests was not everywhere sufficient; in some areas reforestation was necessary. And if the concept of enlightened self-interest had to be stretched to halt deforestation, it would have to be redefined to accomplish reforestation.

The growth of arboreal vegetation is so slow that, though he who buries an acorn may hope to see it shoot up to a miniature resemblance of the majestic tree which shall shade his remote descendants, yet the longest life hardly embraces the seedtime and the harvest of a forest. The planter of a wood must be actuated by higher motives than those of an investment the profits of which consist in direct pecuniary gain to himself or even to his posterity; . . . no generations have ever sown so liberally, and, in their own persons, reaped so scanty a return, as the pioneers of Anglo-American social life. We can repay our debt to our noble forefathers only by a like magnanimity, by a like self-forgetting care for the moral and material interests of our own posterity.[33]

Marsh concluded that a sort of standard in the form of a land ratio should be established:

It is time for some abatement in the restless love of change which characterizes us, and makes us almost a nomad rather than a sedentary people. We have now felled forest enough everywhere, in many districts far too much. Let us restore this one element of material life to its normal proportions, and devise means for maintaining the permanence of its relations to the fields, the meadows, and the pastures, to the rain and the dews of heaven, to the springs and rivulets with which it waters the earth. The establishment of an approximately fixed ratio between the two most broadly characterized distinctions of rural surface—woodland and plough—would involve a certain persistence of character in all the branches of industry, . . . and would . . . help us to become, more emphatically, a well-ordered and stable commonwealth, and not less conspicuously, a people of progress.[34]

In the same year that *Man and Nature* first appeared, the U.S. congress granted Yosemite Valley to the State of California as a public park. Among those appointed to a state commission for managing the park was Frederick Law Olmsted. Olmsted, considered the first American landscape architect, had for seven years been occupied with the design and development of New York's Central Park. His careful study of the needs of big city residents for parks enabled him to offer remarkable insights into the benefits that Yosemite (and other areas of natural beauty) could confer on the people, and the management policies these implied. These are set out in his 1865 report prepared in the official capacity as a commissioner.[35]

Olmsted believed that scenic recreation is especially valuable in restoring and preserving mental health, and was concerned that the English experience of private parks would be repeated in the U.S. To him the provision of recreation opportunities by the government was the solution:

Men who are rich enough and who are sufficiently free from anxiety with regard to their wealth can and do provide places of this needed recreation for themselves. . . . There are in the islands of Great Britain and Ireland more than one thousand private parks and notable grounds devoted to luxury and recreation. . . . their only advantage to the commonwealth is obtained through the recreation they afford their owners . . . and these owners with their families number less than one in six thousand of the whole population. The enjoyment of the choicest natural scenes in the country and the means of recreation connected with them is thus a monopoly, in a very peculiar manner, of a very few, very rich people. The great mass of society, including those to whom it would be of the greatest benefit, is excluded from it. . . .

The establishment by government of great public grounds for the free enjoyment of the people under certain circumstances, is thus justified and enforced as a political duty.[36]

Olmstead concluded that the management policies for Yosemite Valley should be to preserve and maintain the natural scenery as exactly as possible for the enjoyment of all people, and that

. . . in permitting the sacrifice of anything that would be of the slightest value to future visitors to the convenience, bad taste, playfulness, carelessness, or wanton destruction of present visitors, we probably yield in each case the interest of uncounted millions to the selfishness of a few individuals. . . .

This duty of preservation is the first which falls upon the state under the Act of Congress, because the millions who are hereafter to benefit by the Act have the largest interest in it, and the largest interest should be the first and most strenuously guarded.[37]

The final selection on environmental values summarizes the views of many people who participated in the progressive conservation movement including Teddy Roosevelt, Gifford Pinchot, and W. M. McGee. It is a set of excerpts from the opening address by President Roosevelt to a 1908 White House Conference on Conservation.

With the rise of people from savagery to civilization, and with the consequent growth in the extent and variety of the needs of the average man, there comes a steadily increasing growth of the amount demanded by this average man from the actual resources of the country. And yet, rather curiously, at the same time that there comes that increase in what the average man demands from the resources, he is apt to grow to lose the sense of his dependence upon nature. He lives in big cities. He deals in industries that do not bring him in close touch with nature. He does not realize the demands he is making upon nature. . . .

. . . [T]he growth of this Nation by leaps and bounds makes one of the most striking and important chapters in the history of the world. Its growth has been due to the rapid development, and alas that it should be said! to the rapid destruction, of our natural resources. . . .

This nation began with the belief that its landed possessions were illimitable and capable of supporting all the people who might care to make our country their home; but already the limit of unsettled land is in sight, and indeed but little land fitted for agriculture now remains unoccupied save what can be reclaimed by irrigation and drainage—a subject with which this Conference is partly to deal. We began with an unapproached heritage of forests; more than half of the timber is gone. We began with coal fields more extensive than those of any other nation and with iron ores regarded as inexhaustible, and many experts now declare that the end of both iron and coal is in sight. . . .

. . . In the past we have admitted the right of the individual to injure the future of the Republic for his own present profit. In fact there has been a good deal of demand for unrestricted individualism, for the right of the individual to injure the future of all of us for his own temporary and imme- diate profit. The time has come for a change. As a people we have the right and duty, second to none other but the right and duty of obeying moral law, of requiring and doing justice, to protect ourselves and our children against wasteful development of our natural resources . . . [38]

The heritage of environmental thought in America is indeed magnificent. But the statements of environmental interest and concern shared a common fate: their calls for government action were ignored. Catlin's dream of a huge park at the foot of the Rockies was of course never more than that. And not until the final decade of the nineteenth century had any significant effort been made to heed Marsh's plea for forest preservation. Olmsted's proposed policy for managing Yosemite was ignored by California, and the issues he raised remain unresolved today in national park planning. And the progressive conservation movement apparently was too progressive, and died with Teddy Roosevelt's administration.

The following categories are a convenient summary of environmental values today:

1. *Preserve nature*

We should preserve rare and endangered species and their habitats; and protect areas of special ecological, geological, historical, scenic, and recreational significance. We should respect the functioning of ecological systems and the natural hazards to which man is exposed.

2. *Conserve resources*

We should confine resource use to the global steady-state level, by stabilizing populations, shifting to resource-conserving life styles, recycling recoverable resources, shifting energy use to renewable sources, and limiting our calculations of steady-state supplies to proven resources and technologies, not forecasted but uncertain discoveries and advancements.

3. *Control pollution*

We should eliminate damaging, hazardous and noxious pollution of air, water and land.

Many of the values currently articulated are still several steps ahead of public action, but, of course, great progress has been made in the adoption of environmental policies by governments.

For many people environmentalism has become a philosophy, and for some a personal philosophy of life. However, if too narrowly conceived, it tends to become a negative, life-denying conception of society and the world. It has a great deal to say about what we as individuals and society *should not* be doing, but little to say in a positive way about what we *should* be doing to advance the welfare of people.

4.3 HUMANISTIC VALUES

An overly narrow conception can be avoided by joining environmental with humanistic values. Humanist thought is rich with insights into the questions of human welfare, and is quite compatible with environmental views. An extensive discussion of humanistic values would not serve our present purpose, but it will be useful to summarize a few of the key values that apply to modern conditions:[39]

1. *People come first*
It is people that count, not things. A person should be judged by what he is and not what he has.

2. *Meeting basic needs*
All people should have the opportunity to provide themselves and their families with the material essentials of life, and be provided with health and educational services. Aid to the starving, ill and illiterate millions in the world is an essential, but only the first, step in helping all people to provide for themselves.

3. *Human development*
Human not economic development should be the goal. People should be encouraged and provided with the opportunities to develop all of their human capacities and potentials; to think and to feel; to be competent in managing their own affairs and in meeting their responsibilities to others; to develop their interests in arts, crafts, music, creative writing, intellectual pursuits, exploration, and so forth; to be self-reliant and self-confident; and to help other people develop their human potentials. Meaningful work can be essential to one's purpose in life, not only by providing an opportunity for creative expression, but as a way of serving other people; therefore, jobs should be designed to give full expression to these qualities.

4. *Cooperation*
Personal relations should be marked by honesty, sincerity, openness, and helpfulness. Cooperation rather than competition should prevail in community relations.

5. *Decentralization*
Large scale, centralized organizations—in business, labor, government and human settlement—are seen as alienating and destructive of individual initiative, creativity, self-reliance, and self-respect. Decentralization is seen as an important aid to overcoming these problems and serving the goal of human development.

6. *Optimism*
Humanism is optimistic about human nature and the future. It believes that the moral impulse to do good is in each person and will become a guiding force in his life where conditions are right. The evil acts of people are seen as manifestations of ill treatment. Attention to the development of each person

is supported by the confidence that not selfishness but service to others lies at the highest rungs of the human development ladder.

The nonmaterialistic orientation of humanistic values makes them particularly compatible with environmental values. Clearly, if people spent more time developing their creative potentials and participating in community affairs, and spent less time working for and consuming unessential material goods, more nature would be preserved, fewer resources consumed, and less pollution generated. The harmony between the two sets of values can be seen in many ways. It can be seen in the thoughts and lives of certain people. The philosophy of Emerson is a happy combination of the love for people and the love for nature. The life of Albert Schweitzer exemplifies the deepest devotion to these feelings. His concept of "reverence for life" (for human life and all other forms of life), which he advanced as the underlying moral principle unifying all life-affirming philosophies and religions, would be a fitting label for the merger of environmental and humanistic values.[40]

The life and philosophy of Mohandas Gandhi illustrate the highest observance of reverence for life. He was a strict vegetarian, because he abhorred the maltreatment and killing of animals for food, and he swore off all but a minimum of personal possessions. His campaign to re-establish cottage industries in India was a move to return self-reliance and self-respect to his people. Gandhi's complete devotion to helping downtrodden people and uprooting injustice has few comparisons in history.[41]

The harmony between the two sets of values is also revealed by what appears to be a significant trend of the past several years in their merger. This can be found, for example, in Schumacher's remarkable book, *Small Is Beautiful*,[42] and in his work to revive Gandhi's cottage industry ideas in the name of "intermediate" (or "appropriate") technology. It can be found in Rene Dubos's *So Human an Animal*.[43] More importantly, it is seen in the emergence of new life styles, in the back-to-the-land, family farm movement,[44] and in the proliferation of "intentional communities" in rural areas;[45] it is seen in neighborhood and community development programs,[46] and in the revival of the co-op movement.[47] In each of these cases a combination of environmental and humanistic values are consciously being used to guide the formation of new life styles and new community relations.

This newly emerging pattern of thought and action offers sophisticated views on the determinants of social welfare, quite distinct from those of conventional economic thought, which is reviewed in a subsequent chapter. It suggests a very different concept of progress that helps explain why many people today are casting their votes against the continuation of undifferentiated economic development.

4.4 IMPLICATIONS FOR EVALUATION

The implications of the foregoing for evaluation are far-reaching, going way beyond any summary that might be provided here. Nevertheless it will be helpful to list briefly a few of the specific points that will recur in future chapters at the expense of being anti-climactic.

1. *Intangibles*
It is well recognized that certain environmental and social impacts such as aesthetics and the sense of community are intangibles, that is, difficult to express in quantitative terms. The importance of giving adequate representation to intangibles alongside quantified impacts should go without saying.
2. *The qualitative character of values*
Separate from the issue of intangible impacts is the fact that many values have a qualitative character going well beyond a simple feeling of importance. Certain environmental values, for example, express deep moral feelings, religious views, and philosophies of life that cannot be conveyed in numerical ratings. Evaluations should be capable of giving full expression to these values.
3. *Future generations*
A common characteristic of many environmental values is the interest, and, indeed, the perceived ethical obligation to preserve nature and conserve resources for the benefit of future generations. In their treatment of time, evaluation methods must be capable of respecting this view.

4.5 BIBLIOGRAPHY ON ENVIRONMENTAL VALUES

Atkinson, Brooks, (ed.). *The Selected Writings of Ralph Waldo Emerson.* New York: The Modern Library, 1940.

Boulding, Kenneth. "The Economics of the Coming Spaceship Earth." In *Environmental Quality in a Growing Economy.* Edited by Henry Jarrett. Baltimore, Md.: Johns Hopkins University Press, 1966.

Carson, Rachel. *Silent Spring*. Boston: Houghton Mifflin, 1962.

Carter, Vernon Gill, and Tom Dale. *Topsoil and Civilization*. Norman, Okla.: University of Oklahoma, 1955.

Catlin, George, *Letters and Notes on the Manners, Customs, and Conditions of North American Indians*. New York: Dover, 1973, in two volumes.

Commoner, Barry. *The Closing Circle*. New York: Alfred A. Knopf, 1971.

Darling, F. F., and J. Milton (eds.). *Future Environments of North America*. New York: Natural History Press, 1966.

Dasmann, Raymond. *The Destruction of California*. New York: Collier, 1966.

Dubos, Rene. *So Human An Animal*. Boston: Charles Scribner, 1968.

Ehrlich, Paul. *The Population Bomb*. New York: Ballantine, 1968.

Hardin, Garrett. "The Tragedy of the Commons." *Science,* vol. 162 (December 13, 1968), pp. 1243–1248.

Lappe, Francis Moore. *Diet for a Small Planet*. New York: Ballantine, 1971.

Leopold, Aldo. *A Sand County Almanac*. New York: Oxford University Press, 1949.

March, George Perkins. *Man and Nature*. Edited by David Lowenthal. Cambridge, Mass.: Belknap Press of Harvard University Press, 1964.

Muir, John. *Our National Parks*. Boston: Houghton Mifflin, 1901.

Muir, John. *Steep Trails*. Boston: Houghton Mifflin, 1901.

Nash, Roderick. *Wilderness and the American Mind*. New York: Yale University Press, 1967.

Nash, Roderick, (ed.). *The American Environment*. Reading, Mass.: Addison-Wesley, 1976.

Olmsted, Frederick Law. "The Yosemite Valley and the Mariposa Big Trees," *Landscape Architecture,* vol. 43 (October 1952), pp. 12–25.

Osborn, Fairfield. *Our Plundered Planet*. New York: Little, Brown, 1949.

Pinchot, Gifford. *Breaking New Ground*. New York: Harcourt, Brace, and World, 1947.

Stone, Christopher D. *Should Trees Have Standing?* Los Altos, Calif.: William Kaufmann, 1974.

Thomas, W. L., Jr., (ed.). *Man's Role in Changing the Face of the Earth.* Chicago: University of Chicago, 1956.

Thoreau, Henry David. *Walden.* New York: Thomas Crowell, 1961.

Torrey, Bradford, and Francis H. Allan (eds.). *The Journal of Henry D. Thoreau.* Boston: Houghton Mifflin, 1906.

Udall, Stewart L. *The Quiet Crisis.* New York: Holt, Rinehart and Winston, 1963.

White, Lynn, Jr. "The Historical Roots of Our Ecological Crisis." *Science,* vol. 155 (March 10, 1967), pp. 1203–1207.

White, William H. *The Last Landscape.* New York: Doubleday, 1968.

4.6 BIBLIOGRAPHY ON HUMANISTIC VALUES

Atkinson, Brooks, (ed.). *The Selected Writings of Ralph Waldo Emerson.* New York: The Modern Library, 1940.

Dewey, John, and James H. Tufts. *Ethics.* New York: Henry Holt, 1932.

Fisher, Louis. *The Life of Mahatma Gandhi.* New York: Harper and Brothers, 1950.

Fromm, Eric. *The Sane Society.* New York: Holt, Rinehart and Winston, 1955.

Fromm, Eric. *The Art of Loving.* New York: Harper and Row, 1956.

Gandhi, Mohandas K. *An Autobiography: The Story of My Experiments with Truth.* Boston: Beacon Press, 1957.

Maslow, A. H. *Motivation and Personality.* New York: Harper and Row, 1954.

Melville, Keith. *Communes in the Counter Culture.* New York: William Morrow, 1972.

Mumford, Lewis. *The Conduct of Life.* New York: Harcourt, Brace, 1951.

Mumford, Lewis. *The City in History.* New York: Harcourt, Brace, 1961.

Nearing, Helen, and Scott. *Living the Good Life.* New York: Schocken Books, 1970.

Rogers, Carl. *On Becoming a Person.* Boston: Houghton Mifflin, 1961.

Schumacher, E. F. *Small is Beautiful.* New York: Harper and Row, 1975.

Schweitzer, Albert. *Out of My Life and Thought.* New York: Henry Holt, 1949.

Schweitzer, Albert. *The Philosophy of Civilization.* New York: Macmillan, 1950.

Thoreau, Henry David. *Walden.* New York: Thomas Crowell, 1961.

Tolstoy, Leo. *My Confessions and Critique of Dogmatic Theology.* In *The Complete Works of Count Tolstoy,* vol. 13. Translated by Leo Wiener. Boston: Dana Estes, 1904.

Tolstoy, Leo. *The Kingdom of God is Within You.* Translated by Leo Wiener. Boston: Dana Estes, 1905.

II
EVALUATION METHODS AND PROCESSES

5

INTRODUCTION TO EVALUATION METHODS

5.1 INTRODUCTION

Part II marks a major shift in the character of the discussion from general to specific. The discussion of human values, democratic philosophy, and environmental values covers background considerations not traditionally included in the evaluation literature. Its purpose, of course, is to help establish a broader philosophy of evaluation, getting away from the view of planning as a purely technical exercise, and to develop broader criteria for assessing evaluation methods and designing evaluation processes. But the wide ranging discussion cannot be maintained. The methods are quite technical, so descriptions and critiques of them are necessarily more detailed and intensive. This chapter discusses some of the basic characteristics of systematic methods and the context in which they are applied. Several specific methods are discussed in subsequent chapters.

Most proposed public actions are complex, entailing many potential consequences of interest and concern to the public. To understand their possible implications as a whole is very difficult, and therefore a systematic evaluation of them proceeds, analytically, by dividing the whole into parts, or impacts.

The number of separate impacts to be identified in an evaluation can be quite large. To gain a quick visual impression of the quantity of information that might be generated by an impact analysis, consider the table, or matrix, shown in figure 5.1. Various beneficial and adverse impacts are listed separately, and these are further subdivided according to the time periods in which they occur and the people or interest groups on which they fall. If impact information were organized in a table such as this, a separate table of information would be needed for each option being evaluated. Considering the potentially large number of impact types, time periods, people or interest groups, and alternatives, the number of bits of information can be sizable. The quantity of impact information can also be judged by reference to checklists that have been prepared for guiding impact analyses. For example, the Leopold Matrix has 8,330 distinct impact items recommended for consideration in preparing environmental impact statements.[1] If only 2 percent of these were applicable in a particular situation, the impact analysis would cover over 160 environmental items, to which must be added the many social, economic, and political impacts not included.

Clearly, when information on a proposed public action is as detailed as

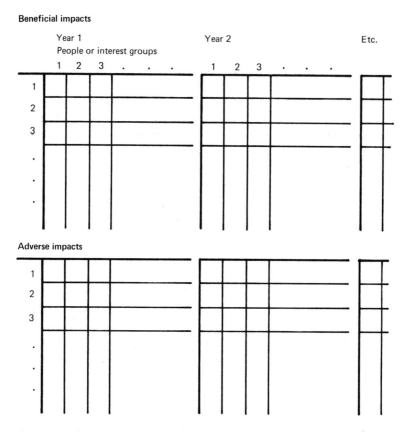

Figure 5.1
Table of disaggregated impacts

this, decision-makers are able to gain keen insights into its advantages and disadvantages. However, it is also evident that to form a judgment on the desirability of a proposed action, decision-makers and citizens face a difficult task of acquiring a holistic view from the many component pieces.

This poses what I refer to as "the evaluation dilemma": to understand the implications of a proposed action it is very useful to divide the impacts into many component parts, but to arrive at a judgment about its desirability it is necessary in some way to reassemble or synthesize the parts into an understandable whole. To eliminate the analytical step of detailing the impacts is obviously unacceptable. Thus the solution must be focused on some means of synthesis. The common way people solve this kind of problem is the informal approach of devoting whatever time is necessary to study the parts and relying on the mind to form a holistic impression. In earlier decades decision-makers often could devote a fair amount of time to reviewing each societal issue, so this approach, augmented by discussion and debate, was used almost exclusively (although the availability of information on impacts was far from ideal). But as the number and complexity of issues has grown, the time allotted to each has greatly diminished, and pressure has mounted for establishing time-saving evaluation aids.

Mathematically the ideal solution to the dilemma is to devise a formula or equation that can summarize all the impacts in a single score or grand index to which a simple criterion can be applied for accepting or rejecting the proposal. If the score for beneficial impacts exceeds that for adverse impacts, the grand index is positive, indicating that the action should be supported; if the grand index is negative, it should not. Many evaluation methods attempt to meet this presumed ideal.

5.2 TRADE-OFFS AND COMMENSURATE UNITS

The notion of trade-offs is fundamental to evaluation. When comparing two alternatives, almost always we find that each has certain advantages over the other: by selecting one, we gain the advantages it provides but forgo the advantages of the other. The beneficial and adverse impacts of alternatives reveal the trade-offs that are made, implicitly if not explicitly, in the selection process.

When the various impacts are described in different terms, the personal process of assessing the trade-offs can be difficult if not frustrating. To the extent that they can be described in similar terms, and especially in the same measurement units (that is, in commensurate units), the comparison of trade-offs is greatly facilitated. The grand index methods of evaluation represent attempts to convert impacts into identical units, so they can all be added into a single score.

Some people, especially those with a strong quantitative orientation, seem to assume that it is impossible to assess trade-offs that are not described in commensurate units. Actually, it *is* impossible, if one assumes the analysis must be confined to the scientific realm of objective proof. But the evaluation of public actions inevitably embodies the subjective realm of human values. It requires judgments of the relative importance, of competing values, of the interests of various people differentially affected by the action, and of the contrasts between immediate impacts and long-term consequences. These judgments might be converted into quantitative expressions, but numbers do not make them objective, for there is no way of proving that one person's numbers are better or more accurate than another's.

Perhaps the quantification of values satisfies the mathematical tendency in us to come up with a precise answer, but clearly it neither makes a judgment more accurate nor more objective. On the other hand, a number scale can be a useful way to summarize a person's feelings of relative importance in a single indicator. No doubt there are people who employ some sort of numerical rating procedure as a personal aid when judging the pros and cons of complex issues. It is this function, as a potential aid in dealing with complex judgments, that quantified values should be seen as serving. Whether or not they are a useful aid in evaluating public actions is one of the key questions we will be considering as we review the methods that use them.

Another misleading assumption about trade-offs is the view, advanced by conventional economic thought, that everything is tradable—that a person will sacrifice anything if the price is right. This unfortunate idea comes from the economic theory of consumer and producer behavior that has clearly been overgeneralized. Certainly there are many people who live by personal, moral, and religious standards that are central to their existence and would not give them up for any price. However, the objects of these standards might be tradable in the context of public decision making, where some values are inevitably sacrificed in the process of serving others. Those whose absolute standards are violated by a public action are not only likely to be angered by the decision but also may totally fail to understand why seemingly meaningless values could take precedence over those that are central to their own view of the world. But such is the nature of human value systems. However, even in public decision making, some things are not tradable. Constitutional rights, for example, are inviolable within the time frame of most planning efforts.

5.3 CONVENTIONS

Certain assumptions or conventions are adopted in conducting evaluations, independent of the methodology that is used. The reference point and boundaries are common subjects of conventions; they should be made explicit but sometimes are only implicit in the way evaluations are conducted.

The reference point concerns the basis for describing impacts. An impact typically represents a comparison between two states. One state is the condition that results from implementing the subject action. The impact description compares this state to some reference point or state, which might be one of the following:

1. The original state existing before the action was taken, commonly referred to as the *baseline state.*
2. The state that would have evolved in the absence of the action. This is the conventional reference point.
3. Some goal or target state.
4. The ideal state.

To illustrate these, the unemployment effect of an action could compare the number of unemployed people estimated to exist following the implementation of an action to (1) the baseline number of people unemployed before the action, (2) the number who would have been unemployed in the absence of the action, (3) some target number of unemployed, or (4) some ideal level, such as zero, or the minimum level resulting from the normal process of switching jobs and occupations.

The conventional reference point—the state that would have existed without the action—is preferred because, when a proposed action is being reviewed, it is simpler merely to study its impacts (so measured or described) alone in order to form an accept-or-reject judgment. That is, with this reference point no comparison needs to be made between the impacts of the subject action and the no-action alternative to judge the acceptability of the action: the comparison between the two is automatically built into the impact measures.[2] Any reference point could be used, so long as it is understood that in order to judge properly the acceptability of an alternative, its impacts would have to be compared to those of no-action. When comparing two alternatives, however, the baseline state is sometimes preferred, because this is the state that people are most familiar with. But when a single alternative is being reviewed for its acceptability, the conventional reference point has the advantage that only one list of impacts rather than two need to be studied.

A second convention of most evaluations is the choice of boundaries for the study area, beyond which impacts are ignored. Whether desirable or not, it is common for the selected boundaries to correspond with the geographical boundaries of the government for which the evaluation is being prepared. Certainly evaluators cannot be expected to prepare global analyses; they aren't given the budgets to prepare them, even if they were feasible, and they have an obligation to address the interests of their clients. Nevertheless, it doesn't seem unreasonable to suggest that if major impacts are expected to occur beyond the boundaries of the chosen study area, these impacts should at least be mentioned in the evaluation report.

5.4 CRITERIA FOR ASSESSING EVALUATION METHODS

The selection or design of an evaluation procedure, itself, poses an evaluation problem for which impact categories, criteria, or goals should be identified. The review of methods in subsequent chapters does not attempt precise measurements, but judgments are formed on the following criteria as well as those established in previous chapters. The criteria are not to be taken as absolute directives but simply as guides.

1. *Systematic*
The method should be systematic so that the results are replecable. That is, it should be possible for different people to follow the procedures and obtain similar results.

2. *Simple*
The method should not be so complicated that only a few people are able to use it or understand the results.

3. *Quick*
People using the method should be able to generate answers within a reasonable length of time.

4. *Inexpensive*
The method should be capable of providing useful information on a reasonable evaluation budget.
5. *Legally acceptable*
The method should conform to the various legal and administrative requirements to which it is subject.
6. *Comprehensive*
The method should be capable of taking into account all of the factors relevant to the decision it is intended to aid.

5.5 SOME CHARACTERISTICS OF EVALUATION METHODS

The manner in which evaluation methods differ from each other can be understood in terms of their distinguishing characteristics. Some of the main characteristics are revealed by the way the following questions are answered:

1. What categories and descriptions are to be used for estimating and reporting the impacts?
2. How are the magnitudes of the impacts to be estimated?
3. How are the ratings, which indicate the relative importance of each impact, to be measured?

Impact Categories and Descriptions
A basic rule for selecting impact categories is that they should be mutually exclusive and exhaustive: in other words, they should not overlap one another (to avoid double counting), and they should cover all the important impacts. The availability of information limits the degree to which these conditions can be met.

In describing impacts, some methods—particularly those that make a special effort to include environmental considerations—focus attention on technical measures of means rather than of ends. Examples are the various measures of air and water pollution, soils, topography, geology, hydrology, and ecological conditions. The importance of these items cannot be judged independent of the ends to which they are linked. Certain experts who work regularly with technical information are knowledgeable about the means-end linkages and therefore are able to make the value judgments the average citizen and decision maker cannot. Nevertheless, some of these measures are the targets of government programs. And in the case of air and water pollution, federal and state standards can form the basis for feasibility tests in screening alternatives.

Nontechnical measures of ends can be used to promote the best possible understanding of the implications of a proposed action among decision-makers and the public. Yet calculating impacts in terms of ends is not always easy, and in some cases scientific knowledge is not ready for the task. Some evaluation methods use techical categories and measurements that are more accurately addressed by scientific procedures, whereas others attempt to describe all impacts as visible ends.

Estimating Impacts

Generally mathematical and statistical procedures represent the ideal approach for estimating the magnitudes of impacts. In some cases, expert judgment is used instead, due to (1) the absence of a scientifically validated procedure, (2) the lack of data needed to implement the procedure, or (3) the high cost of using the procedure. Expert judgment is being increasingly recognized as a reasonable and sometimes necessary approach for estimating objective information. People who have devoted much time to studying a system through which impacts are transmitted (such as ecological, social, or economic systems) can make reasonably accurate judgmental estimates of impacts.

Measuring Ratings

Several distinctions can be made among the different methods used for measuring rating. One is the source of the rating, which can be expert judgment, market prices, and a measurable physical characteristic. Another distinction is the measurement unit: money, points (or votes), and energy are the three most frequently used units. Points typically represent expert judgments obtained through questionnaires, interviews, or meetings. Monetary measures are commonly derived from prices in the marketplace, although citizen judgment is occasionally used. Energy is a measurable physical characteristic.

The final distinction regards the type of rating. The methods reviewed in subsequent chapters use one of the four types: (1) simple, (2) constant "value weight," (3) scaled value weight or (4) rescaled impacts. The hypothetical information on a water project in table 5.1 is used to illustrate their differences. In this fabricated case the rating total for adverse impacts exceeds that for beneficial impacts, suggesting that the proposed project would reduce the social welfare and therefore should be rejected. If the ratings had been determined by a simple rating method, a set of guidelines or standardized procedures would have been followed in assigning judgmental scores of importance to each estimated impact. Unless some standardized procedure is followed, the simple method has an arbitrary, unsystematic character. Thus different evaluators can derive entirely different results, and each might be suspected of biasing the results in favor of his own values.

The constant value weight is a rating that is applied to each unit of a given type of impact. The total rating for a given impact is calculated by multiplying the impact magnitude by the applicable value weight. For example, if the rating for water supply in table 5.1 had been derived by the use of a constant value weight, the value weight would have been 0.8 points per million gallons per day (MGD) of water, which is equal to 40 points (that is, 0.8 x 50 = 40). The quantity, 0.8, is a *constant* value weight, because it applies to each of the 50 MGD, not just some of them.

For reasons that will be given later, values are usually not constant or uniform for each increment of an impact, so *scaled* value weights are sometimes used to avoid the inaccuracy of constant weights. A scaled value weight is a series of value weights (mathematically, a function), each element of which applies to a different range of impact units. To illustrate, take the case of the water supply, again. A scaled value weight might be 1.2 points for each MGD of the first 10 MGD of water supply, 1.0 points each for the second 10, 0.8 points for the third, 0.6 points for the fourth and 0.4 points for the last 10 MGD. In this example the scaled value weights is stair-stepped; others are ramped (that is, graphically they form a smooth, continuous line).

When a panel of experts is asked to assign value weights, the use of scaled value weights greatly complicates the procedure and adds to the time of securing the judgments. A means for overcoming this problem without losing the advantage of a scaled value weight is to *rescale* the impacts so that each increment of impact is equally valued. With this accomplished, a constant value weight can be used, on which it is much easier to secure judgments. Again, using the water project example, the impacts could be rescaled

Table 5.1
Hypothetical evaluation of a water project

Beneficial impacts	Rating
Water supply:	
50 million gallons/day	40
Flood control:	
property damage savings; $200,000/year.	20
human lives saved; 1/year	20
imputed land rent from land opened to farming; $300,000/year.	30
Electricity supply:	
300,000,000 kilowatt-hours	20
Recreation on impounded lake:	
40,000 visitor days	3
Increase in aquatic habitat:	
100,000 fish	0.2
Total score for beneficial impacts:	133.2

Adverse impacts	
Resources utilized for construction:	
$10,000,000	120
Resources utilized for operation:	
$100,000/year	10
Loss of nutrient supply to farm land:	
100 tons/year	5
Loss of sand supply to beaches:	
20 tons/year	5
Loss of wild river recreation:	
1,000 visitor days	5
Loss of terrestrial habitat (submerged):	
1 bear, 50 deer, 1,000 rodents, 5,000 trees,	
500 acres of wildflowers	10
Total score for adverse impacts:	155
Index of public welfare contribution (the difference	
between scores for beneficial and adverse impacts):	−21.8

as follows: the first 10 MGD could be called 12, the second could be retained at 10, the third called 8, the fourth called 6 and the last 10 MGD of water supply could be called 4. It can be verified that, by applying a constant value weight of 10 points to these rescaled impacts, the result is identical to that for the scaled value weight for each 10-unit range of the impact. A mathematical description of these four types is provided in table 5.2.

The table 5.3 summarizes the characteristics of the evaluation methods that are described and critiqued in subsequent chapters: cost-benefit analysis, the planning balance sheet, the goals-achievement matrix, energy analysis, land-suitability analysis, the East Sussex landscape assessment procedure, the environmental evaluation system, and the judgmental impact matrix.

5.6 EVALUATION AS A PROCESS

In most situations today, evaluation is properly seen as a process that includes in-design and post-design assessments, as diagrammed in figure 5.2. Not many years ago, evaluations were conceived as strictly post-design studies. The designers and engineers developed a detailed plan for solving a problem; then the evaluators entered onto the scent to calculate the consequences of the plan so that an accept-or-reject decision could be made. Major redesigns of plans as a result of evaluations were commonly regarded as impractical because the plan itself represented a substantial investment of public funds.

Today, of course, the picture has changed. Plans that took years to develop are scrapped, new designs are developed from scratch, and occasionally projects are even halted during construction. In the words of some observers, projects used to be innocent until proven guilty; now they seem to be guilty until proven innocent.[3] The change in attitude has necessitated extending the formal evaluation process into the design phase of planning. It recognizes that designers make numerous informal evaluations in creating a detailed plan which in aggregate can be more significant to the outcome than the typical post-design evaluation.[4]

Fundamental to this new way of thinking is that a variety of potential planning solutions should be generated—perhaps in a sort of open brainstorming atmosphere—before any evaluation takes place. This early step in the design phase helps avoid the common impulse to latch on to the first

Table 5.2
Mathematical description of the four types of ratings

Simple rating:

$$r_1 + r_2 + \cdots + r_n,$$

Constant value weight:

$$w_1 I_1 + w_2 I_2 + \cdots + w_n I_n,$$

Scaled value weight:

$$\sum_{i=1}^{n} \sum_{j=1}^{m} w_{ij} I_{ij},$$

or

$$\int w_1 I_1 \, dI_1 + \cdots + \int w_n I_n \, dI_n,$$

Rescaled impact:

$$w_1 [S_1^{W*}(S_1^W)_1 - S_1^{R*}(S_1^R)] + \cdots + w_n [S_n^{W*}(S_n^W)_n - S_n^{R*}(S_n^R)_n]$$

where

r_i = rating assigned to impact i (beneficial impacts are assigned a positive r and adverse impacts a negative r),

I_i = the magnitude of impact i, defined as $S_i^W - S_i^R$,

S_i^W = the state of characteristic i *with* the implementation of the subject action,

S_i^R = the reference state for characteristic i,

w_i = the value weight assigned impact i (desirable impacts have a positive w and adverse impacts a negative w),

I_{ij} = the magnitude of impact i for increment j,

w_{ij} = the value weight assigned to the jth increment of impact i,

$S_i^*(S_i)_i$ = the state of characteristic i rescaled in units of S^* (a single function is used to transform all measures of characteristic i).

Table 5.3
Characteristics of evaluation methods

	Cost-benefit analysis	Planning balance sheet	Goals-achievement matrix	Energy analysis	Land suitability analysis	East Sussex landscape assessment	Environmental evaluation system	Judgmental input matrix
1. Type or measure:								
Technical					●	●	●	●
Nontechnical	●	●		●				●
Either			●					
2. Method of estimating impact:								
Scientific	●			●				
Judgmental						●		●
Either		●	●		●		●	
3. Determining of ratings:								
Source								
expert judgment		●			●	●	●	●
market prices	●	●						
physical characteristic				●				
not specified			●					
Measurement unit								
money	●	●						
points or votes			●		●	●	●	●
energy				●				
Type of rating								
simple					●	●		
constant value weight			●	●				●
scaled value weight	●	●						
rescaled impacts							●	

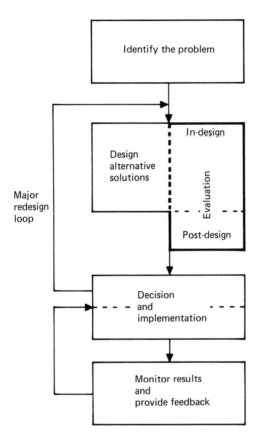

Figure 5.2
Evaluation in the planning process

seemingly agreeable idea and become close-minded about other possible solutions.

The initial list of options, which usually includes the no-action alternative, can be quite long, so the first step in the formal evaluation is to screen out all but the few ideas most likely to yield acceptable solutions. The no-action alternative is automatically passed through the screens. Two frequently used screening criteria are feasibility and effectiveness. How feasible is an idea in terms of absolute constraints such as legal requirements? Are the institutional and financial arrangements attending its implementation legally permissible? Will it pass air and water quality standards? Will it violate legally recognized property rights? These are the sorts of questions that are asked in testing the feasibility of alternatives. The evaluators will also want to determine how effective each alternative is likely to be in solving the subject problem. Naturally, when the initial list of alternatives is long, the amount of time that can be devoted to screening each idea will be quite limited, so evaluators must rely on judgments. Several of the methods presented in subsequent chapters are specifically intended to meet the needs, such as these, of in-design evaluation.

After the list of alternatives is narrowed down to one or a few design considerations, the post-design phase can begin. In this phase more careful attention can be given to the full range of potential impacts, and scientific procedures for estimating impacts can be utilized more fully.

5.7 A SELECT BIBLIOGRAPHY ON PLAN EVALUATION

Arnstein, Sherry R. "A Ladder of Citizen Participation." *Journal of the American Institute of Planners,* vol. 35 (January 1969), pp. 216–224.

Bishop, B. A. "An Approach to Evaluating Environmental, Social and Economic Factors in Water Resources Planning." *Water Resources Bulletin,* vol. 8 (1972), pp. 724–734.

Chapman, P. F. "Energy Costs: A Review of Methods." *Energy Policy,* vol. 2 (June 1974), pp. 91–103.

Dalkey, Norman C. *Studies in the Quality of Life.* Lexington, Mass.: D. C. Heath, 1972.

Dasgupta, Ajit K., and D. W. Pearce. *Cost-Benefit Analysis: Theory and Practice.* New York: Barnes and Noble, 1972.

Dee, Norbert, et al. "An Environmental Evaluation System for Water Resource Planning." *Water Resources Research,* vol. 9 (June 1973), pp. 523–535.

Dinius, S. H. "Social Accounting System for Evaluating Water Resources." *Water Resouces Research,* vol. 8 (October 1972), pp. 1159–1177.

Dorfman, R., (ed.). *Measuring the Benefits of Government Investments.* Washington, D.C.: Brookings Institution, 1965.

Fines, K. D. "Landscape Evaluation: A Research Project in East Sussex." *Regional Studies,* vol. 2 (September 1968), pp. 41–55.

Gilliland, Martha W. "Energy Analysis and Public Policy." *Science,* vol. 189 (September 26, 1975), pp. 1051–1056.

Hill, Morris. "A Goals-Achievement Matrix for Evaluating Alternative Plans." *Journal of the American Institute of Planners,* vol. 34 (1968), pp. 19–28.

Hill, Morris. "Planning for Multiple Objectives." Monograph Series Number 5. Philadelphia: Regional Science Research Institute, 1973.

Holmes, J. C. "An Ordinal Method of Evaluation." *Urban Studies,* vol. 9 (June 1973), pp. 179–191.

Hudson, Barclay M., Martin Wachs, and Joseph L. Schofer. "Local Impact Evaluation in the Design of Large-Scale Urban Systems." *Journal of the American Institute of Planners,* vol. 40 (July 1974), pp. 255–265.

Isard, Walter, et al. *Ecologic-Economic Analysis for Regional Development.* New York: The Free Press, 1972.

Klee, Albert J. "The Role of Decision Models in the Evaluation of Competing Environmental Health Alternatives." *Management Science,* vol. 18 (October 1971), pp. B52–B67.

Krutilla, John V., and Otto Eckstein. *Multiple Purpose River Development.* Baltimore, Md.: Johns Hopkins University Press, 1958.

Krutilla, John, and A. C. Fisher. *The Economics of Natural Environments.* Baltimore, Md.: Johns Hopkins University Press, 1975.

Leopold, L. B. "Quantitative Comparison of Some Aesthetic Factors Among Rivers." U.S. Geological Survey, Circular 670. Washington, D.C.: Government Printing Office, 1969.

Leopold, Luna, et al. "A Procedure for Evaluating Environmental Impacts." U.S. Geological Survey, Circular 645. Washington, D.C.: Government Printing Office, 1971.

Lichfield, Nathaniel. "Cost-Benefit Analysis in Town Planning: A Case Study of Cambridge." Cambridgeshire and Isle of Ely County Council, 1966.

Lichfield, Nathaniel, Peter Kettle, and Michael Whitbread. *Evaluation in the Planning Process.* Oxford: Pergamon Press, 1975.

McHarg, Ian. *Design with Nature.* New York: Natural History Press, 1969.

McKean, R. N. *Efficiency in Government through Systems Analysis.* New York: John Wiley and Sons, 1958.

Mishan, E. J. *Cost-Benefit Analysis.* New York: Praeger Publishers, 1976.

Moffit, Leonard. "Value Implications for Public Planning: Some Thoughts and Questions." *Journal of the American Institute of Planners,* vol. 41 (November 1975), pp. 397–405.

Nash, Christopher, David Pearce, and John Stanley. "Criteria for Evaluating Project Evaluation Techniques." *Journal of the American Institute of Planners,* vol. 41 (March 1975), pp. 83–89.

Peterson, George L., Robert S. Gemmell, and Joseph L. Schofer. "Assessment of Environmental Impacts: Multidisciplinary Judgments of Large-Scale Projects." *Ekistics,* vol. 37 (January 1974), pp. 23–30.

Prest, A. R., and R. Turvey. "Cost Benfit Analysis: A Survey." *The Economic Journal,* vol. 75 (December 1965), pp. 683–735.

Shafer, Edwood L., Jr., John F. Hamilton, Jr., and Elizabeth A. Schmidt. "Natural Landscape Preferences: A Predictive Model." *Journal of Leisure Research,* vol. 1 (Winter, 1969), pp. 1–19.

Steinitz, Carl, et al. "A Comparitive Study of Resource Analysis Methods." Department of Landscape Architiecture, Harvard University, Cambridge, Mass, 1969.

Suchman, Edward A. *Evaluative Research.* New York: Russell Sage Foundation, 1967.

Wachs, Martin, Barclay M. Hudson, and Joseph L. Schofer. "Integrating Localized and Systemwide Objectives in Transportation Planning." *Traffic Quarterly,* vol. 28 (April 1974), pp. 159–184.

Warner, Maurice L., and Edward H. Preston, "A Review of Enviromental Impact Assessment Methodologies." Prepared for the U.S. Environmental Protection Agency. Washington, D.C.: Government Printing Office, 1974.

Weiss, Carol H. (ed.) *Evaluating Action Programs.* Boston: Allyn and Bacon, Inc., 1972.

Wenger, Robert B., and Charles R. Rhyner. "Evaluation of Alternatives for Solid Waste Systems." *Journal of Environmental Systems,* vol. 2 (June 1972), pp. 89–108.

U.S. Water Resources Council. "Establishment of Principles and Standards for Planning Water and Related Land Resources." *Federal Register,* vol. 38 (September 10, 1973), pp. 24, 778–24, 869.

6

THEORY OF COST-BENEFIT ANALYSIS

6.1 INTRODUCTION

Cost-benefit analysis (CBA) is an evaluation methodology in which impacts are measured in nontechnical terms and estimated principally by scientific methods. Its most distinctive characteristic is that the ratings represent estimates of the monetary (or monetized) value of the impacts. It utilizes scaled value weights that are derived principally from market information on the expressed demand for goods and services.[1] The monetized value of a beneficial impact is called a "benefit" and the monetized value of an adverse impact is called a "cost." If the sum of the benefits exceeds the sum of the costs, it is presumed that the proposed action should be adopted, otherwise not. An advantage of CBA over other evaluation methodologies is that no additional analysis is required to derive ratings for some of the important adverse impacts because they are measured directly in dollar terms (that is, they involve dollar expenditures). Another advantage is that the dollar, as a unit of measure for ratings, is readily understood by everyone, rather than being a technical measure that only specialists can comprehend.

CBA is probably the most frequently used systematic evaluation method and clearly has the most fully developed theoretical foundation. Yet this foundation for the most part remains scattered throughout the welfare economic and microeconomic literature, and is written for an audience of advanced economists, so that it is virtually impossible for someone who has not studied economics to understand it. Thus it is very difficult for the vast majority of those who must make decisions on the basis of CBA to become familiar with the theoretical strengths and weaknesses of the methodology. The purpose of this and the following chapter is to provide a theoretical overview of CBA including its underlying assumptions, cast in the least technical manner.[2] Chapter 8 covers applications of CBA in monetizing various environmental impacts.

6.2 THE SOCIAL WELFARE FUNCTION

The theory of welfare economics suggests that the welfare of society depends on the well-being (or "utility") of the individuals in society. A common representation of this relationship, and one that CBA is based on, states that the social welfare *(SW)* is equal to the weighted sum of the utilities of all individuals. Mathematically this is expressed as

$$SW = w_1U_1 + w_2U_2 + \ldots + w_nU_n, \tag{1}$$

where

U_i = the utility of person i, which depends on the quantity and quality of goods he or she consumes during a given period of time (such as a year),

w_i = the weight attached to U_i, reflecting the relative importance of U_i in determining SW.

The typical evaluation problem seeks to estimate the change in social welfare resulting from a public action, so the following variation of equation (1) is more directly relevant for our purposes:

$$\triangle SW = w_1\triangle U_1 + w_2\triangle U_2 + \ldots + w_n\triangle U_n, \tag{2}$$

where

$\triangle SW$ = the change in social welfare brought about by some program or project,

$\triangle U_i$ = the change in utility of individual i resulting from some program or project.

In words, equation (2) states that the change in social welfare due to a public action is equal to the weighted sum of each person's change in utility due to the impacts of the action. To make use of this concept in the practical affairs of evaluation, methods must be available for measuring its two basic components: the utility changes and the weights.

6.3 THE MEASUREMENT OF UTILITY

For over a hundred years economists defined utility as a measure of individual well-being or happiness and assumed it could be quantified. The entire body of microeconomic theory rested on the uncomfortable assumption that happiness could be measured in "utils," until the late 1930s when Hicks[3] demonstrated that the theory did not depend on an absolute measure of utility but only a ranking.

Since no one was able to demonstrate that the intensity of utility was directly measurable, economists gladly switched to the less threatening assumption that utility could be ranked. The notion of utility as a measure of individual happiness or well-being was also abandoned and replaced by the testable notion of preference. Thus, according to the reformed definition of utility, a person's utility for items can be determined by simply having the person rank his preferences for them. For example, if good x is preferred over good y then, by definition, the utility of x exceeds the utility of y.

An important behavioral postulate regarding utility is the law of diminishing marginal utility, which states that the more a person has of something, the less he or she desires having an additional unit.

Although the change in the definition of utility strengthened the positive (or descriptive) theory of microeconomics, it served to highlight a major weakness in normative (or prescriptive) welfare economics. Indeed, if the social welfare function is to have any value for assessing public actions, utility must be quantifiable, directly or indirectly.

The concept of utility as a preference ranking poses another interesting problem for the normative application of welfare economics: namely, the translation between the concepts of individual preference and individual well-being. Assuming, as welfare theory does, that social welfare is determined by the *well-being* of individuals, then individual preference should be a good indicator of individual well-being; but is it? In other words, if a person prefers good x over good y, can we be certain that the well-being of the person is better served by x than by y?

There is no definitive scientific answer to this question. However, a basic value of democracy is the view that each person is the best judge of his or her own welfare, so it is assumed that preference and happiness are usually equivalent. Yet even in democratic societies, where the majority have the right to make their own decisions, certain groups are usually denied this right, such as children, the senile, and the mentally ill. Among individuals who have the right of self-determination, the equivalence between preferences and well-being is recognized to be imperfect. One reason for divergence is the lack of information regarding the personal consequences of some types of actions; that is, the lack of knowledge about certain means-ends linkages. Health decisions are a good example of this. We go to a doctor when faced with a major health problem because we do not have the specialized knowledge required to make important medical decisions on our own. We usually follow the doctor's advice because we are confident that the two of us have the same end in mind.

Decisions that have personal consequences for the distant future also seem to be problematical. It is observed, for example, that most people do not save a sufficient portion of their income in preparation for retirement. Hence social security programs have been adopted that in effect establish a minimum savings for use in old age. It is also believed that most people do not make wise decisions in situations involving a very low probability of a large loss. The decision to use an auto seat belt is an example. We frequently hear that the use of seat belts substantially reduces the likelihood of death in an accident, but only a fraction of the people make the small effort of buckling-in to reduce their chances of being killed. The decision to build a home in a flood plain or in the zone of an active earthquake fault provides another example. Thus in adopting the view that personal preferences are the best indicator of personal well-being, it is recognized that there are probably some exceptions to the rule.

An Attempted Direct Measure of Utility

Although the idea that utility could be measured in utils was eliminated from economic theory, several methods for direct measurement have nevertheless been attempted in recent decades. Perhaps the most interesting of these is the gaming approach of Von Neumann and Morganstern.[4] Using their approach, one can devise a relative scale of utilities for different items by posing a series of gaming choices to the person whose change in utility is being estimated.[5] The major theoretical criticism of the gaming method of measuring utility is that some people like to gamble. Thus, when given the option of selecting something with certainty or a game involving risk, the choice will be biased toward the game to the extent that the person enjoys taking a chance. A major obstacle for the practical use of the method is the large quantity of data it requires.

No method of directly measuring utility has been developed to the point of being operational for evaluation purposes, although research continues in this area and breakthroughs may be achieved eventually.

Willingness-to-Pay as an Indirect Measure of Utility

In order to apply the concept of a social welfare function in evaluations, some method of measuring utility, however indirect, is necessary. CBA uses the willingness-to-pay criterion as the basis for measuring both increases and decreases in utility, and the theory of welfare economics has been expanded to support this approach. The maximum willingness-to-pay to secure a desired change is a benefit; the maximum willingness-to-pay to avoid an undesired change is a cost. There are two general types of benefits: one, the subject of traditional economic theory, the other, of more recent concern. The traditional benefit is the *gain in something desired.* Examples in the fields of environmental quality and natural resources are water supply, recreation, energy, protection of landscape aesthetics, and preservation of wildlife. Theoretically, this type of benefit can be measured by reference to a demand curve, which identifies the maximum willingness-to-pay for various quantities of the subject good or service. The theoretical aspects of this method are discussed in the following section.

The second type of benefit is the *reduction in something not desired.* Examples are air pollution, water pollution, noise, and risks from natural hazards such as fires, floods, and earthquakes. The willingness-to-pay criterion applies in the measurement of these benefits also, but the method of implementing the criterion varies from case to case, and use of the demand curve is only one method. Examples of the methods that have been used in attempting to measure these benefits are described in chapter 8.

Analogous to the benefit side of the picture, there are two general types of costs: one, of traditional concern in economic theory, the other, of more recent concern. In traditional economic theory, cost is defined as *the lost opportunity for a benefit* and arises because economic resources, such as land, labor, and materials, used in a subject project could have been put to alternative uses which also would have generated benefits. This definition of cost may seem strange by comparison to the common-language definition of the term, but actually the two are closely related. As explained in a subsequent section, the willingness-to-pay for lost opportunities due to the use of economic resources in a particular project often can be measured by the dollar expenditure for acquiring these resources in the marketplace.

The second type of cost is the *increase in something not desired.*

Environmental examples are air pollution, water pollution, noise, and radiation hazards. The methods of measuring these costs are sometimes identical to those for the second type of benefit, which parallel these. The willingness-to-pay is the usual criterion for measurement, but, as discussed later, the willingness-to-accept-compensation sometimes is more appropriate.

6.4 THEORY OF MEASURING BENEFITS IN PERFECT MARKETS

The analyst typically tries to measure benefits using market information on the prices and quantities of goods and services to derive demand curves, which in effect are scaled value weights expressed in money units. Theory suggests that the accuracy of market information will depend on whether or not market conditions approximate the perfect market ideal.[6] Although the private market, in general, does not approximate the ideal, sometimes the analyst can draw information from specific sectors that do. Even if the information he obtains comes from highly imperfect markets, he may be forced to use it because it is all he has. Thus the theory on measuring benefits in perfect markets is the usual basis for benefit measurement.

The theory of consumer choice states that a consumer's utility will be maximized when the marginal utility (that is, the change in utility) derived from the last dollar spent on each good consumed is the same for all goods.[7] The logic behind this equality is that if the marginal utilities from the last dollar spent on each good were not the same, the person could increase his total utility by reducing his purchases of items for which the marginal utility (from the last dollar spent) is relatively low and increase his purchases of items for which it is high. These substitutions will be halted when equality is reached.

Another way of describing the same equilibrium condition is that the ratio of marginal utilities for different goods will be equal to the ratio of their respective prices.[8] This implies that the market price is a useful *relative* measure of the marginal utility derived from the last increment of a good. So, for example, if an individual buys and consumes 6 oranges in a month at a price of 10 cents each, then 10 cents is a relative measure of the marginal utility derived from the sixth orange. In CBA it would be referred to as the benefit of the sixth orange. If the same individual also purchases 4 apples at 5 cents each, then the theory indicates that he values the sixth orange twice as much as the fourth apple. Hence we can add the value of the sixth orange and the fourth apple by simply weighting each by its price. The total, 15 cents (1 X 10¢ + 1 X 5¢), is the benefit of the sixth orange plus the fourth apple. This is a simple illustration of how cost-benefit measures utility indirectly and uses the measures to add apples and oranges. In other words, it is a simple example of how cost-benefit analysis determines ratings for apples and oranges.

It cannot be stressed too strongly that the market price represents the maximum willingness-to-pay *only for the last unit consumed.* This can be understood graphically by reference to a demand curve. An individual demand curve traces a person's maximum willingness-to-pay for each unit of some object good or service for a specified period of time. A demand curve is usually downward sloping to the right, indicating that the more one has the less he is willing to pay for an additional unit. This follows, of course, from the law of diminishing marginal utility. An illustration of a demand curve for the oranges example cited above is shown in figure 6.1. Note that the willingness-to-pay is 30 cents for the first orange, and it tapers down to 10 cents for the sixth.

By definition there is no price discrimination in perfect markets; therefore everyone can buy an item for the same price. It follows then that, if the ratio of prices is equal to the ratio of marginal utilities for one person, as already established, it will be equal to the ratio of marginal utilities for all people.[9] However, this does not mean that prices are good relative measures of the marginal utilities of different people because the marginal utilities of some people for *all goods* may be higher than others. More will be said on this in a later section on equity.

The theory of benefit measurement discussed to this point has focused on the benefit of the last unit consumed. In general, it can be concluded that benefits representing small changes, relative to what people already have, can be approximated by multiplying the change in quantity by the market price (assuming one exists). This procedure, however, will yield gross underestimates if applied to relatively large changes.

The willingness-to-pay for large changes should be estimated by reference to the full sweep of the demand curve rather than to a single point on it. The benefit of a large change is represented by the area under the demand curve, bracketed by the quantity change. For example, in figure 6.1 the benefit of all 6 oranges in the previous illustration is measured by the area under the

Evaluation Methods and Processes

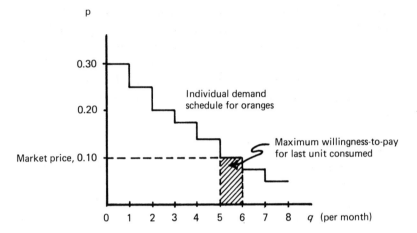

Figure 6.1
An individual's demand schedule for oranges illustrating the willingness-to-pay for the last orange consumed

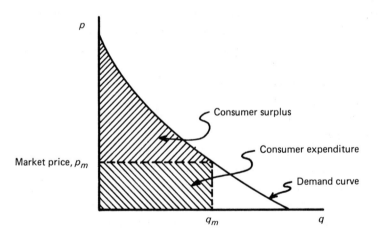

Figure 6.2
The areas under the demand curve representing consumer expenditure and consumer surplus

demand curve between the quantities 0 and 6. The logic of this relationship is best understood by examining the willingness-to-pay for each of the 6 oranges separately. The willingness-to-pay for the first is 30 cents, and the area under the demand curve between the quantities 0 and 1 is equal to 30 cents (that is, it is a rectangle with a height of 30 cents and a width of 1; 30¢ × 1 = 30¢). The willingness-to-pay for the second orange is 25 cents and the area under the demand curve between 1 and 2 is equal to 25 cents. Similarly, the willingness-to-pay for the third, fourth, fifth, and sixth is 20, 17, 14, and 10 cents, respectively. Thus the benefit of all 6 oranges is equal to $1.16, which corresponds to the area under the demand curve between 0 and 6.

Sometimes the area under the demand curve is called the "consumer benefit." It is useful to distinguish between two components of consumer benefit: consumer expenditure and consumer surplus. These are shown graphically as areas under a demand curve in figure 6.2 (It will be noted that the custom of drawing smooth rather than stair-stepped demand curves will be followed from this point forward.) The consumer expenditure, as the term suggests, measures the consumer's dollar outlay on the subject good (that is, the quantity, q_m, multiplied by the price, p_m). The consumer surplus is that portion of the consumer benefit that the consumer retains after paying for the good. One might think of it as the net benefit of the good to the consumer; it is the excess of the total benefit (or consumer benefit) over the total cost (or consumer expenditure). The existence of a consumer surplus is due to the fact that people are usually able to buy goods for less than they would be willing to pay if compelled to. Competition holds prices down, enabling buyers to retain their consumer surplus, but when a seller monopolizes a market he is able to extract at least some of this surplus from consumers by charging higher prices.

A few examples will help to clarify how the willingness-to-pay criterion can be used to measure the benefits of a proposed action. These examples make reference to market demand curves rather than individual demand curves, which have been the subject of the previous illustrations. A market demand curve is simply the total of all individual demand curves. It measures the total quantity of a particular good that would be purchased at each price *by all people* in the marketing territory. Alternatively, it can be described as showing the maximum willingness-to-pay for each unit offered the consuming public, without reference to who buys which unit.

The subject of the first example of measuring benefits is a project that reduces the cost of water for municipal supply, enabling the public water company to reduce the price and increase the quantity of water, as shown in figure 6.3a.

The annual benefits of water *without* the project are measured by the area under the demand curve between the quantities 0 and $q_{w/o}$; the annual benefits of water *with* the project are measured by the area under the demand curve between the quantities 0 and q_w. The benefits of the project are equal to the difference between the two, which is indicated by the shaded area in the figure. It can be noted that the smaller the change in price and quantity resulting from the project, the closer will $p_{w/o}$ reflect the benefit per unit of the additional quantity. This observation coincides with the previous point that the market price measures the benefit of the last unit, and justifies the use of the market price to evaluate small changes.

The second example is a project to develop and operate a new recreation facility that will be available to the public at no charge. The benefits of the project are measured by the total area under the demand curve in figure 6.3b.

The last example is the development of a new highway that reduces the travel time to an existing regional recreation facility. The benefits of recreation *without* the highway are measured by the area under the demand curve without the highway, shown in figure 6.3c; the benefits *with* the highway are measured by the area under the demand curve with the highway. The benefits of the highway are measured by the difference between the two areas, shown as the shaded area in the figure.

Some public actions create consumer benefits indirectly, by enhancing production opportunities. Examples include water projects that increase the supply of irrigation water and power plants that provide additional electricity to industry. The basic principle for measuring benefits described above applies to these cases also. The increased output of consumer goods (and services) attributable to the change in production opportunities is valued by reference to the market demand for the goods. If the change is comparatively small, the market price of the good can be used to approximate the consumer benefit. For example, if a water project provides additional water to farmers, enabling them to expand rice production, the value of the irrigation water can be approximated by the market value of the additional rice (less the extra production costs), provided the change in rice output is small compared to

Theory of Cost-Benefit Analysis

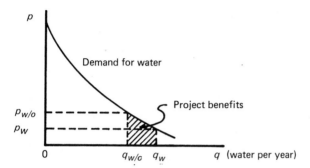

Figure 6.3a
Benefits of a project that reduces the price of water

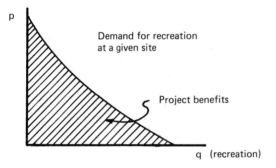

Figure 6.3b
Benefits of a project that provides a new recreation opportunity

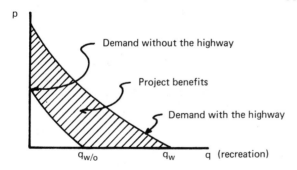

Figure 6.3c
Benefits of a project to construct a highway that would lead to an existing
recreation facility

the total market volume of rice. However, when the change is relatively large, the benefit is better measured by reference to the demand curve for the good.

6.5 THEORY OF MEASURING COSTS IN PERFECT MARKETS

All projects require the use of scarce resources which, if not used in the subject project, would yield benefits in alternative uses. The cost of these resources, sometimes referred to in economics as the "opportunity cost," is their value in the highest valued alternative use. Therefore the cost of a resource used in a project is the maximum willingness-to-pay for it in another use.

If the lost opportunities for the resource are concentrated in one or a few alternative uses, resulting in a large change, the cost of the resource should be measured by the reduction in the areas under the demand curves for the alternatives. If the lost opportunities for the resource are widely diffused among many alternative uses, resulting in very small changes for each use, then the cost of the resource can be closely approximated by its market price. For example, in evaluating a proposal for strip mining of coal, we may wish to establish the opportunity cost of the large quantity of water necessary for land reclamation. If the use of the water were to foreclose its use for only one alternative, say the municipal supply of a single city, the impact could be relatively large, as shown in figure 6.4a. In this case the market price, p_m, is well below the average value of the water withheld from the city (that is, the quantity between q_w and $q_{w/o}$). But if the use of the water for land reclamation foreclosed its use for four alternatives and is evenly spread among them, as shown in figure 6.4b, the market price for each use closely approximates the average value of the foregone water for each.

Estimating the cost in the case of large changes can pose serious operational problems of identifying alternative uses and estimating the demand curves for each. Fortunately, this is seldom required because most resources have many alternative uses. Therefore, even if a large quantity of a resource is used in a given project, the effect on each alternative is generally very small. Thus the opportunity cost of a resource can usually be measured by its price in the marketplace when conditions approximate perfect markets.

It is important to note that in some situations cost should be measured by the willingness-to-accept-compensation, rather than the willingness-to-pay.

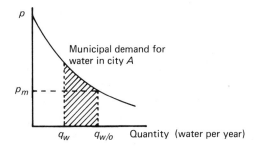

Figure 6.4a
The opportunity cost of water for one alternative

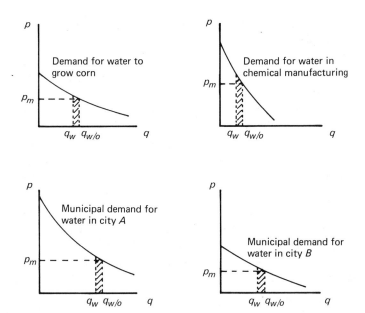

Figure 6.4b
The opportunity cost of water for four alternatives

This is proper whenever the cost is the loss of something *to which a person has a right.* For example, if a person has the right to freedom from excessive noise in his home, then the cost of excessive noise created by the operation of a nearby airport should be measured by his willingness-to-accept-compensation for it, not his willingness-to-pay. The difference is more than one of semantics, because the willingness-to-accept-compensation is usually larger, and may be a great deal larger, than the willingness-to-pay. To take an extreme example, Thoreau's willingness-to-pay for preventing the pollution of Walden Pond would have been very low because he lived on a very meagre income, but his willingness-to-accept-compensation for the pollution no doubt would have been infinitely high.[10]

6.6 SOME FINAL COMMENTS ON THE THEORY OF MEASURING BENEFITS AND COSTS

Only the bare bones of the theory of measuring benefits and costs have been presented. The theoretical literature on the subject is extensive, and there are many unresolved technical issues that serve to qualify a summary presentation such as the above.[11]

A basic premise to the theory is that market information used for computing costs and benefits is drawn from perfect markets, where sufficient competition prevails and externalities (or uncompensated spillovers) do not exist. To the extent monopolies and externalities prevail, market prices will be biased measures. In monopolistic markets, prices are excessively high; that is, they are higher than the opportunity cost of the resources used to make the products would justify. When an externality exists, such as the air pollution caused by paper mills, the market price, of paper for example, will be too low because it does not include the cost of the externality, such as the pollution imposed on people.

Since externalities are pervasive and competition is absent in many markets, the economist has little opportunity to obtain completely unbiased market data. Typically, the only reasonable option open to the analyst is to use market information as if it fit the ideal conditions. If adjustments can be made to correct the biases, all the better, but this is seldom attempted because often the magnitudes of the biases are not known.

6.7 TREATMENT OF EQUITY IN CBA

The concept of equity is concerned with the distribution of costs and benefits among the members of society. No universal definition of optimal equity exists, but the norm of equality is usually assumed to be a good guidepost. Because CBA uses dollars to measure benefits and costs, it is not surprising that these are totaled for groups of people rather than on a person-by-person basis. Thus the typical CBA study ignores equity considerations—a practice that is not supported by welfare economic theory but by a more practically oriented welfare criterion.

In terms of the social welfare function, the practice of CBA implies that all the weights in the equation should be set equal to one. On the surface this might seem very equitable because it gives equal weight to all people, but it must be tested against the fact that utility changes are being measured by the willingness-to-pay, which is greatly affected by the *ability* to pay. With weights set at one, and utility changes measured by the willingness-to-pay, the CBA version of the social welfare function could be described as a sort of "dollar democracy" in which each person's vote is weighted by his income. In pursuing the equity issue, we will begin by briefly reviewing the traditional views on the subject contained in the welfare economic literature.

The Traditional Economic View on the Treatment of Equity.
The proper measure for the weights in the social welfare function (that is, the w_i) has been long debated. Some political economists in the eighteenth and nineteenth centuries argued that the weights should be inversely proportional to income; in other words, the utility of a low-income person should be multiplied by a larger weight than the utility of a high-income person. This was usually justified on the grounds that the basic needs of the impoverished are more important than the frivolous desires of the wealthy. Thus it was frequently argued that social welfare could be increased by transferring money from the rich to the poor.

As the normative aspects of economic theory were weeded out during the current century in the interest of establishing economics as an objective science, the presumed measurability of the weights was not overlooked. It became apparent that in the absence of an acceptable method of measuring utility directly there was no way of *proving* that a dollar gives more utility to the poor than the rich. In the absence of any other means of determining the relative importance of each person to the social welfare, it was argued convincingly that the selection of the weights is subjective and not capable of objective verification. This remains the dominant view among welfare economists today.

But if the weights are unknown, can anything be salvaged from the social welfare function that is useful for evaluation? Pareto asked this question at the turn of this century and advanced what is now referred to as the "Pareto criterion" for judging an increase in social welfare. The criterion states that if some societal action (such as a project) makes nobody worse off and one or more people better off, then social welfare has increased. But, if even one person is made worse off, it cannot be asserted that an improvement in social welfare has occurred, *even if everyone else is made better off by the action.*

It can be noted that the Pareto criterion is akin to the unanimity role in voting—assuming that those who are unaffected by the change do not vote. In effect, the criterion gives veto power to every person in society. Clearly, the criterion is an extremely restrictive method of judging the desirability of a proposed public action: there probably has never been a public action that did not make someone worse off, and probably never will be.

It is important to note that the equity impacts of many proposed projects can be lightened by redesigning the project, changing the method of financing and providing for the compensation of easily identifiable losers. However, even the best designed program or project will inevitably make some people worse off. To eliminate all losers would probably involve costs (including those for identifying, quantifying, and administering the compensations) that exceed the project benefits.

Thus it would appear that the Pareto criterion provides no practical help to the public evaluator. Recognizing this, Kaldor and Hicks set aside their scientific hats, briefly, and advanced what is now referred to as the "potential Pareto criterion." Seeking to take a practical approach to the problem, it states that if an action generates sufficient benefits that the gainers can compensate the losers and still be better off, then social welfare is judged to increase *even if the compensation is not paid.* In effect, the criterion supports the conventional CBA procedure of aggregating dollars and ignoring equity impacts. It is interesting to note that when this criterion is applied to actions that have only monetary effects, it is equivalent to evaluating the action for its impact on the Gross National Product (GNP). If GNP goes up, then so does social welfare; if GNP goes down, then social welfare goes down. Indeed, most applications of CBA in the 1950s were couched in precisely these terms.

Economists have since abandoned reference to GNP in evaluations, recognizing the importance of the environmental, social, and other welfare factors that are not counted in it. Many, however, have not yet abandoned the position that the distribution of gains and losses is unimportant, although there is a trend now away from this view. Those maintaining the position usually argue that progressive income taxes can be used for redressing the equity problems caused by dollar-oriented public decisions. However, this argument suffers from several weaknesses. First, this author is not aware of a single case in which the income tax structure was altered to meet the inequities caused by a public action, or a group of public actions. Furthermore, tax relief to impoverished groups, who pay virtually no income tax, is meaningless. Also, tax relief is only a monetary compensation, but there are many things that money can't buy. For example, to the person who loses a job, is disabled, or becomes chronically ill as a result of a public action (or inaction), money cannot offset the suffering nor replace the lost sense of dignity and self-respect that comes from honest work to support one's self and one's family. Finally, the inequities of public actions that are not income related cannot be redressed at all by changes in income taxes.

Discussion of the Equity Issue

To people who are more sensitive to equity issues, the potential Pareto criterion is less than satisfactory, but few are willing to substitute the more restrictive Pareto criterion. It could be argued that the use of the Pareto criterion would eliminate any possibility of improvement in society, whereas the potential Pareto criterion represents a policy for long-term improvement. Indeed, this position is consistent with various points of law. For example, the law of nuisance protects people from the imposition of annoying noise, odors, dirt, and so forth, by others, and provides a mechanism whereby one can receive compensation for a nuisance loss. However, the law does not give people the right of absolute freedom from nuisances; only nuisances that are judged to be beyond reasonable bounds can serve as the basis for compensation. Accordingly, a certain amount of nuisance is deemed normal and acceptable in the progress of society.

The restrictiveness of the Pareto criterion can also be seen from another perspective. If it is applied at too small a scale of decision making, welfare may be reduced rather than increased. For example, it might be applied to the decision of whether or not to install an individual traffic signal. Because a traffic signal (and its enforcement) requires some people to stop so that others may go, it will not pass the Pareto criterion. Does this mean that traffic signals should not be installed and enforced? The answer, of course, is "not necessarily." The evaluation should also consider the system-wide effects of traffic signals on people over a period of time. While it is true that a person must stop periodically in a system even when there is no cross-traffic, as he passes through the system over time, he is usually made better off by the system rather than worse off.

In a similar manner a person may be made worse off by a particular public program, but, as he "passes through the system" of public programs, he may be made better off by the entire system rather than worse off. In a sense, a set of public programs that provide services to different groups of people serve to compensate the losers of one program with the services of another.

Viewed from this macro-perspective, the serious equity problem arises when biases in the selection, design, evaluation, and operation of programs cause some people to be consistent losers. Biases of this sort are likely to be present in conventional cost-benefit analysis because its criterion for value is the willingness-to-pay, which is greatly affected by the ability to pay. Thus conventional cost-benefit gives more attention to the values of the rich than of the poor. The possibility that some poor people may become consistent losers is particularly bothersome.

It will be recalled that these same issues were discussed in chapter 2, on the Philosophy of Democracy, although in different terms. The social contract theories of Locke and Rousseau suggested that man in the state of nature was better off joining a political society—*all things considered*—than remaining on his own. In the terms of the above argument, they suggested that man is better off joining the system than not. The problem of consistent losers is analogous to the problem of tyranny over the minority.

The view that the equity effects of a proposed action should be taken into account in conducting CBA has been gaining ground among economists in recent years. Several methods have been proposed for determining weights that would be applied to the costs and benefits received by people at different income levels. One of the most interesting of these methods is to determine the weights from the schedule of income tax rates by income level.[12] The basis for this approach is the notion that society takes a smaller percentage of the last dollar earned by the low-income person for taxes than the high-income person, because a dollar is judged to be more valuable to the low- than the high-income person. Accordingly, the tax rate schedule reflects society's judgment of the difference in the value of a dollar to people at different income levels. The weights can be calculated from tax tables by taking the inverse of the (marginal) tax rate. To give a simple illustration, if the tax rates for low-, middle-, and high-income groups were 0.2, 0.4, and 0.6, respectively, the weights would be 5 (i. e., 1/0.2), 2.5 (i. e., 1/0.4), and 1.67 (i. e., 1/0.6).

Another method for addressing equity impacts is simply to report separately the costs and benefits affecting different groups and leave the equity weighting to the judgment of the decision-makers.[13]

The resolution to the issue of equity treatment in CBA should not be addressed independent of many other issues that will be raised about CBA and other evaluation methodologies. Therefore the continuation of this discussion will be postponed to a later chapter.

6.8 BIBLIOGRAPHY OF COST-BENEFIT THEORY, PART I

Arrow, Kenneth J., and Tibor Scitovsky. *Readings in Welfare Economics,* Homewood, Ill.: Irwin, Inc., 1969.

Baumol, William J. *Welfare Economics and the Theory of the State.* Cambridge, Mass.: Harvard University Press, 1967.

Coase, Ronald H. "The Problem of Social Cost." *Journal of Law and Economics,* vol. 3 (October 1960), pp. 1–44.

Dasgupta, Ajit K., and D. W. Pearce. *Cost-Benefit Analysis: Theory and Practice.* New York: Barnes and Noble, 1972.

Freeman, A. Myrick, III, Robert H. Haveman, and Allen V. Kneese (eds.). *The Economics of Environmental Policy.* New York: John Wiley, 1973.

Friedman, Milton. *Price Theory*. Chicago: Aldine, 1962.

Graff, J. de V. *Theoretical Welfare Economics*. Cambridge, England: Cambridge University Press, 1957.

Hicks, J. R. *Value and Capital*. Oxford: Clarendon Press, 1939.

McKean, R. N. *Efficiency in Government through Systems Analysis*. New York: John Wiley and Sons, 1958.

Mishan, E. J. *Cost-Benefit Analysis*. New York: Praeger Publishers, 1976.

Myrdal, Gunnar. *The Political Element in the Development of Economic Theory*. Translated by Paul Streeten. New York: Simon and Schuster, 1969.

Pigou, A. C. *The Economics of Welfare*. London: Macmillan, 1924.

Prest, A. R., and R. Turvey. "Cost-Benefit Analyses: A Survey." *The Economic Journal*, vol. 75 (December 1965), pp. 683-735.

Scitovsky, Tibor. *Welfare and Competition*. Homewood, Ill.: Irwin Inc., 1971.

Stigler, George. *A Theory of Price*. New York: Macmillan, 1966.

Turvey, Ralph. "On Divergencies Between Social Cost and Private Cost." *Economica*, vol. 30 (August 1963), pp. 309-313.

7

MORE THEORY OF COST-BENEFIT ANALYSIS

7.1 TREATMENT OF TIME IN CBA

The common practice in CBA for adding the benefits and costs occurring in different years is to discount future quantities to their present value. The theoretical basis for the procedure is the fact that people are not willing to pay as much for something they are to receive at some future date than if they can have it immediately. Another way of describing this time preference is that people are willing to sacrifice gains in the future in order to receive more in the present. A common means of accomplishing this is to buy goods and services on credit. The fact that most people do not put their entire future in hock for present consumption indicates that the willingness to sacrifice the future is not unlimited. According to the theory, there exists a quantitative ratio between present and future gains to which a person is indifferent, and this ratio can be expressed by a rate of interest. Thus, if a person's rate of interest is 6 percent, he would be indifferent to receiving $100 today or $106 one year from today.[1]

It is usually presumed that the various points of indifference between present and future quantities can be represented by a compound interest equation:

$$V_t = V_0 (1 + r)^t,$$

where

V_t = value at the end of year t,
V_0 = present value,
r = rate of interest,
t = time in years.

These results are usually tabulated as shown in table 7.1: each quantity in the table represents an amount at the end of some future year which is equivalent to $10 today at a given rate of interest. For example, $10 today is equivalent to $17.91 in 10 years at 6 percent interest. This, in fact, is what it would accumulate to if left in a savings account for 10 years at 6 percent interest, compounded annually.

Table 7.1
Values at the end of year *t*, equivalent to $10 today at rate of interest *r*

Year (t)	Rate of interest (r)			
	4 percent	6 percent	8 percent	10 percent
1	10.40	10.60	10.80	11.00
5	12.17	13.38	14.69	16.11
10	14.80	17.91	21.59	25.94
15	18.01	23.97	31.72	41.77
20	21.91	32.07	46.61	67.28

Source: Samuel M. Selby (ed.), *Standard Mathematical Tables* (Cleveland, Ohio; The Chemical Rubber Co., 1971).

Table 7.2
Present value equivalent of $10 at the end of year *t*, using discount rate *r*

Year (t)	Discount rate (r)				
	4 percent	6 percent	8 percent	10 percent	12 percent
1	$9.62	9.43	9.26	9.09	8.93
5	8.22	7.47	6.81	6.21	5.67
10	6.76	5.58	4.63	3.86	3.22
15	5.55	4.17	3.15	2.39	1.83
20	4.56	3.12	2.15	1.49	1.04
50	1.41	0.54	0.21	0.09	0.03
100	0.20	0.03	0.004	0.0008	0.00009

Source: Harley H. Hinricks and Graeme M. Taylor, *Program Budgeting and Benefit-Cost Analysis* (Pacific Palisades, Calif.: Goodyear, 1969).

In order to provide present value information that is more useful for our analysis, the quantities can be transformed using the following rearranged equation:

$$V_0 = \frac{V_t}{(1 + r)^t} \ .$$

The transformed information shown in table 7.2 is obtained, indicating the present value equivalent of $10 at the end of certain years for a given interest rate. In this case the interest rate is called the "discount rate." For example, the discounted present value of $10 in 15 years, using an 8 percent discount rate, is $3.15. This is so because, if $3.15 were placed in a savings account at 8 percent interest, it would grow to $10 in 15 years.

Since benefits and costs occurring at different points in time are not equally valued, they are like apples and oranges, requiring some adjustment in their measurement before they can be added together. The usual adjustment procedure in CBA is to discount all future values to their present value equivalent, using a social discount rate. The adjusted values are added to arrive at the total present value of the stream of future values. Tables of discounted present values, such as table 7.2, are used for this purpose.

On the Selection of the Correct Social Rate of Discount
The mathematical equations and numerical tables give to the discounting procedure an aura of preciseness that it does not deserve. Actually, there is substantial disagreement among economists regarding the theoretically correct approach to measuring the social rate of discount. Some argue that the time preferences of consumers or taxpayers should be used. Others argue that a social time preference should be used, based upon the collective will of society to invest for the benefit of future generations. Still others argue that the social opportunity cost of capital should be used, based on what private enterprise is willing to pay for funds to expand future production.

The implications that these concepts have for the level of the social rate of discount varies widely. Rates from 4 to 12 percent are commonly encountered in the literature, and more widely divergent rates are occasionally advocated. It can be shown that a variation of only 2 or 3 percentage points can make the difference between accepting or rejecting many large-scale public projects.

The projects most sensitive to variations in the discount rate are those for which benefits and costs coincide least in time. The most common example is the project entailing heavy initial costs for constructing facilities that generate a steady stream of benefits over a long period of time.

A simplified example of a proposed hydroelectric project will help illustrate the effect of a small variation in the discount rate in such cases. Assume that a dam is proposed to be built at time zero at an estimated cost of $28 million and that the electricity benefits, beginning in year one and continuing for fifty years, are estimated at $2 million a year.[2] Now let's consider the present value of the costs and benefits using alternative discount rates of 6 and 8 percent. The present value of the costs are unchanged by discounting, because they are incurred initially. The present value of the benefits, at a 6 percent discount rate, is $31.5 million, and at 8 percent is $24.5 million. Thus at 6 percent the (present value of the) benefits exceed the (present value of the) costs, suggesting that the proposed project would increase social welfare and therefore should be accepted. However, using an 8 percent social rate of discount, the benefits fall short of the costs, suggesting that the project should be rejected.

The fact the costs and benefits of this proposed project do not coincide closely in time makes it quite vulnerable to variations in the discount rate, because the discounting process affects the costs and benefits disproportionately. Public policies, programs, and projects for which the costs and benefits coincide closely in time are much less sensitive to variations in the discount rate, and, in the extreme case of perfect coincidence, completely insensitive.

A range of uncertainty usually exists regarding the correct discount rate to use in a particular evaluation. This is due both to differences in the theoretically correct approach to its measurement and to the sampling errors that are inevitable in statistical estimation procedures. The method that some cost-benefit analysts have used for dealing with this range of uncertainty is to conduct a sensitivity testing[3] in which two or more alternative present value computations are made, each with a different assumption about the correct discount rate. In some cases sensitivity testing reveals that the outcome is unaffected within the range of uncertainty. For example, if it is decided that the appropriate discount rate for evaluating a particular proposed action lies somewhere between 5 and 8 percent, the use of each may reveal that in either case the proposal would be accepted (or rejected). Thus sensitivity testing can be a useful evaluation tool when uncertainty exists regarding the best quantity to use. Even if the results in a particular application reveal that the acceptance of a proposal importantly depends on the quantity used within the range of uncertainty, this, too, is important information; it can serve to (1) identify the need for further investigation to narrow the range of uncertainty, and (2) reveal to decision-makers the tenuousness of their choice.

Societal Implications of Alternative Discount Rates

The arguments among economists supporting and opposing the alternative approaches for determining the best social rate of discount are directed principally at the implications of lower-versus-higher rates for factors such as the efficiency of the national economy, the conservation of nonrenewable resources in short supply, the protection of the environment from irreversible impacts, and the equitable treatment of present and future generations.

The use of lower rates will increase the number of long-term, capital-intensive public projects. The major arguments in favor of this are (1) the present generation should invest more of its resources for the benefit of our children and theirs, and (2) the present generation should devote more of its resources to long-term programs and projects for protecting the natural environment and conserving natural resources.

On the other hand, the use of a higher social rate of discount will reduce the number of long-term, capital-intensive public projects and make more money available for private business investments and for short-term public programs. Some major arguments in support of this alternative (and in opposition to lower rates) are (1) higher rates will increase business investments that serve to expand the capacity for producing private goods and services that in aggregate are more highly valued (and therefore will make a greater contribution to the social welfare than the long-term public goods and services that would be sacrificed), (2) higher rates will make funds available to deal with the more immediate social problems that are urgently in need of attention, and are far more important than making long-term investments for the benefit of future generations (who, it is argued, will have a much higher per capita income than we and therefore will be quite able to take care of themselves without our help), and (3) higher rates will reduce the number of large-scale public projects destroying the natural environment, hastening the depletion of nonrenewable resources and foreclosing future options.

These arguments, which summarize the thoughts of several economists who have participated in the debate, are puzzling.[4] Some suggest that environmental protection and resource conservation are promoted by long-term projects, while others claim the exact opposite. The problem is that the arguments are overgeneralized. Some long-term projects tend to protect the environment, whereas others tend to damage it. Similarly, some long-term projects tend to be resource conserving, and others tend to be resource consuming. Thus the choice of the social discount rate has little effect on the desirability of project features.

The rate of discount is a mighty crude tool for achieving such goals as nature preservation, pollution control, resource conservation, and the alleviation of social problems. The best way to address them is to place high priority on plans and programs directed at them, rather than arguing about the correct discount rate.

On the Appropriateness of Time Discounting

More fundamental, though, is the issue of whether discounting is appropriate *at all*. It will be recalled that in chapter 4 the concern for the distant future appeared as a common thread running through many environmental values. And it was concluded, there, that evaluation methods should be capable of representing the interests of future generations. The question that must be raised, then, is whether the CBA practice of time discounting passes this criterion.

In the arguments over lower versus higher discount rates, there is the suggestion that lower rates give adequate weight to long-term considerations, but the meaning of long-term is not revealed. The distinction between short- and "long-term" in CBA typically applies only to a time period of roughly fifty years. If one defines a generation as covering, say, twenty-five years, the distinction concerns only the current and the next generation of people. Thus the "long-term" is not very long!

Cost-benefit evaluations seldom consider impacts beyond fifty years, because however large the impacts might be, once they are discounted to present value using even a comparatively low discount rate, they don't amount to much. For example the data in table 7.2 reveal that at the modest rate of 4 percent, a $10 benefit or cost occurring fifty years hence has a present value of only $1.41, and a $10 impact in 100 years has a present value of only 20 cents. At 10 percent, a rate much closer to current usage, $10 discounted fifty years equals 9 cents, and discounted 100 years amounts to less than one-tenth of a cent. It has been noted that at 10 percent, a time stream of one million dollars a year beginning in fifty-one years and *continuing each year to the end of time* has a total present value of only $185,000.[5] It is not surprising, then, that the common practice in CBA is to use a *cutoff point,* usually at around fifty years, beyond which *all impacts are totally ignored.*

Already, one conclusion seems inescapable: the practice of discounting third generation impacts and beyond (impacts beyond fifty years) is unacceptable. Ignoring the interests of people who will be alive fifty and one hundred years hence is not exactly showing concern for future generations.

Even the practice of discounting impacts on the next generation is questionable. To establish an order of magnitude in the matter, consider the following: at a 4 percent discount rate (the lowest that is seriously considered) $10 in 37½ years has a present value of only $2.30;[6] and at 10 percent, a much more realistic rate, the present value is only 28 cents. Is it unreasonable to conclude from this that discounting second generation impacts is also unacceptable?

Finally, we should address the appropriateness of discounting present generation impacts. The choice is not as clear in this case. Discounting does not reduce to insignificance the impacts occurring within twenty-five years. Also, the ethical problem of people not being able to represent their own interests is less severe. When the present generation makes a decision affecting future generations, only a small minority of the affected people are able to influence it. But when the current electorate makes a decision affecting people over the next twenty-five years, the great majority of those affected have an opportunity to participate in it. I conclude from this that no serious ethical problem arises when citizens choose to discount first generation impacts. But, summarizing the prior conclusions, it is not appropriate to compute the present value of impacts on future generations. These impacts deserve serious consideration, which is denied when they are discounted.

Alternatives to Conventional Time Discounting
The conclusion that has been reached, stated in other terms, is that the CBA practice of collapsing an entire time stream of benefits and costs into a single

index of monetized impacts, using a discount rate, is inappropriate. What is the alternative? Many can be devised. The essential ingredient is that impacts on future generations should be reported separately and remain undiscounted. Two alternatives satisfying this condition are the following:

1. Report the impacts in two distinct, nonoverlapping categories: the first representing impacts on the present generation; the second, impacts on future generations. The present generation impacts would be discounted and totaled; the future generation impacts would also be totaled but not discounted. It would be up to the decision-makers to weigh in their minds the relative importance of the two classes of impacts in making their selection.

This idea is analogous to the approach mentioned in the last chapter that some economists have suggested for dealing with the equity problem in CBA; that is, to report impacts on different income groups separately and not combine them in a single index, weighted or unweighted. Indeed, the similarity to the solution is not surprising. The discounting of distant impacts poses a kind of equity problem; it is an "inter-generational" equity problem not essentially different from the traditional equity concern is welfare economics.

2. A second alternative is to report the impacts in two distinct but overlapping categories: the first measuring the rate of return for all monetized impacts, present and future generations combined; the second representing the total undiscounted impacts on future generations. The rate of return, discussed more in the following section, is that particular discount rate which equates the present value of benefits to the present value of costs. If the time stream of costs is viewed as an investment and the benefits as the payoff, the rate of return measures the interest rate earned on the investment.

The great advantage of utilizing the rate-of-return calculation is that it avoids altogether the theoretically sticky and operationally time-consuming task of trying to estimate the social discount rate. The time stream of impacts is not discounted, it is simply used to compute the rate of earnings it implies. The computed rate can be compared to various market rates of interest in judging its magnitude.

Again, in reviewing the evaluative information thus organized, decision-makers would weigh the comparative importance of the two classes of information in reaching their decision.

No single method is advocated here for solving the discounting problem. Indeed, the appropriate approach is probably better decided for each particular case rather than in general. But the conclusion bears repeating: the consequences of present actions for future generations are too important to be hidden behind mathematical calculations containing a fundamental ethical flaw; they should be brought out into the light of day and addressed directly.

7.2 TREATMENT OF RISK AND UNCERTAINTY IN CBA

Sometimes an impact and its monetary value cannot be stated with certainty, because its magnitude depends upon the occurance of events that cannot be predicted precisely. When the probability of such events occurring can be estimated, it is referred to as a "risk" situation; when the probability cannot be estimated, it is referred to as an "uncertain" situation. A formal method exists for treating risk in CBA, but not uncertainty.

A good example of a risk situation is a natural hazard that threatens damages. Some types of government actions are explicitly designed to reduce such damages. Examples are flood control projects, and various policies that serve to limit or exclude urban development from potential slide areas, earthquake zones, and flood plains. In each case an important benefit of the action is the reduced damages that it secures. The standard CBA approach to evaluating this type of action is to estimate the benefits (as well as the costs) for each year during the duration of the action, and then to discount them to their present value. The problem of estimating the reduction in damages in a given year is that the occurrence of the event is not known. However, if the probability of the event can be estimated, the "expected damages" can be estimated, with and without the public action. The difference between the two values represents the annual benefits of the action. The expectation is calculated with the following equation:

$$E(X) = \sum_i X_i p(X_i),$$

where

$E(X)$ = the expectation of X,
X_i = the outcome of (for example, the damage caused by) event i,
$p(X_i)$ = the probability that i will occur.

Most people, whether or not they realize it, use this formula, or some variant of it, when playing games of chance. For example, if someone offered to enter a coin-flipping game with you in which he would pay you $1 for a head and take $1 from you for a tail, you would consider this a fair offer, because on average you should break-even, or in terms of the present discussion the expectation of each flip of the coin is zero. On the other hand, if he offered to pay you $1 for each head and take $3 from you for each tail, you would not consider it a fair offer, because on average you would stand to lose $2 (that is, $3 less $1) for each pair of heads and tails. In this case the expectation of each coin flip is minus $1.

To give a simple illustration of the use of the expectation equation, this last case will be used. The information is tabulated in table 7.3. The events (i) are heads and tails, the probability of each is ½, the outcome of heads is +$1 and the outcome of tails is —$3. The product of the outcome times the probability of each is shown in the third row of the table, and they sum to —$1, the expectation of each coin flip.

The same general procedure can be used for calculating the annual damage prevention benefits of a flood control project. Assume that historical records reveal that the recurrence of flooding in a hypothetical river valley is as shown in figure 7.1. Every ten years, on the average, a flood will occur within the 10-year flood zone, the peak level represented in the figure by the "10-year flood level." The damage that would result from the average 10-year flood, if it were to occur in the subject year, is shown to be $5 million. Every 20 years, on the average, a flood will rise above the 10-year level and reach as high as the "20-year flood level." The average 20-year flood would result in $20 million in damages. Every 50 years, on the average, a flood will rise above the 20-year level, possibly reaching as high as the 50-year flood level and cause $100 million in damages. Assume there is no evidence that floods have ever risen above the 50-year flood level.

This completes the information needed to calculate the expected damages from floods of different severity. The data are tabulated in table 7.4 to facilitate the calculation. The calculations reveal that the expected flood damage in the current year without flood protection is $3.5 million. If a flood control project were built that eliminated the risk of 10-year floods, it would save an average of $500,000 in annual damages, and if a project eliminated the risk of both 10- and 20-year floods, it would save an average

Table 7.3
Probabilities and payoffs for a coin flip

	Events (i)	
	Heads	Tails
X_i	+$1.00	−$3.00
$p(X_i)$	1/2	1/2
$X_i p(X_i)$	+$.50	−$1.50
$E(X) = -\$1.00$		

Table 7.4
Data on flood occurrences and damages (in millions of dollars)

	Floods (i)			
	Fifty-year	Twenty-year	Ten-year	No flood
X_i	$100	$20	$5	0
$p(X_i)$	0.02	0.05	0.10	0.83
$X_i p(X_i)$	$2	$1	$.5	$0
$E(X) = \$3.5$				

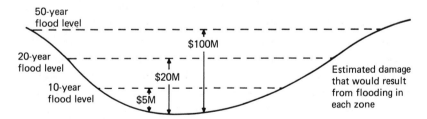

Figure 7.1
Cross section of hypothetical river valley showing flood levels and the estimated current damage that would result from flooding in each zone

of $1.5 million (that is, $0.5 million + $1 million) in annual damages. In order to calculate the present value of flood protection benefits, the damage figures (and possibly the probabilities) would have to be re-estimated for various points in the future so that the expected annual damages in future years could be estimated and discounted to present value.

Of course, this example has been highly simplified in order to demonstrate the standard procedure in cost-benefit analysis for calculating monetary values in a risk situation. In reality estimates of probabilities and outcomes usually are difficult to derive. Probability data for some cases do not exist, and, when they do, they usually require modifications due to historical changes. For example, historical data on flood probabilities usually must be adjusted for the effect of developments in the watershed. Upstream dams reduce the probability of downstream floods, but upstream urban development (that covers the land with impervious surfaces) and channelization increase the probability of downstream floods. Estimating outcomes requires forecasting the population, income, property values, and other similar factors. For example, to estimate the damage prevention of a flood control project requires forecasts of factors such as population, land-use, and property values (including potential open space values) in the flood plain over the lifetime of the proposed project.

It is well known that the expected value of an action provides only a rough estimate of the aggregate willingness-to-pay. In some loss avoidance situations it is likely to underestimate the willingness-to-pay, as evidenced by the fact that people buy insurance despite the fact most insurance companies operate at a profit and therefore must charge more than the expected loss for their policies. On the other hand, the fact that many people reside in natural hazard zones is sometimes taken as evidence that people are not sufficiently cautious of risk situations involving a very low probability of a very large loss.

In the absence of a better operational method that can overcome these limitations, the expectation approach continues to be the standard method for treating risk in CBA.

When the probability of events affecting the magnitudes of impacts cannot be ascertained, the expected loss cannot be calculated. There is no accepted method in CBA to address these uncertain situations, but a couple of approaches to the problem have been taken. One method is to use sensitivity testing in which upper and lower boundaries of the probabilities are selected.

The expectation is calculated and reported for each, giving a high and low estimate for the monetary value of the impact. Another approach is simply to report the best and worst case outcomes. Actually this is equivalent to sensitivity testing in which the probability of an event is judged to range from 0 to 1.

7.3 DECISION CRITERIA IN CBA

After all the impacts in a cost-benefit evaluation are computed, the question that must be addressed is how are the results to be organized or added together to reach a decision. The decision criterion chosen for the analysis answers this question. Decision criteria are used in CBA for two types of decision situations: (1) accept-reject decisions and (2) ranking a list of alternative actions so that the best proposal, or the top several proposals, can be identified.

The standard CBA criterion for accepting or rejecting a proposed public action is very simple: if benefits exceed costs, the proposed action should be accepted; if not, is should be rejected. Another way of stating this criterion is, If net benefits (that is, the difference between benefits and costs) are positive, the action should be accepted; otherwise not. Despite the fact that this criterion ignores equity effects, as discussed in the previous chapter, it is widely used in CBA evaluations today.[7]

The appropriate criterion for ranking is a more controversial subject among economists, and in the following pages, several alternatives will be presented. It is important to note, first, that there are two types of ranking situations. One involves ranking *alternative* proposals for addressing the same goal so that the best alternative can be selected. The other involves ranking *nonsubstitutable* proposals (that is, proposals for addressing different goals, or for addressing the same goal, but in different geographical areas) so that limited resources can be allocated to the most important ones.

It might be thought that the net benefit criterion would be useful for either type of ranking, but usually it is not. This is illustrated by the hypothetical data on benefits and costs of three proposed actions in table 7.5. Assume, first, that the three proposals are alternatives for addressing the same issue or problem. It will be noted that the net benefits of all three are positive, so they all pass the accept-reject criterion. The net benefits of X are

Table 7.5
Benefits and costs for three hypothetical proposed actions (in millions of dollars)

Proposed action	Benefits (B)	Costs (C)	Net benefits (B − C)	Benefit-cost ratio (B/C)
X	$150	$75	$75	2.0
Y	$120	$50	$70	2.4
Z	$ 70	25	$45	2.8

highest with Y second and Z last. Thus it might appear that X should be ranked first and selected as the best alternative. The problem with this selection is that, although X provides the highest net benefits, it also costs the most. And, if we are concerned with how much we are getting for our money —which certainly we are—then we should be comparing the alternatives in terms of how much we get versus how much we pay. A simple indicator of this is the benefit-cost ratio, shown in the last column in table 7.5. This ratio measures the average benefits per dollar of cost for a proposed action. The data show that alternative Z would provide $2.8 of benefit and X would provide $2.0 of benefit. Thus the ranking of the three according to the benefit-cost ratio would be Z first, Y second, and X last—just the reverse of that suggested by the net benefit criterion.

Without introducing any other complications, Z would ordinarily be selected as the best. However, it might be felt that Z does not go far enough in meeting the intended goal, as revealed by the low level of benefits achieved. If so, then Y would be the next candidate in line. But, if Y also is considered inadequate, then X might be chosen. Another method of dealing with the problem that the alternative with the highest benefit-cost ratio is too small is to redesign it to make it larger while attempting to retain its desirable features.

Now let's consider the problem of ranking nonsubstitutable proposals. Utilizing the data in table 7.5, again, let us assume that the proposed actions address different goals and that the decision-makers are limited by a budget of $75 million in supporting them. With $75 million they could adopt X and get benefits of $150 million. Alternatively, they could support both (Y and

Z), and get combined benefits of $190 million. Clearly the second alternative is preferred, indicating again that the net benefit criterion is not the best for ranking proposals.

Although the benefit-cost ratio is a commonly used index for ranking alternatives, it is not the only one. A limitation of the simple benefit-cost ratio is the fact that it doesn't separate out the initial investment cost from the continuing operating costs of a proposed action. When selections are being made from a fixed budget, the initial cost of a proposed action often is the most critical. The capital-output ratio is an indicator that is better suited to this type of situation. It is computed by the following equation:

$$\text{capital-output ratio} = \frac{C_0}{\displaystyle\sum_{t=1}^{n} \frac{B_t - C_t}{(1 + r)^t}}$$

where

$C_0 =$ the initial cost of the proposed action,
$C_t =$ the annual continuing cost in year t,
$B_t =$ the annual benefit in year t,
$r =$ the social rate of discount,
$n =$ the duration of the action, in years.

It should be noted that the costs and benefits are inverted in this ratio, so that lower values are better than higher ones. The capital-output ratio has been used widely by international aid organizations such as the Agency for International Development (AID) and the World Bank.

The social rate of discount must be determined in order to calculate either the benefit-cost or the capital-output ratio. The uncertainty of this rate is a source of concern to many analysts but can be avoided in the task of ranking by calculating some rate-of-return factor. The internal rate of return is a popular decision rule among economists. It is defined as the interest rate that equates the present value of benefits to the present value of costs. In equation form it is the i that satisfies the following equality:[8]

$$\sum_{t=0}^{n} \frac{B_t}{(1+i)^t} = \sum_{t=0}^{n} \frac{C_t}{(1+i)^t} .$$

A limitation of the internal rate of return is that, like the benefit-cost ratio, it does not single out the initial investment cost as a critical factor. An alternative that does is the investment rate of return. Like the internal rate of return, it can be calculated without determining the social rate of discount. In the investment rate-of-return equation, i equates the initial cost, C_0, with the present value of net benefits (excluding C_0):

$$C_0 = \sum_{t=1}^{n} \frac{B_t - C_t}{(1+i)^t} .$$

The investment rate of return has been used for years in the business community as an important indicator of investment desirability, and deserves more attention in the evaluation of public actions.

Other types of rates of return might also be considered. As the supplies of certain types of nonrenewable resources dwindle, they could become more limiting than investment funds (particularly if rationed). For example, a nonrenewable energy rate of return might become a useful evaluation indicator.

Economists are generally not in agreement as to the best index for ranking proposed actions. The author contends that no single index should be used, either for ranking or making accept-reject decisions.

7.4 COST-EFFECTIVENESS ANALYSIS

Cost-effectiveness analysis (CEA) is a form of CBA in which dollar costs are compared to units of output, rather than dollar benefits. It is a very useful technique for evaluating alternative proposals that address the same goal and can be compared by a single measure of output. For example, water supply alternatives can be compared by the gallons of water per day they produce, and urban recreation alternatives can be compared by the daily attendance they generate. The most cost-effective alternative usually is defined as the one that either (1) maximizes the output for a fixed cost or (2) minimizes the cost of producing a fixed level of output, depending upon the nature of the decision situation.

Sometimes it is assumed that CEA overcomes the CBA problem of having to monetize outputs and therefore is superior to CBA, but this is not true. Whenever some or all of the outputs of a proposed action are not monetized, the accept-reject decision is complicated by the necessity of comparing unlike units—specifically, comparing dollar costs (assuming that all the undesirable impacts can be monetized) to units of output (such as gallons of water or recreation attendance). However, there are many situations in public decision making in which the accept decision has already been made, so the evaluation problem is narrowed to that of selecting the best action for meeting the specified objective. These situations fall into one of two categories: one is the case in which a standard or a level of output is fixed, and the evaluation problem is to select the least-cost method of achieving it. An example in the environmental field is the task of meeting a standard for air or water quality at the least cost. The other is the case in which a fixed budget is set aside for a specific purpose, and the evaluation problem is to choose the highest output method that does not exceed the budget. Many public service sectors, such as education, police protection, fire protection, recreation, and library services, are examples. It should be clear that in these cases cost-effectiveness analysis cannot take the credit for avoiding the difficulties of monetizing outputs; instead, the difficulties are avoided by the fact that *the accept-reject decision has already been made.*

Many cost-effectiveness evaluations are conducted using methematical optimization models. On the surface the advantage of this approach is that the *full range* of alternatives can be assessed and the "optimal" solution identified. This is in contrast to the conventional evaluation in which only a limited number of alternatives is assessed, and the "best" among them is selected. One must be more than cautious, however, in accepting "optimal" solutions. They can only be derived when all evaluative criteria are reduced to a mathematical expression. Questions should be asked such as; How are the apples and oranges added? Does the objective function include all the important quantifiable factors? Are there intangible factors important to the decision that are necessarily excluded from the model? How does the model deal with equity issues? How is the discounting issue resolved?

In some cases, such as in certain engineering studies, these questions do not uncover any serious problems, but in any significant evaluation of a public action they are bound to. Some cost-effectiveness modelers are careful to represent the results of their work only as evidence to be weighed in reaching a decision, but too many are inclined to state their findings as the *optimal solution.*

CEA is a useful evaluation tool when its limits are respected.

7.5 BREAK-EVEN ANALYSIS

Break-even analysis is widely used for investment evaluation in the private sector—when demand cannot be accurately estimated. It is occasionally used in CBA for valuing intangibles, that is, impacts which cannot be quantified or monetized (although users apparently have not recognized that the tool has a private investment analogy, because the term, "break-even analysis," is seldom used in connection with CBA applications). It is a simple method to implement, requiring the same type of information used in cost-effectiveness analysis.

The basic idea of break-even analysis is, in the absence of hard data on monetized benefits, to calculate the minimum monetary value per unit of output that would be required to justify acceptance of the proposed public action. If the level of service can be accurately estimated, then only a single break-even figure is necessary. For example, a study tentatively estimated that the level of dissolved oxygen in the Delaware estuary could be raised to 3 milligrams per liter at a total cost of $22.4 million, and that this would create a total demand for boating of 8.8 million boater days.[9] The researchers were unable to place a dollar value on the water quality project, so instead they calculated the break-even value. The above quantities suggest that if boater days were worth a minimum of $2.55 each (the break-even value), the benefits of the water quality project would exceed the costs.[10] This would seem to be a reasonable value, particularly considering the fact that the water quality project would generate many other desirable impacts in addition to the boating activity.

The usefulness of break-even analysis derives from the fact that it organizes information in a form that decision-makers can conveniently test against their personal experience. For example, in the estuary illustration, the decision-makers can ask themselves, Would the average boating enthusiast be willing to pay $2.55 a day to go boating on an estuary? The general principle of organizing information to facilitate judgments has been barely explored in the field of evaluation.

7.6 BIBLIOGRAPHY OF COST-BENEFIT THEORY, PART II

Time Discounting

Baumol, William J. "On the Social Rate of Discount." *American Economic Review,* vol. 58, (June 1968), pp. 788–802.

Feldstein, M. S. "The Social Time Preference Discount Rate in Cost Benefit Analysis," *Economic Journal,* vol. 74 (June 1964), pp. 360–379.

Marglin, Stephen A. "The Social Rate of Discount and the Optimal Rate of Investment." *Quarterly Journal of Economics,* vol. 77 (March 1963), pp. 95–111.

Marglin, Stephen A. "The Opportunity Costs of Public Investment." *Quarterly Journal of Economics,* vol. 77 (May 1963), pp. 274–289.

Nash, C. A. "Future Generations and the Social Rate of Discount. *Environment and Planning,* vol. 5 (1973), pp. 611–617.

Risk and Uncertainty

Friedman, M., and L. J. Savage. "The Utility Analysis of Choices Involving Risk." *Journal of Political Economy,* vol. 56 (August 1948), pp. 279–304.

Luce, R. D., and H. Raiffa. *Games and Decisions: Introduction to Critical Survey.* New York: John Wiley, 1967.

Schlaiffer, R. *Probability and Statistics for Business Decisions.* New York: McGraw Hill, 1969.

8
APPLICATIONS AND CRITIQUE
OF COST-BENEFIT ANALYSIS

8.1 MONETIZING ENVIRONMENTAL IMPACTS

The typical context for applying CBA is the evaluation of a public project or program; the purpose of the methodology is to monetize each of the anticipated impacts so that a grand index of net benefits—or benefit-cost ratio, or rate of return—can be computed. Some impacts are naturally measured in dollars, whether or not CBA is used. The best example is the resources used to build and operate a project, which are commonly measured by their money cost rather than the quantities and qualities of materials, energy, labor, and land. The greatest challenges and difficulties are in monetizing impacts that don't have dollar tags directly attached to them.

While the theory of CBA represents the ideal approach for monetizing impacts, frequently the limitations of data, time, and resources impose gaps between theory and practice. Perhaps the central problem in implementing the theory is the limited market information on the willingness-to-pay for impact items. Indeed, this problem could be stated as a fundamental dilemma: according to economic theory, the reason public actions are often necessary is because the private market fails to value properly all the consequences of its actions. Thus it is obvious that private market information for monetizing certain values connected with public actions will be sparse if not nonexistent. Theory does not indicate how this problem can be solved in any particular situation; it is up to the ingenuity of the analyst to scrape together whatever evidence is available on the willingness-to-pay in each case.

The purpose of this section on applications of CBA is to provide an overview of the methods analysts have used for monetizing a variety of environmental impacts and to identify the limitations of the results. Covered are environmental concerns such as recreation, landscape aesthetics, wildlife, unique natural areas, natural resource supplies, noise, air and water pollution, and a brief summary of social impacts. The goal is not to present the detailed, step-by-step procedures for monetization, only the general concepts upon which the measures are based. The valuation of public outdoor recreation is singled out for a more lengthy presentation because it offers an excellent illustration of how the economist tries to infer market values from information on a nonmarket resource. However, the reader should be forewarned that the case is not typical; the attempts to monetize many other nonmarket resources have not been so successful.

Outdoor Recreation

In evaluating a public action that would provide or destroy recreation opportunities, CBA attempts to place a dollar value on the recreation impact. Several approaches for doing this have been developed over the past twenty years; they are applicable mostly to regional (or resource-based) outdoor recreation sites. The fact that most public recreation opportunities are provided at a zero or nominal price means that there is little direct evidence on willingness-to-pay. However, in using public facilities, people incur expenditures for equipment, transportation, food, and lodging in route, which give some indication of their willingness-to-pay for recreation experiences. Most approaches utilize this kind of information.

According to economic theory, the ideal approach to valuing a regional park site would be to (1) estimate the demand curve—representing the willingness-to-pay by recreationists to utilize the site—for each of many time periods in the future, (2) calculate the area under each of the demand curves to obtain the total willingness-to-pay for each time period, and (3) discount these future values and sum the results to obtain a present value total. If the park site is being made available by the proposed action, the total represents the measured benefit of the recreation; if it is being removed by the action, the total represents a cost. The key here is to estimate the demand curves. Several methods have been used for doing this; most are variants of the Clawson, or travel-cost, approach.[1]

A demand curve traces the quantity of a good or service that people would be willing to buy at each of a range of alternative prices. At any given time most markets provide information for only one point on the curve: the point representing the single current price and the quantity purchased at that price. But since users of a regional park travel different distances to visit it, and therefore incur different costs associated with the trip, the analyst has an opportunity to measure how the quantity demanded varies with cost. The Clawson method takes advantage of these cost differentials to derive a demand curve. It is important to note that the demand curve used for calculating benefits (or costs) does not relate *total expenditures* by the recreationist, only the (hypothetical or real) price the recreationist would be willing to pay as an *entrance fee*. Travel cost is used to infer the willingness-to-pay an entrance fee, but it is not included in the fee or in the demand schedule.

In a simplified explanation of how the Clawson method works, the first step is to take a survey of the visitors at the subject park site to determine the number of trips coming from a variety of origin zones. Assume that the results of this survey are as shown in column one of table 8.1. The recreationists come from one of three cities, *A, B,* and *C;* they all travel by automobile: 1,600 trips coming from city *A*, 6,000 from *B*, and 2,400 from *C*. No entrance fee is charged.

The second step is to gather some additional data and draw a curve that relates the trip-making rate to travel cost. Information is gathered on the population of the three cities, the round trip mileage between each city and the park, and the travel cost per mile. This information is used to complete the table. The information on trips per thousand population and travel cost is plotted for each city in figure 8.1, a line connecting the points is drawn, as an estimate of the relationship between trips and cost.[2] The line in fact describes the relationship between trips and travel cost, but utilizing the assumption that recreationists are indifferent between a dollar expended for travel and a dollar paid at the gate, the curve is used as an indicator of the relationship between trips and total cost, travel and entrance fee combined. Based on this assumption, the line can be used to simulate what would happen to park utilization (in terms of trips) if different entrance fees were charged.

In the third step, the line in figure 8.1 is used to estimate the number of trips that would come from each city for each of several alternative entrance fees. For example, take city *A*. At a $0 fee, which is the base case, we know from figure 8.1 that 1,600 trips are made. This is recorded in table 8.2. Alternatively, if the fee were $5, then *A* residents would incur a total cost of $10 in using the park (that is, $5 for travel plus a $5 fee). The line in figure 8.1 tells us that at $10, 600 trips per thousand population would be made, and, since the population of *A* is 2,000, we can estimate that at $10, 1,200 trips (2 x 600) would come from *A*. This simulation process is continued for alternative prices and for each city. The completed results are shown in table 8.2.

The final step is to total the trips for each entrance fee in table 8.2, plot the results on figure 8.2, and connect them to form the estimated demand curve.

This hypothetical example of how to derive a demand curve for recreation has been greatly simplified. If the proposed action is to provide a new park, then a user survey of the site would be irrelevant.[3] In addition future demand

Table 8.1
Hypothetical data on park use, population of origin cities, and travel cost

City	Trips (annual)	Population	Trips per 1,000 population	Miles (round trip)	Travel Cost (total)
A	1,600	2,000	800	50	$ 5.00
B	6,000	10,000	600	100	$10.00
C	2,400	6,000	400	150	$15.00

Table 8.2
Estimated schedule of trips from each city at alternate entrance fees

Price (entrance fee)	City A	B	C	Total
$ 0	1,600	6,000	2,400	10,000
$ 5	1,200	4,000	1,200	6,400
$10	800	2,000	0	2,800
$15	400	0	0	400
$20	0	0	0	0

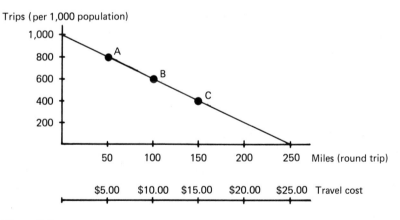

Figure 8.1
Estimated relationship between trips and cost

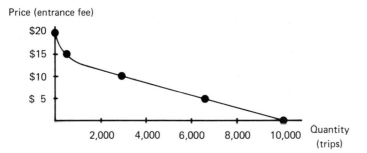

Figure 8.2
Estimated demand curve

must be estimated. Thus instead of a simple univariate procedure, it is necessary to develop a multivariate forecasting model capable of predicting the use of a potential site for various future time periods. Many suitable models have been developed for forecasting recreation activity; they include such predictive variables as population, income, age distribution, park characteristics, distance, and competition.[4] The inclusion of distance as a variable in these models makes it possible to derive a demand curve by the Clawson method.

The accuracy of the monetized values derived by the Clawson method is limited by a variety of factors. First, there is a margin of error to the model forecasts, and sometimes the error can be quite large. Second, there is a great deal of uncertainty regarding the correct cost-per-mile figure used to convert the model results to a demand curve. Several factors are responsible, including the difficulty of forecasting future gasoline prices, the disagreement as to whether vehicle operating costs alone should be used or whether fixed costs such as insurance and depreciation should also be included, and the question of whether the value of time in transit should be included as a travel cost.

Another limitation of Clawson-based values is that in some cases people owning residences adjacent to the site benefit a great deal from it, but are virtually ignored by the travel cost calculations. However, there is a way of monetizing these benefits and adding them to the travel demand figure. Residential properties that benefit from a park often have higher market values than otherwise equivalent properties. When this occurs or is expected, the land value differentials can be estimated. In fact, some CBA studies have used these differentials as the primary basis for monetizing recreation sites.[5]

Another problem with most monetized recreation values is that they fail to reflect the fact that recreation is not the only reason for establishing regional parks. Wildlife preservation, nature education, and ecological research are additional purposes probably not included in the recreationist's willingness-to-pay. Also missing is a measure of the option value—a term economists use to reflect the view that many nonusers of certain services such as recreation are probably willing to pay something to preserve the option to use them in the future rather than let them disappear for lack of financial support.[6] However, no one has developed a proven operational method for measuring option value. Furthermore, it should be emphasized that the practice of computing the present dollar value of a park greatly discounts and, beyond the cutoff point, totally ignores future users, contrary to the human value expressed by Frederick Law Olmsted and many people since, that parks should be provided and preserved to meet the needs of future generations as well as the present one. This limitation, of course, is not unique to recreation monetization but applies to CBA in general.

Finally, while the Clawson method can provide partial monetary measures for regional parks, its applicability to local parks and playgrounds and to wilderness areas is very doubtful. Since a high proportion of the users of local urban recreation centers either walk or ride bikes to them, travel cost information is quite limited. No analyst has tried to add up shoe leather and bicycle tires! In the case of visually attractive urban parks, the property value approach can be used, but it is not likely to work for recreation centers, because of the noise and other disadvantages associated with being near active playgrounds.[7] A serious limitation to both the Clawson and property value approaches is that among the special targets of urban recreation planning are poor youth and elderly people whose willingness-to-pay is severely limited by their ability to pay and is a totally irrelevant indicator of the importance of serving them.[8]

Although users may travel long distances to reach wilderness areas, the low level of use is an inadequate measure of their significance to society. Option demand, nature preservation, future generations, and the uniqueness of the wilderness experience seem more relevant to wilderness evaluation.

Landscape Aesthetics

Landscape aesthetics can be damaged and destroyed by many public actions, such as power plants, water projects, forest management, strip mining policies, overhead utility lines, and urban development zoning, but the impact is usually treated as an intangible in cost-benefit studies, incapable of being monetized. Actually, the methods of monetizing recreation impacts should be applicable to landscapes, considering that in terms of time spent the most popular outdoor recreation activity is pleasure driving, of which landscape (also, seascape and skyscape) is presumably a major attraction.[9] But for the most part landscape vistas lie scattered across the country, outside park boundaries. No one has figured out how to secure a traveler's willingness-to-pay for scenery, let alone the general public's monetary value (if indeed this is even a relevant concept). Only recently have models for predicting park use included measures of park attractiveness, and no known model is sensitive enough to be able to predict how travel along various highways is affected by the vistas highways provide. There may be some opportunities to merge modeling efforts with landscape assessment procedures, but almost nothing along these lines has been tried as yet.

Aside from the aesthetics within parks, the main empirical evidence on the dollar value of landscapes is provided by residential land values. Housing tends to be higher priced in areas with picturesque views of a river, lake, ocean, or mountain, for example, than in areas without such views but otherwise comparable. The premiums on scenic views can be very high in big cities but may not be measurable in some rural areas where the supply is high relative to demand.

It is a sad commentary on our priorities that in areas where residential developers build lakes, parks, golf courses, and other amenities into their projects to capture the buyer's willingness-to-pay for them, the broader resources of the region are frequently ignored in public planning. Is it not peculiar that urban development attracted to areas of great natural beauty is so often allowed to proceed unrestrained, destroying in its path the very resources that made the areas unique places to live, work, and play?

Wildlife

As in the case of landscapes, many public projects can be harmful to wildlife, but CBA typically ignores it. Nature preservation is highly valued by many people for various reasons, including the ethical view that native plants and animals have a right to live, the religious view that nature is God's work, and the ecological view that man's welfare is inextricably bound up with the welfare of nature. The self-centered calculating man who forms the basis of economic thinking would not, according to economic theory, voluntarily pay to protect wildlife even if he shared these values; he would be a free rider—preferring to wait for others to support wildlife preservation out of their own pockets—thus enjoying the benefits without paying any of the costs. Fortunately, not all people behave according to this theory; many nonprofit programs for wildlife protection are supported by voluntary donations. Nevertheless, the level of support is probably an inadequate reflection of full public sentiment on the matter.

The few cost-benefit studies that have attempted to place a money value on wildlife have used some variant of the Clawson method to measure the willingness-to-pay of hunters. Moose, deer, and migratory waterfowl have been valued in this way, as if their main value is to be stalked and killed by sportsmen![10] Again, the limits of CBA in measuring human values is painfully evident.

Unique Natural Areas

The valuation of unique natural areas that combine recreation, aesthetics, wildlife, and unusual ecological features has been an especially challenging problem for certain environmentally sensitive economists. John Krutilla made an heroic attempt to prove the economic superiority of preserving Hell's Canyon rather than developing its hydroelectric potential.[11] First, in the Hell's Canyon analysis, and later in a coauthored book of case studies, he has attempted to shape and mold CBA into a preservationist tool, bending it as far as it will go.

Because certain natural areas like Hell's Canyon are unique, and therefore have no substitutes, Krutilla argues that the recreation benefits will grow at a very rapid pace as population and income rise in the future. On the other side of the balance, he argues that continued technological advances in the future will expand our production alternatives, serving to slow the growth of benefits from projects developed in natural areas such as for electricity generation or resource extraction. The combination of these effects suggests to him that the net benefits of preserving unique natural areas could exceed those for development, and his empirical analysis of Hell's Canyon lends support to this view. His reasoning is sophisticated and complex; only a trained economist would be able to understand his Hell's Canyon evaluation. Decision-makers and citizens would have to accept his results on blind faith. But this problem is not peculiar to Krutilla's analysis; it is common to many cost-benefit studies.

Since the key to Krutilla's argument is the future, he is compelled to make some extremely shaky forecasts. In attempting to overcome this problem, he uses sensitivity analysis to test how the conclusions would be affected by alternative model assumptions. But the results are not particularly helpful because there is little basis for judging whether *any* of the sets of model assumptions are likely to approximate the future. Subsequent events best illustrate this problem. His model takes no account of changing fossil fuel and nuclear energy costs, which weren't apparent when he originally made his computations. Yet, the now rapidly rising costs of these fuels if continued into the future could easily reverse his conclusion that preservation is more economical.

Although Krutilla is sensitive to the issue of future generations, he nevertheless persists in clinging to the traditional economic doctrine that the future must be discounted. With all due respect to Krutilla for the major contributions he has made to the evaluation literature over the years, his analysis of unique natural areas does far more to reveal the fundamental inadequacies of cost-benefit analysis than to overcome them.

Natural Resource Supplies

In evaluating projects that supply resources, such as water, minerals, coal, timber, or electricity, monetizing the benefits of the supply is a straightforward application of the theory presented in chapter 6. If the amount provided by the project represents a large increase relative to that already supplied to the market, the demand curve should be estimated so that the area under the curve, representing the maximum willingness-to-pay, can be computed. This is much easier to say than to do, however. Econometric procedures must be used to estimate the statistical relationships between price and quantity, based upon data somewhat analogous to the recreation example in which behavioral responses to different prices are revealed. Good data are often not available, and the statistician must do the best that he or she can under the circumstances.

The monetization task is vastly simplified when the proposed increment in supply is relatively small. In this case the increased quantity can be valued using the price paid for the existing resource. In other words, this approach calculates the benefits as the revenue to be received from selling the additional supply.

If the project has more than one type of benefit, such as in the case of multiple purpose water projects (which frequently offer flood protection, water supply, electricity, and recreation), each type is monetized.

The cost of a resource development project includes the direct dollar costs for construction and operations. To these, the analyst might attempt to add certain monetized values of adverse environmental impacts following the concepts described in this section for valuing environmental damages. Those that can't be monetized are naturally left out of the calculation.

An alternative to resource development is resource conservation, but this is almost never explored in cost-benefit studies. It might be thought that the no-action alternative gives adequate attention to conservation, but it really doesn't. A key concern in conserving natural resources is the equity issue of retaining resources for future generations. The standard practice of discounting gives doubtful attention to the coming generation and none to generations beyond fifty years. Thus the importance of conserving our natural resources for the future of mankind is virtually ignored.

Another equity issue in the use of natural resources is right sharing among all people. Many believe that the world's resources should be shared fairly among all people, not dominated by the wealthy. CBA is in direct conflict with this value because its willingness-to-pay criterion has the effect of weighing the importance of people by their income (or wealth). Thus the higher is a society's income, the higher will be the benefit-cost ratio of supplying them natural resources.

Noise
As in the case of most other environmental elements, there is no established market for the purchase and sale of noise (or quiet). Thus the cost-benefit

analyst must infer the willingness-to-pay for no noise from whatever evidence he can garner. Noise, as well as air and water pollution, has both direct and indirect effects; either may provide useful information. The direct effects of noise are damage to environmental aesthetics, disruption of social, educational, religious, recreational, and commercial activities, and short-and long-term hearing loss and other health damages. The indirect effects result from the attempts by people to avoid some of the direct effects, including the cost of shifting activities to less noisy locations, the cost of noise insulation, the cost of moving to a quieter neighborhood, the changes in property values, and so on.

By far the greatest interest in monetizing noise has occurred in Great Britain—as a result generally of their serious noise problems in urban areas and particularly of the Roskill Commission's cost-benefit evaluation of alternative sites for the third London airport. Most of the attention has been directed at residential property values, which should be higher in quieter locations, reflecting the willingness-to-pay for quiet. A great deal of care is needed in designing a statistical model for measuring the difference so that the results are reasonably accurate. Of course, the analysis of house prices does not reveal the cost of noise impacts on commercial and public activities. In the case of schools, libraries, hospitals, and other public institutions, market values of properties do not exist, but the expense of providing insulation can be used for measuring the noise cost. However, this approach excludes the cost to outdoor activities, including the many forms of active and passive recreation.

An additional difficulty with the methods of monetizing noise is that they provide estimates of the willingness-to-pay, which in some cases is not the appropriate criterion. In the case of airport noise many courts have ruled that surrounding residents have a certain right to peace and quiet, which means that the monetization question is not how much people would be willing to pay to have airport noise reduced but how much they would be *willing to accept* as *compensation.* No practical method has been developed for measuring this. The most obvious approach is to conduct questionnaire surveys in which people are asked how much compensation they would require, but in general responses concerning compensation are suspected of being exaggerated.

In sum, the methods for monetizing noise impacts yield only partial measures at best, and the research can be time consuming and expensive.

Air and Water Pollution

The benefits of reduced air and water pollution and the costs of increased pollution are estimated by reference to the effects of the change. The monetization methods are generally the same irrespective of whether the change is an increase or a decrease. Pollution control is not an end in itself, but rather a means linked in a causitive chain to a variety of ends. In estimating its monetary value, economists look to the effects of pollution, including human health, commercial production, materials damage, recreation, aesthetics, and the health of endemic plants and animals. Thus the methods of monetizing pollution impacts boil down to the methods of monetizing each of these effects.

There are three major steps to the monetization procedure: first, estimates are prepared of the types of pollutants and their intensities as caused by the subject action. Second, the effects of the estimated pollution are forecasted by reference to "dose-response" (or damage) functions. Third, the effects are monetized, discounted, and totaled. The purpose of the first two steps, of course, is to estimate the impacts. With a few exceptions the knowledge and data available for impact estimation are still quite weak. We are only beginning to gather good information on the types and quantities of pollutants emitted by various sources. After emission occurs, the manner in which pollutants move through their medium (of air, water, or both) and react chemically with each other can have an enormous influence on their effects. The flows and reactions, too, are not well understood. From laboratory experiments, episodic events, and personal experiences we know the types of effects pollution is likely to cause, but estimating their magnitudes in the full complexity of the real environment poses serious research problems of isolating the effects caused by a particular public action independent of all the other potential causitive agents.

Sometimes impacts are measured directly in dollar terms and sometimes not. It is of course only in the later case that monetization is necessary. In general, the data and procedures for valuing impacts are as weak as those for estimating them, and economists are constantly emphasizing the need for more government-supported research to advance the state of the art.

The available evidence suggests that pollution has a substantial effect on human health, although a great deal more research is needed to determine the breadth and magnitude of the problem. It is quite clear that air pollution causes illness and death from respiratory diseases. And water pollution is believed to cause certain forms of cancer which are probably linked to the industrial chemicals and pesticides that are either dumped or wash into our rivers, lakes, bays, and oceans.

The typical approach to monetizing the health effects is partly based on the human capital concept in economics, which views people as inputs to production processes and values these inputs in terms of the dollar value of the output that can be attributed to their effort. If people become ill or die, and therefore cannot work, production is reduced. The dollar loss is measured by the wages the people would have received if they had been working, which theoretically is equal to their production contribution. Thus, for each estimated sickness and premature death attributed to pollution, the loss of wages is computed as one of the dollar measures. It should be noted that according to this approach, low-income people aren't worth as much as high-income earners. Also, the death of a child counts very little because the lost earnings in the distant future when discounted to present value don't amount to much. Housewives are also problematical; occasionally, to avoid the implication that they are worthless (because they don't earn a wage), economists value their illnesses and premature deaths on the basis of the average wage of domestic servants. According to the practice, retired people apparently have no value. In addition to wages, monetized health impacts include the expenses of hospitals, doctors, drugs, and so forth.

Despite the obvious fact that pain, suffering, and loss of loved ones are left out of their calculations—which means that their monetized values represent the least significant aspect of the problem—some economists will go to great lengths to sharpen their estimates of production and consumption losses. For example, one analyst developed a sophisticated procedure for calculating the economic loss due to the premature use of resources for burials.[12]

Recently, a few economists have begun to question the human capital approach to valuing health effects. They argue that wages may not be a good measure of the willingness-to-pay to avoid death or illness (or to avoid the probability of these occurring). Accordingly, more direct approaches for measuring the willingness-to-pay need to be devised. However, the thinking on this matter has still not come to grips with the fact that willingness-to-pay, being based on the ability to pay, places less value on the life of poor people than the rich. But far more fundamental than this is the narrow persistence in trying to interpret everything in terms of market exchange values. When will economic science recognize that people are more important than things, that human life lies above dollar values, that indeed *life is the most fundamental value,* that life cannot be made more significant by hanging dollar signs on it? If ever decision-makers need dollar signs on human life to give it due weight in their deliberations, we will have reached a mighty sad state of affairs!

The issue raised here is not whether monetization should be completely discarded; certainly it has its place. The point to be made is that monetary measures should be applied only to those impacts the meaning of which can be adequately communicated by dollar magnitudes. Medical expenses pass this test, the loss of life does not.

Pollution can affect a variety of economic production activities. Agricultural output and costs are affected by high salinity and sediment levels in water. Laboratory research and field surveys show that air pollution can cause widespread damage to crops, and the emissions of certain industrial processes have caused illness and death to range animals. These effects are monetized by computing the attending change in farm income, considering the changes in both sales and production costs. The effects of water pollution on commercial fishery yields of shellfish and finfish, which have been shown to be sizable in some instances, are monetized by calculating the change in fishery income.

The impacts of water pollution on processing costs for municipal water supply, for cooling, and for direct use in production activities, such as paper, textile, chemical, beverage, and food processing are well documented. In most cases these can be measured directly in dollar terms, so no further monetization is necessary. Pollution also damages materials. Water pollution causes corrosion and chemical buildup on pipes, equipment, household appliances, boats, piers, and so forth; and air pollution can damage electrical contacts, rubber, paints, dyes, and other materials. Although laboratory experiments can confirm these effects, establishing their statistical significance in field research has not proven easy. These effects, when measurable, are monetized by computing the extra cost of manufacturing resistant materials, of maintenance, and of premature replacement. Closely related is the soiling effect of air pollution, which can require extra effort in cleaning and maintenance, but the measurable economic implications of this have been difficult to validate in field research. Somewhat analogous to this is the effect of high sediment loads in water, which upon settling can obstruct navigation in waterways, reduce water storage in reservoirs, and increase hazards in flood plains. If these effects can be measured, they would be monetized either by computing the cost of removal or the cost of the resulting damage.

Pollution also affects recreation, aesthetics, and endemic plants and animals. Water-related activities such as fishing, swimming, and boating are among the most popular outdoor recreation pursuits. Although these sports are obviously sensitive to the quality of water, there is little empirical evidence to estimate how water quality changes would affect them in magnitude. There is even less evidence linking air pollution to recreation. This, of course, poses serious problems for monetization, which typically would follow the Clawson method.[13] A few analysts have resorted to using questionnaire surveys in which recreationists are asked how much they would pay for improved water quality in recreation areas. Most economists, however, are skeptical of survey responses from a concern that respondents are likely to play a strategy, either overstating their willingness-to-pay, if they believe this will lead to improved conditions at no cost to them, or understating their preference, if they believe they might be asked to contribute to the cause.

Ironically, although according to the Clawson model an *increase* in travel to a recreation area would be associated with increased recreation benefits, some analysts suggest that a *decrease* in travel also indicates a benefit in certain situations. These cases occur where pollution at urban or near-urban recreation sites is reduced, with the result that people reduce their travel expenditures in reaching suitable recreation opportunities. However, there may be an inconsistency here, which economists will have to resolve.

In addition to the benefits of clean water that are reflected either by the Clawson method or by reduced travel expenditures, research has shown that the values of residential properties within view or walking distance of water bodies are influenced by water quality. The higher values of properties near clean water probably measure its aesthetic as well as recreational advantages to the residents.

Several empirical studies have used models to measure the association between residential property values and certain air pollutants, notably sulfates and particulates. The research supports the view that people are willing to pay for reduced air pollution, but the magnitude is difficult to interpret, for several reasons: first, in order to isolate the effect of air pollution from all the other factors that determine property values, the models include a large number of variables; this raises questions about the reliability of the measured magnitudes. Second, even if a model is properly specified, the revealed monetary value of air pollution applies to small but not large changes. Third, it is not known which effects of air pollution are incorporated in the measured values. Presumably property value differentials reflect (1) the aesthetic effects of greater visibility and less soiling (of plants, porches, balconies, and window sills, for example) and (2) noticeable health effects such as shortness of breath and eye burn. But do they also measure the cumulative health effects that can lead to illness and death? The question, which has not been answered, is more than academic. The two main sources of information on the willingness-to-pay for reduced air pollution are health impacts and property values. To the extent that property values reflect health considerations, the two monetized values cannot be added without double counting. Economists emphasize the need for more research to overcome these problems.

Pollution also affects the health of endemic plants and animals. In the case of water pollution aquatic species are the most obvious victims, but many terrestrial species are also likely to be harmed. Air pollution has been linked to massive die-offs of Jeffrey and Ponderosa pines, and is suspected of causing lung cancer and lead poisoning in zoo animals, which are not exactly endemic to cities but cannot be overlooked. The difficulties of monetizing impacts on native life, as discussed earlier, are severe. To the extent that the health of plants and animals can be linked to hunting, fishing, hiking, camping, and other recreation activities, the economist might be able to place a dollar sign on them, but even if a wealth of data were available for the task, many values that lie behind the urgings for nature preservation would be left out of the calculus.

Social Impacts

The approaches used in CBA to value environmental impacts reveal fairly completely the methods of monetizing social impacts as well. Monetization of health effects has already been discussed. Housing can also be viewed as a human capital input, so housing impacts have been valued by reference to their implications for health, productivity, and medical expenses.[14] Education, drug addiction, alcoholism, crime, and poverty impacts are also valued in terms of their effects on economic production as well as on public revenues and expenses.[15] Generally, there is a growing recognition that the dollar measures of social impacts do not reflect equity and other important values that must be taken into account in decision-making.

Some Conclusions on Monetizing Impacts
In conclusion, it should be clear that among the environmental impacts and the derivative effects of pollution, some factors are monetizable and some definitely are not. The factors that are definitely monetizable are the ones having direct dollar implications, including agricultural production, industrial processing, municipal water treatment, and materials damage. Recreation is monetizable to a degree, but not without extensive research in most cases. However, the primary difficulty is estimating the *impacts* of public actions on recreation activities, which should be attempted whether or not the impacts are monetized. Monetized values, when estimated, should reflect the likely margin of error they contain and the human values (such as nature preservation) they exclude.

The factors that are definitely not monetizable are the preservation of human life (human life, wildlife, and plant life), the pain and suffering from illness, equity in resource use, and conservation for future generations. Aesthetics should be included in this list also, but it should be recognized that useful dollar measures of certain aesthetics factors have occasionally been estimated.

Estimating the environmental impacts of a public action is usually a major research task, even without monetization. Rather than use scarce research resources attempting to monetize factors that can't be adequately represented by dollar measures anyway, they would be better spent on improving the impact estimates.

8.2 SUMMARY AND CRITIQUE OF CBA

CBA, usually represented as a comprehensive evaluation methodology, attempts to solve the evaluation dilemma by calculating a grand index of the social welfare implications of proposed actions. The ratings that form the index are measured by the willingness-to-pay criterion. Benefits are measured by reference to market information on the willingness-to-pay to acquire desired items and avoid undesired items. Costs are measured by market information reflecting the willingness-to-pay—and occasionally by the willingness-to-accept-compensation—for resources sacrificed and undesired items received.

The costs and benefits to different people are typically added without attempting to adjust for the likelihood that a dollar is valued differently by people at different income levels. Costs and benefits occurring in different years are totaled in an index of present value, utilizing a discounting procedure based on the fact that people are not willing to pay as much for something received later rather than sooner. Some types of impacts have obvious dollar translations because they are regularly exchanged in markets. Others do not, so indirect evidence must be collected and analyzed in order to derive some indication of their dollar value.

CBA has several important assets supporting it as a useful evaluation tool:

1. It is based on an established theory of value that has been scrutinized and debated by many economists during its lengthy evolution and adjusted to meet some of its theoretical and operational shortcomings.

2. It attempts to reflect the values of all people rather than a select few, insofar as these values are revealed by the behavior of people in the marketplace.

3. It uses impact categories and measurement units that are understandable to decision-makers and the average adult.

4. There is an extensive body of literature on applications of CBA, covering a wide variety of evaluation problems, that serves as a valuable resource to the evaluation community.

On the other side of the ledger, CBA has several important liabilities that underline caution in its use:

1. The willingness-to-pay criterion for placing values on impacts violates the democratic principle of equality, because willingness-to-pay is greatly affected by the ability to pay. An essential value to a democratic system of government is that public issues should be settled by a political process in which each adult has an equal vote, irrespective of income, wealth, education, and other factors. In some applications the use of the criterion does not unduly violate the equality principle because the interests of different income groups are not in conflict, or because the proposed action is especially

designed to deal with a social equity problem, such as poverty. However, there are many other cases in which the equality principle is seriously violated. Thus as a general rule a CBA should always be scrutinized for the likelihood of giving insufficient attention to the values of the poor.

2. In its attempt to monetize all impacts, CBA has adopted a set of very technical procedures that are difficult for decision-makers and the public to understand. Thus it is not uncommon for decision-makers and interested citizens, after having read a CBA evaluation, to find themselves in a position of either having to accept *on faith* the estimated monetary impacts or ignoring them.

3. The accuracy of many monetized environmental impacts is highly questionable due to the paucity of willingness-to-pay information on environmental factors. Usually the dollar values placed on environmental impacts are only partial estimates and therefore represent minimum values, with no indication of the maximum values.

4. Some types of environmental impacts have almost entirely eluded attempts to estimate their dollar value, and others frequently escape any form of quantification. Unmonetized and intangible impacts cannot be included in a net-benefit calculation, and therefore are given unequal treatment in CBA reports, with the possible consequence that decision-makers and others reviewing these reports give insufficient attention to them in forming their opinions.

5. The monetization of some types of impacts is a step backward rather than a step forward. For example, there is nothing more basic to human understanding and more central to the concept of public welfare than human life. The CBA practice of converting the loss of human lives to a dollar value confuses rather than enlightens the decision-maker's task of forming a judgment regarding the wisdom of a proposal.

6. There is serious doubt that dollar values can or should be placed on many types of environmental, social, and political impacts. These impacts relate to issues and problems that people do not equate with money. The willingness-to-pay criterion is useful for valuing items that can be and are acquired in the marketplace, and therefore provide people with adequate experience to form good judgments regarding their dollar values. But many human values are formed totally outside the scope of the market, so people in their roles as consumers and producers do not confront them in such a way

that their monetary equivalents are assessed. Even if monetary values were secured, say by personal interviews, their usefulness must be questioned. Many societal concerns are long-term collective issues for which the uncoordinated willingness-to-pay of individuals cannot be considered an accurate or an appropriate guide. Also, because money is the primary mode for dealing with private wants, questions about the willingness-to-pay may place people in a mode of thought that blocks their perspective from broader public issues.

7. The cost of conducting a CBA can be very high. One of the prime reasons is that extensive research is necessary to derive monetary values for impacts that do not have immediate dollar equivalents. Due partly to their high cost, CBA is seldom used in local government.

8. The procedure of discounting future costs and benefits creates serious intergenerational equity problems, placing virtually no importance on long-term environmental damages and resource depletion.

9. People who live by strong environmental and humanistic values place less emphasis on making high incomes. Thus their willingness-to-pay is lower because their ability to pay is lower, which means that their views and wishes will be selectively discriminated against by CBA evaluations.

10. CBA usually is conducted by economists who tend to be more aware of and sensitive to monetary than nonmonetary impacts, with the result that CBA evaluations often give insufficient attention to estimating noneconomic impacts.

For years certain proponents of CBA have been selling it as a completely comprehensive evaluation method, capable of incorporating in its grand index all the factors important to public decisions. This they have done despite its many weaknesses on the unrealized hope that further research would solve the problems. But some of its serious limitations are inherent to its fallacious premise that all important human values can be adequately represented by money, which no research can overcome. The inevitable conclusion is that CBA is not and cannot become a completely comprehensive evaluation method. However, this does not mean that the method should be thrown away. Economic factors are and will always be important in decision making and CBA is well suited for addressing the strictly economic impacts of public actions.

8.3 SELECT BIBLIOGRAPHY OF CBA APPLICATIONS

General

Chase, Samuel B., (ed.). *Problems in Public Expenditure Analysis.* Washington, D.C.: Brookings Institution, 1968.

Dorfman, R., (ed.). *Measuring the Benefits of Government Investments.* Washington, D.C.: Brookings Institution, 1965.

Harberger, Arnold C., et al. (eds.). *Benefit Cost and Public Policy Analysis.* Chicago: Aldine Press, 1971–1974.

Haveman, Robert H. *The Economic Performance of Public Investments.* Baltimore, Md.: Johns Hopkins University Press, 1972.

Kneese, Allen V. "Economics and the Quality of the Environment: Some Empirical Experiences." In *Social Sciences and the Environment.* Edited by M. Garnsey. Boulder, Colo.: University of Colorado Press, 1967.

Prest, A. R., and R. Turvey. "Cost-Benefit Analysis: A Survey." *The Economic Journal,* vol. 75 (December 1965), pp. 683–735.

Recreation

Clawson, Marion, and Jack Knetsch. *Economics of Outdoor Recreation.* Baltimore, Md.: Johns Hopkins University Press, 1966.

Clawson, Marion. "Methods of Measuring the Demand for and Value of Outdoor Recreation." RFF reprint no. 10. Washington, D.C.: Resources for the Future, 1959.

Knetsch, J. L., and R. Davis. "Comparison of Methods for Recreation Evaluation." *Water Research.* Edited by Allen V. Kneese and Stephen C. Smith. Baltimore, Md.: Johns Hopkins University Press, 1966.

Knetsch, J. L. "Outdoor Recreation Demands and Benefits." *Land Economics,* vol. 39 (November 1963), pp. 387–396.

Mansfield, N. W. "The Estimation of Benefits from Recreation Sites and the Provision of a New Recreation Facility." *Regional Studies,* vol. 5 (July 1971), pp. 55–69.

McAllister, Donald M. "Planning an Urban Recreation System: A Systematic Approach." *Natural Resources Journal,* vol. 15 (July 1975), pp. 567–580.

McAllister, Donald M., and Frank Klett. "A Gravity Model of Regional Recreation Activity with an Application to Ski Trips." *Journal of Leisure Research,* vol. 8 (January 1976), pp. 21–34.

Merewitz, Leonard. "Recreational Benefits of Water Resource Development." *Water Resources Research,* vol. 2 (1966), pp. 625–664.

Wennergren, E. Boyd, and D. B. Nielsen. "Probability Estimates of Recreation Demands." *Journal of Leisure Research,* vol. 2 (Summer, 1970), pp. 112–122.

Wildlife

Capel, R. E., and R. K. Pandey. "Estimation of Benefits from Deer and Moose Hunting in Manitoba." *Canadian Journal of Agricultural Economics,* vol. 20, (July 1972), pp. 7–16.

Hammack, Judd, and G. M. Brown, Jr. *Waterfowl and Wetlands: Toward Bioeconomic Analysis.* Baltimore, Md.: Johns Hopkins University Press, 1974. Also reported in chapter 9 of John V. Krutilla and Anthony C. Fisher. *The Economics of Natural Environments.* Baltimore, Md.: Johns Hopkins University Press, 1975.

Pattison, W. S., and W. E. Phillips. "Economic Evaluation of Big Game Hunting: An Alberta Case Study." *Canadian Journal of Agricultural Economics,* vol. 19 (October 1971), pp. 72–85.

Unique Natural Areas

Isard, Walter, et al. "Case Study of a Marina Development in Plymouth Bay." In *Ecologic-Economic Analysis for Regional Development,* New York: Free Press, 1972.

Krutilla, John. "Evaluation of an Aspect of Environmental Quality: Hell's Canyon Revisited." *Proceedings of the Social Statistics Section American Statistical Society* (1971), pp. 198–206.

Krutilla, John, and A. C. Fisher. *The Economics of Natural Environments.* Baltimore, Md.: Johns Hopkins University Press, 1975.

Natural Resource Supplies

Howe, Charles W. *Benefit-Cost Analysis for Water Systems Planning.* Washington, D.C.: American Geophysical Union, 1971.

Krutilla, John V., and Otto Eckstein. *Multiple Purpose River Development.* Baltimore, Md.: Johns Hopkins University Press, 1958.

Noise

Starkie, D., and D. Johnson. *The Economic Value of Peace and Quiet.* London: Saxon House, 1975.

Walters, A. A. *Noise and Prices.* Oxford: Clarendon Press, 1975.

Air Pollution

Anderson, R., and T. Crocker. "Air Pollution and Residential Property Values." *Urban Studies,* vol. 8 (October 1971), pp. 171–180.

Benedict, H. M., Miller and Olson. "Economic Impact of Air Pollutants on Plants in the U.S." Stanford Research Institute, Menlo Park, Calif. 1971.

Freeman, A. Myrick, III. "National Estimates of Pollution Control Benefits: A General Overview." Prepared for Enviro-Control, Inc., Rockville, Md., September, 1975.

Heintz, H. T., Jr., and A. Hershaft. "National Estimates of Benefits of Controlling Air and Water Pollution." EPA, Washington Environmental Research Center, Washington, D.C., 1975.

Ridker, R. G., and J. Henning. "The Determinants of Residential Property Values with Special Reference to Air Pollution." *Review of Economics and Statistics,* vol. 49 (May 1967), pp. 246–257.

Ridker, R. G. *The Economic Costs of Air Pollution.* New York: Praeger, 1967.

Waddell, T. E. "The Economic Damages of Air Pollution." EPA, Washington Environmental Research Center, Washington, D.C., 1974.

Water Pollution

Abel, Fred H., Dennis P. Tihansky, and Richard G. Walsh. "National Benefits of Water Pollution Control." EPA, Washington Environmental Research Center, Washington, D.C., 1975.

Davidson, P. F., G. Adams, and J. Seneca. "The Social Value of Water Recreational Facilities Resulting from an Improvement in Water Quality: The Delaware Estuary." In *Water Research.* Edited by Allan V. Kneese and Stephen C. Smith. Baltimore, Md.: Johns Hopkins University Press, 1966.

Davis, Robert. "Planning a Water Quality Management System: The Case of the Potomac Estuary." In *Water Research.* Edited by Allan V. Kneese and Stephen C. Smith. Baltimore, Md.: Johns Hopkins University Press, 1966.

Heintz, W. T., Jr., and A. Hershaft. "National Estimates of Controlling Air and Water Pollution." EPA, Washington Environmental Research Center, Washington, D.C., 1975.

Kneese, Allen V. "Economics and the Quality of the Environment: Some Empirical Experiences." In *Social Sciences and the Environment.* Edited by M. Garnsey. Boulder, Colo.: University of Colorado, 1967.

Peskin, Henry, and Eugene Seskin (eds.). *Cost-Benefit Analysis and Water Pollution Policy*. Washington, D.C.: The Urban Institute, 1975.

Stevens, J. B. "Recreation Benefits from Water Pollution Control." *Water Resources Research*, vol. 2 (1966), pp. 167–182.

Stevens, Joe B. "A Critical Overview of the State-of-the-Art in Assessing Benefits of Water Pollution Control." Prepared for Enviro-Control, Inc., Rockville, Md., September, 1975.

Tihansky, D. P. "An Economic Assessment of Marine Water Pollution Damages," In *Pollution Control in the Marine Industries*. Edited by T. F. P. Sillivan. Proceedings of the Third International Conference on Pollution Control in the Marine Industries, Montreal, 1973.

Tihansky, D. P. "Damage Assessment of Household Water Quality." *Journal of the Environmental Engineering Division, American Society of Civil Engineers*, vol. 100 (1974), pp. 905–918.

Tihansky, D. P. "Recreational Welfare Losses from Water Pollution along U.S. Coasts." *Journal of Environmental Quality*, vol. 3 (1974), pp. 335–342.

9
PLANNING BALANCE SHEET AND
GOALS-ACHIEVEMENT MATRIX

9.1 INTRODUCTION

Most of the evaluation methods that have been developed since the onset of cost-benefit studies have been attempts to overcome certain weaknesses in CBA. This is certainly true of the two methods described in this chapter. The planning balance sheet (PBS) stresses the importance of recording all impacts, whether monetizeable or not, and analyzing the distribution of impacts among different community groups. These features make it sufficiently different from traditional CBA to justify its separate treatment here. The goals-achievement matrix (GAM) defines and organizes impacts according to a set of explicit goals that the public action is attempting to meet and identifies the consequences for different interest groups. It, too, is designed to accommodate unmonetizeable impacts, but unlike PBS it utilizes a set of nonmonetary value weights for computing a grand index.

9.2 THE PLANNING BALANCE SHEET

PBS is a method for conducting systematic evaluations devised by Nathaniel Lichfield and applied by him on several occasions to town and regional plans in Great Britain. It is an adaptation of cost-benefit analysis and shares with CBA its basic theory and methods. PBS goes beyond traditional CBA in two ways: first, to record detailed information on the distribution of costs and benefits among different groups of people affected by a proposed plan and, second, to accommodate formally intangibles and other unmeasured impacts by designating symbols for recording them in evaluation tables alongside monetized impacts.

Description of the Method
In PBS as in CBA, impacts are measured in nontechnical terms and estimated where possible by scientific methods. However, in contrast to CBA the evaluator is given wide latitude in making judgmental estimates because PBS seeks to determine impacts at a more detailed level, which therefore is less amenable to scientific estimation procedures.

Lichfield's idealized evaluation method would calculate a grand index of social welfare so that it could be used as an optimizing tool, but PBS falls short of this ideal.[1] Impacts are monetized whenever possible, but nonmonetizeable impacts are also recorded. This means that a net benefit total cannot be calculated. Instead, the evaluator is required to determine the plan alternative most advantageous to the public interest for each impact category. Thus the rating method yields a set of simple subindices: one for each impact category.

The impacts of a plan, referred to as "transactions," are recorded as in table 9.1. The impacts are categorized according to the people or groups who produce them, called "producers," and those who receive them, called "consumers." A "transaction" may be a typical maket transaction, such as the sale of homes by a developer (the "producer") to families (the "consumers"); or it may be a nonmarket transaction, such as the provision of educational services by a public school (the "producer") to families in the school district (the "consumers") or the imposition of noise caused by the operation of an airport (the "producer") on the nearby populace (the "consumers"). The producer (or producers) involved in a set of interrelated transactions constitutes a "sector"; the same applies to consumers. A "sector" is important because it constitutes the impact category in PBS, for which both "benefits" and "costs" can occur, monetary or otherwise.

According to Lichfield, each cost and benefit can be one of three kinds:[2]

1. *Direct or indirect, or private or social in the conventional terminology*
Private relates to costs that the producer or consumer must bear and to benefits they can appropriate under current law and custom. Social relates to the diffused costs suffered by others which need not be compensated and benefits enjoyed by others for which payment cannot be exacted.

2. *Real or transfer*
Real relates to the use of real (economic) resources, that is, land, men, and materials; whereas transfer relates to financial resources that are simply transferred from one section of the community to another as a result of a transaction, without using up or adding to real resources. The purchase of land is an example of a transfer.

3. *Real (technological) or pecuniary*
These relate in the main to changes in the value of established as opposed to new goods and services brought about externally. Real costs and benefits arise where there are changes in actual quality (such as the atmosphere of an office building when a new park is created nearby). Pecuniary changes in value arise simply because of relative changes in the supply or demand of

Table 9.1a
Planning balance sheet showing a comparison of costs and benefits of alternate plans

Producer	Plan A Benefit	Plan A Cost	Plan B Benefit	Plan B Cost	Consumer	Plan A Benefit	Plan A Cost	Plan B Benefit	Plan B Cost
1					2				
3					4				
5					6				
7					8				

Source: Adapted from Nathaniel Lichfield, *Cost-Benefit Analysis in Town Planning: A Case Study of Cambridge,* Cambridgeshire Isle of Ely County Council, 1966, pp. 58–62.

151

Planning Balance Sheet and Goals-Achievement Matrix

Table 9.1b
Planning balance sheet showing net difference in annual costs and benefits between plan A and plan B

Producer	Plan A minus Plan B				Consumer	Plan A minus Plan B			
	Benefit	Cost	Net	Net Advantage to		Benefit	Cost	Net	Net Advantage to
1					2				
3					4				
5					6				
7					8				

Source: Adapted from Lichfield, *Cost-Benefit Analysis in Town Planning*, 1966, pp. 58–62.

goods and services (for example, the change in values of established houses when new up-to-date houses are built).

Thus PBS like CBA seeks to assess social as well as private costs and benefits. However, unlike CBA, PBS records transfer and pecuniary costs and benefits. These are excluded in CBA on the grounds that they merely represent redistributions of costs and benefits among members of society, and not a change in their totals (as reflected, for example, in net benefits or GNP). Lichfield includes redistributions because he believes that they should be taken into account in designing and evaluating alternative town plans.

To illustrate how impacts are categorized in PBS, take the case of a plan for developing a new industrial park where manufacturers would make products for local consumption but also cause air pollution. The manufacturers would constitute a sector as shown in table 9.2. They would receive as a benefit the dollar revenue from selling their products and incur dollar costs in producing them. The product-consuming public would constitute another sector. Their benefit would be measured by the consumer benefit (using conventional CBA procedures); their cost is the dollar expenditure for the products, which is a quantity identical to the benefit received by the manufacturer. The public exposed to the air pollution is another consumer group; it may include consumers of the manufactured products, but is just as likely to include nonconsumers of the product as well. These consumers receive no benefit but incur the adverse effects of air pollution, which may be partially monetized but otherwise represented in terms of the suffering from illness and death, aesthetic damage, and so forth.

To illustrate how the impact of an environmental plan would be recorded in PBS, take the simplified case of a plan that calls for public agency regulation of industrially caused water pollution. One of the sectors in this case would include two producers: the industries causing the pollution and the regulating agency. As summarized in table 9.3, the polluting industries might possibly receive a benefit in the form of increased dollar revenue from higher prices,[3] but they would have dollar costs for the capital and operating expenditures to reduce their discharge of effluents. The regulating agency would receive as a benefit tax dollars to support its operations and would incur dollar costs for conducting its regulating activities. The consumers of the water (actual and potential) would constitute a second sector, and this

Table 9.2
Illustrative transactions for an industrial park

Sector	Benefit	Cost
Producer		
Manufacturers	Revenue from sale of products.	Cost of manufacturing products
Consumer		
Consumers of products	Consumer benefits of of products	Dollar expenditures for for manufactured products
Consumers of air pollution		Increased exposure to air pollutants

Table 9.3
Illustrative transactions for water pollution regulation

Sector	Benefit	Cost
Producer		
Industries causing water pollution	Possible increased revenues	Expenditures to reduce effluent discharges
Regulating agency	Tax receipts supporting regulatory activities	Expenditures for regulatory activities
Consumer		
Recreationists	More higher quality recreation activities	Tax payments to support regulations
Sightseers	Improved landscape aesthetics	Tax payments to support regulations
Water consumers	Better tasting water	Tax payments to support regulations
Fish and other forms of life.	Better health and fewer mortalities	
Other taxpayers		Tax payments to support regulations

sector would include such groups as active recreationists, sightseers, the water-drinking public, and—I would add—fish (although Lichfield might protest that including acquatic animals takes excessive liberty with his concept of "consumer"). The consumers would gain by the reduced cost (or increased benefit), measured when possible in money units and otherwise in physical units or recorded as an intangible. The consumer groups as well as other tax payers, would incur as a cost the tax payments that support the regulatory agency.

The costs and benefits of alternative plans are compared in adjacent columns of table 9.1a. Although only two alternatives are shown, columns can be added for as many alternatives as are to be evaluated. Each cost and benefit represents a forecast of what would occur with implementation of the plan as compared with no-action.

The measurement unit of each cost and benefit, whether it be money, time, or physical units, is recorded next to the quantity. Money is, of course, the preferred measurement unit, but if monetization is not possible, time and physical units are acceptable. In cases where the magnitude of a measurable impact cannot be estimated, an M, T, or P is recorded to indicate that a money, time, or physical impact is expected to result from the plan; or if the expected impact is an intangible, an I is recorded. A numerical subscript is assigned to each of these letters, keying it to a verbal description of the impact. Negative quantities are underlined to distinguish them from positive ones. Capital items (that is, durable property involving a one-time expenditure) are distinguished from annually recurring items. All future quantities are discounted to their present value.

After the detailed impact information is recorded in table a, it is "reduced" to summary form. The benefits and costs are annualized and totaled for each sector. Thus, if a sector includes more than one producer or consumer, the benefit and cost for each are totaled. Similarly, if a producer or consumer experiences more than one kind of benefit or cost, these are totaled. The reduction process derives a single total, for benefits and costs, for each sector. Totals formed from like units, such as dollars, are expressed as a single quantity; totals formed from mixed items reflect this fact.

The reduced information recorded in table a is transferred to another table such as table 9.1b. This table is organized to facilitate the comparison of alternative plans. For each sector, the benefits and costs of one plan are subtracted from those of the alternative plan, and the net benefits of one plan over the other are calculated. Finally, for each sector, the evaluator records his judgment regarding which plan is more advantageous to the public interest.

The evaluator's judgment regarding the most advantageous plan for each sector can include both objective and subjective considerations. This fact is best understood by reference to a real example. The information listed in table 9.4 shows the reduced impacts that Lichfield derived in evaluating alternative plans for Cambridge, as prepared by the county and by the university. It can be seen that for most sectors the "net" column includes a mixture of different types of impacts; some are monetized quantities, others are items measurable in various units that have not been quantified, and still others are intangibles. In order to judge the most advantageous plan under these conditions, the evaluator must make objective judgments regarding the magnitudes of the unquantified impacts, then make subjective judgments regarding the relative importance of each to the welfare of society. Thus the evaluator is required to make wide-ranging judgments in conducting his or her work, although the summary judgment, "not conclusive," is acceptable when it is felt that no alternative is clearly advantageous.

Critique of PBS

PBS, being a variant of CBA, shares most of the strengths and weaknesses of CBA. However, it has a couple of advantages over CBA:

1. PBS establishes a formal procedure for recording unmonetized and intangible impacts alongside monetized impacts, increasing their visibility to reviewers of the evaluation report. This is a major advance over CBA, in which unmonetized impacts cannot be incorporated in the formal evaluation and, at best, are treated as unimportant afterthoughts in the text of the typical CBA report.

However, it should be noted that the manner of recording impacts in PBS still leaves unquantified impacts at somewhat of a disadvantage. Quantified impacts are fully communicated in the PBS tables whereas the alphabetical symbols for unquantified impacts requires that a reviewer of the evaluation report make reference to a verbal description of them provided elsewhere. Thus, to the extent that a reviewer—either a decision-maker or a concerned

Table 9.4a
Summary planning balance sheet for Cambridge evaluation (in £0000)

(a) Net difference in annual costs & benefits between university & county plan

Producers/operators		Number		University plan minus county plan			
Item number	Sector reduction	City	University	Benefit	Cost	Net	Net advantage to
1.0	City council as developers				120	120	County
3.0	Current landowners						
3.1	Displaced						Neither
3.3	Not displaced			$m_3 m_5$ $m_1 m_5^+$	$m_4 375$ m_2	$m_3 m_5$ $m_1 m_5^+$ $\dfrac{m_4 375}{m_2}$	Probably county

(b) Net difference in annual costs & benefits between university & county plan

Consumers		Number		University plan minus county plan			
Item number	Sector reduction	City	University	Benefit	Cost	Net	Net advantage to
4.2	Occupiers displaced	n	n^+	£130	$\dfrac{p_5+p_6+p_7}{p_5 p_6 p_7^+}$	£130 $\dfrac{p_5+p_6+p_7}{p_5 p_6 p_7^+}$	Not conclusive
4.4	Occupiers not displaced			$m_{18} m_{16}$	$\dfrac{m_{19} m_{20}}{m_{17}}$	$\dfrac{m_{18} m_{16}}{m_{19} m_{20}}$ m_{17}	Probably county

2.02	New occupiers	n	$n+$	$i_2 i_1$	$m_7 m_6$	$\dfrac{i_2 i_1}{m_7 m_6}$	University
2.04	Vehicle users	n	$n+$		$\dfrac{m_9 m_{10}}{m_9+m_{10}}+$	$\dfrac{m_9 m_{10}}{m_9+m_{10}}+$	University
2.06	Car park users	n	$n+$	$i_5+\underline{i_5}$	$\dfrac{m_{11}+t_1+t_3}{m_{11}t_1 t_2}$	$\dfrac{i_5+i_5}{m_{11}+t_1+t_3}$ $\overline{m_{11}t_1 t_2}$	Not conclusive
2.08	University faculty and students	n	n		$\dfrac{i_6 t_3+}{i_6+t_3}$	$\dfrac{i_6 t_3+}{i_6+t_3}$	Not conclusive
2.10	Shopping public	300th	400th	$\underline{i_7+i_7}$	$\dfrac{t_4 i_7 t_6 t_6+}{t_4+i_7+}$ t_6+t_7	$\dfrac{i_7+i_7}{t_4 i_7 t_6}$ $\dfrac{t_7}{t_4+i_7+}$ t_6+t_7	Probably university
2.12	Public at large	n	n	$\dfrac{i_8 i_9 i_{11}}{p_1+p_2 p_4}$ $\dfrac{i_8+i_9+i_{10}}{p_1 p_2+p_4}+$		$\dfrac{i_8 i_9 i_{11}}{p_1+p_2 p_4}$ $\dfrac{i_8+i_9+i_{10}}{p_1 p_2+p_4}+$	County

Source: Nathaniel Lichfield, "Costs-Benefit Analysis in Town Planning," 1966, p. 62.

citizen—has limited time to look over the information, he or she may not take the extra time to look up the descriptions and thereby may judge the alternatives on the basis of quantified information only.

2. Central to PBS is the accounting of impacts according to transactions, revealing the distribution of costs and benefits among particular groups, which is not included in a conventional CBA. The classification of impacts according to producer and consumer groups is unique to PBS. This kind of information can aid decision-makers in judging the equity effects of alternative plans, and also can be very useful during redesigning to reduce adverse equity effects and moderate interest group resistance. The fact that an action may have important equity implications for producers is entirely overlooked in the conventional CBA literature.

The organization of impact information around transactions, however, often may fail to reveal the most important equity effects: namely, the adverse impacts on disadvantaged groups in society, who seldom constitute a unified producer or consumer group. Naturally, this kind of information can be added to a PBS evaluation, but it can be added just as easily to a traditional CBA.

It is worth mentioning that the cost of conducting an evaluation can be greatly increased when impacts must be estimated for each of several groups in society, rather than for society as a whole. The PBS requirement of estimating impacts on producers and consumers separately may be viewed as too rigid—in the sense that it adds to the cost of conducting an evaluation but in many cases may be foreseen to provide unimportant equity information.

PBS is not superior to CBA in all respects. Two disadvantages are important to note:

1. In CBA the evaluator has a free hand in choosing the impact categories that seem (or prove) most important to each evaluation problem, which can be done by reference to the values of the public and their elected representatives. By contrast, the procedures for PBS require that the evaluator select the impact categories on the basis of "transactions." If financial transactions dominate the selection, as they often do, certain types of environmental, social, and political impacts may be slighted or even ignored. This is a special problem for impacts such as pollution and aesthetics that can occur in several sectors and form an aggregate effect that is worthy of independent considera-

tion. To illustrate the problem, a proposed action may cause air pollution in several different sectors. PBS would consider the emission in each sector separately, together with the other impacts that occur within the sector. Thus, while the aggregate air pollution impact may be serious, the total effect might not be reported in a PBS evaluation, and seemingly small emissions from each sector might be treated as unimportant.

Actually, Lichfield has recognized this problem and dealt with it by augmenting his definition of sector to include groups to which explicit planning goals apply. For example, he added the "public at large" as a consumer sector in the Cambridge evaluation in order to assess the impact of alternative plans on the university character of the town, the preservation of which was a major objective of the planning action.[4] Unfortunately, this definitional departure makes the impact categories that characterize PBS appear arbitrary and unimportant.

2. In using PBS the evaluator is permitted to make major value judgments when determining for each sector the most advantageous plan. This violates the criterion stated in chapter 3 that evaluators take care to avoid using their own values on the assumption that theirs are a good indicator of what the values of their clients are or ought to be. CBA does not formally permit the evaluator to insert his or her personal value judgments into the evaluation, although certainly this may occur by subtle informal means.

9.2 THE GOALS-ACHIEVEMENT MATRIX

GAM is an evaluation method, devised by Morris Hill, that attempts to overcome the weaknesses of CBA and PBS. In recent years it has been used frequently for evaluating town plans in Great Britain and elsewhere.

In GAM impacts are categorized according to a set of explicitly stated community goals, and further subdivided according to the community groups that are affected. The quantification of impacts is stressed in GAM, but not monetization. Each impact is estimated by scientific methods when possible and measured in whatever unit most closely describes the goal to which it corresponds. A grand index of "goals-achievement" can be calculated for each alternative action by multiplying the impacts by a set of value weights.

GAM is intended to surmount four major criticisms Hill voices of CBA: (1) intangibles cannot be incorporated into the analysis, (2) the theoretical assumptions on which CBA is based are seldom met in reality, which means that CBA seldom is capable of accurately measuring the social welfare as affected by a proposed action, (3) CBA ignores equity effects, and (4) the conversion of impacts into monetary terms and the focus of attention on net benefits "may lead to an erroneous decision resulting from the confusion of the original purpose of a course of action with its secondary consequences."[5] He is suggesting here that a public action designed to deal with a specific problem may pass the net benefit test even though it is totally or partially ineffective in solving the problem. This can occur when an action has desirable impacts, other than those which it is designed to generate, representing sizable monetized benefits. For example, a flood control project may be ineffective in controlling floods yet be acceptable according to the cost-benefit criterion because it generates large recreation benefits from water impoundments.

Hill's one major objection to PBS is similar to the last criticism of CBA, although stated differently. He takes the position that "benefits and costs have meaning only in relation to a well-defined objective."[6] Therefore he concludes that, because PBS does not require reference to community objectives, "there is no means of knowing whether the costs and benefits listed are relevant for inclusion in the balance sheet. . . ."[7]

Description of the Method

The "rational planning process" seems to represent a guiding set of values which Hill used to construct GAM and assess other evaluation methods. He defines rational planning as "a process for determining appropriate future action by utilizing scarce resources in such a way as to maximize the attainment of ends held by the system."[8] This definition leads him to the conclusion that the "ends" or "goals" of planning must be established and used as the basis for evaluating alternative actions.

A central feature of GAM is the set of community goals by which impacts are organized. Hill defines three types of goals—ideals, objectives and policies—which can be arranged in a hierarchy, from general to specific:

An ideal is like a horizon allowing for indefinite progression in its direction but always receding, such as equality, freedom, or justice. An "objective" denotes an attainable goal that has instrumental value in that it is believed to lead to another valued goal rather than having intrinsic value in itself. Objectives are defined operationally so that either the existence of a desired state or the degree of achievement of this state can be established. . . . A "policy" is the specification in concrete details of ways and means for the attainment of planned objectives.[9]

The goals in GAM are expressed as objectives whenever possible, so that progression toward and regression from their achievement can be measured. The goals should be those held by the community, because the community is the client of the planning process and the group that will be affected by the planning actions. Each goal statement is accompanied by a recommended unit by which achievement of the goal can be measured. The following are examples of a few goals and measurement units proposed by Hill for evaluating transportation plans:[10]

1. *Increase of accessibility*

Measured in average travel time and, when valid, in monetary terms.

2. *Accident reduction*

Measured in terms of numbers of fatalities and injuries; injury costs and property damage measured in monetary terms.

3. *Economic efficiency*

Measured in monetary terms.

4. *Income distribution*

Measured in monetary terms.

5. *Reduction of air pollution*

Measured in terms of the amount of pollutants per unit volume of air.

6. *Noise reduction*

Measured in decibels or sones.

In addition to being organized by goals, impacts are classified according to the community groups that are affected by them. The groups are delineated by the evaluators in a way that will reveal the most important equity effects of the alternative plans.

The impact information is recorded in a matrix similar to that shown in table 9.5. For each goal and each group a goals-achievement account is established to distinguish between impacts that represent a regression from a goal (Hill's definition of costs) and impacts that represent a progression toward a goal (Hill's definition of benefits). The impacts for each quantifiable goal are measured in the same units, permitting an objective comparison

Table 9.5
The goals-achievement matrix

Goal description	Goal 1			Goal 2			Goal 3		
Value weight	2			3			5		
	Value weight	Impacts Benefits	Costs	Value weight	Impacts Benefits	Costs	Value weight	Impacts Benefits	Costs
Incidence									
Group a	1	A	D	5	E	—	1		N
Group b	3	H		4	—	R	2		—
Group c	1	L	J	3	—	S	3		—
Group d	2	—		2	T	—	4	M	—
Group e	1	—	K	1	—	U	5		P
		Σ	Σ		Σ	Σ		Σ	Σ

Source: Adapted from Morris Hill, "A Goals-Achievement Matrix for Evaluating Alternative Plans," *Journal of the American Institute of Planners*, 34 (1968): 23.

between costs and benefits, and facilitating the comparison of alternative actions. Intangible impacts are also recorded in the matrix, although by definition they are not described in quantified units. Uncertain impacts are treated with probability formulations, as in CBA, or are recorded as range rather than point estimates. Future impacts are discounted to present values, using conventional CBA procedures, which can be applied to all quantified impacts, monetized or not.

Value weights are set for each goal and each group to reflect their relative importance in terms of the community's values. For example, in table 9.5, goal 2 is shown to be 50 percent more important than goal 1 because it has a value weight of 3 by comparison to the value weight of 2 for goal 1. The value weights for groups reflect the comparative importance of a goal to different groups. For example, taking goal 1, group b has a value weight of 3 and group a of 1; thus group b considers this goal 3 times as important as group a. Although the weights are shown as constants, Hill indicates they could be scaled instead.

The weights are multiplied by the impacts to derive a grand score of goals-achievement for each alternative being evaluated. The computations begin by applying the group weights to the impacts for each goal to derive a weighted index of achievement for each goal. Then the goal weights are applied to the goal scores to derive the overall goals-achievement score. Naturally, intangibles cannot be included in these calculations.

Capital letters in table 9.5 represent estimated impacts. The braces indicate where an impact applies to several groups combined. A blank implies that no impact is expected, and a dash that the estimated impact is negligible. The summation sign at the bottom of a column indicates that all the impacts for the corresponding goal are quantified and therefore can be totaled.

Since a separate matrix of impact information is required for each alternative being evaluated, it can be seen that GAM is very demanding of detailed impact information, perhaps more so than PBS. PBS requires impact information for sectors only, whereas GAM requires it for both goals and groups.

In order to better demonstrate the contrasts between his method and PBS, Hill applied GAM to the two Cambridge plans previously evaluated by Lichfield. Unfortunately, the lack of properly detailed data severely limited the attempt. He derived a set of goals from several planning reports for Cambridge and from Lichfields's evaluation report. However, existing data did not permit him to assess the incidence of impacts on different groups. Instead he analyzed incidence for the major land-use groupings in central Cambridge, such as the university colleges, residential districts, public buildings, open space, and transportation routes.

Data limitations also prevented him from estimating the magnitudes of impacts. He was forced to adopt a simple three-point, ordinal scale of +1 for progression on a goal, −1 for regression, and 0 for no change.

Hill had no information on community values with which he could form value weights, so he proceeded with two experimental approaches: one was to take the completely arbitrary assumption that all goals and all land-use groups were equally valued. Accordingly, all value weights were set equal to one. The computed goals-achievement scores indicated that the university plan was superior to the county plan. The second experiment was to conduct sensitivity tests, varying the value weights to see how the conclusion would be affected.

In recent years several town- and regional-planning efforts in Great Britain have chosen the GAM over PBS and other evaluation methods, including the Brighton Urban Structure Plan, the Ipswich Structure Plan, the Staffordshire County Plan, the Worcestershire County Structure Plan and the West Central Scotland Regional Plan. The Coventry-Solihull-Warwickshire Study, conducted between 1968 and 1971, is an interesting example, utilizing GAM from an early stage in the design process.[11] The task was to prepare a recommended strategy for urban and rural development in the subregion to the end of the century, indicating the location of key land-uses, such as major residential developments, shopping and employment centers, and rural conservation areas.

The goals selected by the planning team were based on information from a variety of sources. Interviews were conducted with public officials, planning reports from previous studies were examined and local news and editorial columns were read. A public opinion survey was also conducted to test a tentative list of goals, elicit additional goal ideas, and secure priorities. When interviewed following the conclusion of the work, the study director indicated that more attention should have been devoted to formulating goals, particularly to involving the public more directly in the process.[12]

No attempt was made to forecast impacts according to community groups.

It was estimated that this would have added 40 percent to the cost of the study, which was considered more than it was worth.

The value weights for the objectives were determined by the planning team. Each member submitted a set of weights representing his or her professional judgment of the appropriate values. These were used to calculate an average, weighting those of each member by the length of professional experience. The public opinion survey provided some information on citizen values in the form of personal rankings of the five top-priority goals, but it is unclear how this information was used by the planning team.

The goals and value-weights were used not only to evaluate the few major alternatives that issued from the design process, but also to generate a long list of design options in an early design state. Using different sets of value weights, including those of planning team members, outside planners and community interest groups, "development potential indices" were calculated for different areas in the subregion. This enabled the study team to identify several dozen design alternatives. The consistency with which evaluation issues were approached throughout the design and evaluation stages of the study added a margin of confidence that all the important options had been considered.

Critique of GAM
The organization of impact information according to community goals is one of the central features of GAM. The feature is quite useful, although Hill seems to exaggerate the importance of goals statements to the effect that benefits and costs have meaning only in relation to a well-defined objective. A measured cost or benefit estimated by sound cost-benefit procedures represents an impact for which some people are willing to sacrifice personal resources. Should such an impact be ignored by evaluators just because the set of goals established for the planning exercise fails to include it? How should planners react to citizens at a public hearing arguing against a proposed plan on certain personal grounds not covered by the formal goals statements of the plan? Should they tell the citizens that their values are meaningless? Clearly the answer to these questions is that formally prepared goals statements should not be used as a rigid set of criteria for evaluation. Throughout the design and evaluation stages of planning, new information

about impacts is acquired that should be judged on its own merits and not whether it is covered by the existing goals statements. Goals should be augmented when important additional information on impacts is acquired. Hill, himself, hints at this conclusion when he states, "Even in the rational planning model, the goals should be viewed as tentative statements subject to the other elements in the planning process. Initial objective-setting is inevitably provisional and general and thus the rational planning model should also be considered as relating to an iterative process.[13]

A major advantage of goals statements, assuming that citizens and their elected representatives play an important role in preparing them, is that evaluators are forced to see the problem in terms of the community's values rather than their own. Another advantage is that they help organize impact information into categories of like elements, making it easier to compare the advantages and disadvantages of alternatives. For example, unlike PBS, all air pollution impacts would be assessed in one category, making it easier to compare alternative plans for minimizing air pollution. Goals statements also provide important background information for selecting the best descriptors of impacts. Naturally, impact descriptions should coincide as closely as possible with their corresponding goals.

Although Hill stresses that the community's goals should be used, he neither defines what are and what are not community goals, nor does he recommend criteria or procedures for preparing them. Must a goal, in order to qualify as a community goal, have the support of the majority of the people in a community or the majority of the elected representatives? If so, a goal of a minority group would not be a community goal, and thus would not be included in the evaluation. This would hardly be consistent with Hill's purpose of recording the distribution of impacts. Any goal, interest, issue, problem, or concern that is important to a group in society, whether a minority or a majority, deserves to be considered in an evaluation. The manner in which goals are identified and defined, and particularly the manner in which community members are selected to participate in the process, is critical to developing a set of community goals appropriate for evaluation purposes.

The quantification of impacts is emphasized in GAM.[14] The emphasis derives from the fact that only quantified impacts can be included in the grand index of goals achievement. Although Hill criticizes CBA for not considering intangibles, his own method has the same weakness. However, there is a difference: GAM includes unmonetized impacts in its grand index, whereas CBA does not.

Quantification has important advantages: it provides an easy means of describing the magnitude of an impact; it permits the net effect of positive and negative impacts measured in like units to be calculated precisely; and it can be used to compare quickly the effectiveness of alternative actions in meeting a goal. However, quantification can be carried too far, and there is a danger of this when using GAM. Quantification is not useful when the measurement unit leaves out a great deal of important information. In such cases a verbal, graphical, or pictorial description may be vastly superior.

Another danger of overemphasizing quantification is the adoption of measurement scales and indices that are too complex to be understood by most people, including most decision-makers. For example, in a paper on goals-achievement for outdoor recreation planning, Hill suggests using the following six objectives: (1) increase national economic benefits, (2) increase regional economic benefits, (3) equitable distribution of recreation benefits, (4) high quality recreation facilities, (5) increase the proportion of the public served, and (6) preservation of natural areas.[15] His proposed measurement unit for goals 3, 4, and 6 are very difficult to interpret. For example, he presents the following index for measuring the preservation of natural areas:[16]

$$N_j = (1 - F_k)(1 - e^{-f_{jk}}),$$

where

F_k = the percentage of region k in a natural state,

f_{jk} = the percentage of site j in region k that is in a natural state.

How could affected citizens or decision-makers possibly determine the importance of an impact measured by this index?

The value weights are another main feature of GAM. Hill states, "The key to decision-making by means of the goals-achievement matrix is the weighting of objectives, activities, locations, groups, or sectors in urban areas. By the application of relative weights, it is possible to arrive at a unique conclusion."[17] Although the value weights are supposed to reflect the values of the community, Hill does not recommend a specific method for determining them. However, he outlines the following possible alternatives:[18]

1. The decision-makers may be asked to weigh objectives and their relative importance for particular activities, locations, or groups in the urban area.
2. A general referendum may be employed to elicit community valuation of objectives.
3. A sample of persons in affected groups may be interviewed concerning their relative valuation of objectives.
4. The community power structure may be identified, and its views on the weighting of objectives and their incidence can be elicited.
5. Well-publicized public hearings devoted to community goal formulation and valuation can be held.
6. The pattern of previous allocations of public investments may be analyzed in order to determine the goal priorities implicit in previous decisions on the allocation of resources.

Among his conclusions, Hill cautions the reader that "The goals-achievement matrix is not very useful if weights cannot be objectively determined or assumed. The development of methods for the determination of weights is thus of first priority for the successful application of the goals-achievement matrix."[19] This seems to place GAM on very shaky grounds. Valid methods for determining value weights have not been developed yet, and are not likely to be developed. Although value weights are technically a neat solution to the evaluation dilemma, the exercise of having citizens or decision-makers express their value weights is a very abstract process. How confidently can people answer questions such as, Which is more important to you, reducing traffic accidents or reducing noise? How much more important is it: twice, three times, four times? Such questions are very general. They don't indicate the severity of existing conditions, the magnitudes of the changes, the precise locations of the improvements, the people who would be affected, and so on. People must be presented with more specific information for them to be able to accurately express their values. In the process of over-emphasizing the importance of the weights, Hill, unfortunately, under-emphasizes the great worth of the detailed impact information organized in his matrix.

GAM has several advantages over CBA:

1. It establishes a formal procedure for assessing the equity effects of public actions, although it must be recognized that the procedure will raise the cost of conducting the evaluation.

2. It is designed to include all quantified impacts in its grand index, not just monetized impacts.

3. It emphasizes the importance of organizing impacts in categories that relate directly to community goals, which is consistent with one of the criteria established in chapter 3 that evaluators consult the values of the people or their elected representatives in selecting the impact categories to be employed.

GAM has two advantages over PBS worth noting:

1. In GAM the evaluator has a freer hand in selecting the community groups to be used in assessing equity effects. The groups can be selected for the sole purpose of isolating the important equity impacts, whether or not they conform to the (PBS) definition of a sector.

2. The evaluator also has a freer hand in selecting the impact categories. Rather than being bound to sectors, the evaluator can organize the impact information around the issues and problems important to citizens and their elected representatives. High priority environmental, social, and political impacts are more likely to be placed in independent impact categories rather than submerged piecemeal in numerous financial sectors.

Advocates of PBS and CBA cite as the one main disadvantage of GAM its method of calculating an index of goals-achievement not being based on any accepted theory of social welfare.[20] It could be further noted that procedures for measuring point-type value weights have not been validated. These criticisms are accurate, but GAM is not necessarily at a disadvantage because of them. While there are some people who accept the theoretical base for CBA, there are others who do not, pointing to its many shortcomings. One might take the position that an evaluation method based on a sophisticated but erroneous theory of social welfare is more dangerous than one without a theory at all.

9.3 CONCLUSION

PBS demonstrates a systematic approach to evaluating alternatives without forcing all factors into a grand index of net benefits (or benefit-cost ratio). It provides valuable ideas for representing equity and nonmonetizeable impacts, but its emphasis on transactions as the basis for organizing impact information is unnecessarily restrictive and can force the evaluator to perform useless double-entry bookkeeping, thus diverting attention away from the key issues surrounding the planning action.

The main contribution of GAM is its emphasis on organizing impact assessments around community goals and issues. Both CBA and PBS overlook the importance of focusing explicit attention on the key issues as identified by the people who will be affected by a plan. GAM offers a view different from CBA on how impacts can be summed into a total score. Whether or not its formal mathematical approach for solving the evaluation dilemma is useful, however, is not established.

9.4 BIBLIOGRAPHY ON PLANNING BALANCE SHEET

Lichfield, Nathaniel. "Cost-Benefit Analysis in City Planning." *Journal of the American Institute of Planners,* vol. 26 (November 1960), pp. 273–279.

Lichfield, Nathaniel. "Cost-Benefit Analysis in Plan Evaluation." *Town Planning Review,* vol. 35 (July 1964), pp. 160–169.

Lichfield, Nathaniel. "Cost Benefit Analysis in Town Planning: A Case Study of Cambridge," Cambridgeshire and Isle of Ely County Council, 1966.

Lichfield, Nathaniel. "Cost-Benefit Analysis in Urban Expansion: A Case Study, Peterborough." *Regional Studies,* vol. 3 (September 1969), pp. 123–155.

Lichfield, Nathaniel. "Evaluation Methodology of Urban and Regional Plans: A Review." *Regional Studies,* vol. 4 (August 1970), pp. 151–165.

Lichfield, Nathaniel, Peter Kettle, and Michael Whitbread. *Evaluation in the Planning Process.* Oxford: Pergamon Press, 1975.

9.5 BIBLIOGRAPHY ON GOALS-ACHIEVEMENT MATRIX

Hill, Morris. "A Method for the Evaluation of Transportation Plans." *Highway Research Record,* no. 180 (1967), pp. 21–34.

Hill, Morris. "A Goals-Achievement Matrix for Evaluating Alternative Plans." *Journal of the American Institute of Planners,* vol. 34 (January 1968), pp. 19–28.

Hill, Morris, and M. Shechter. "Optimal Goal Achievement in the Development of Outdoor Recreation Facilities." In *Urban and Regional Planning.* Edited by A. G. Wilson. London: Pion Press, 1971.

Hill, Morris, and Yigal Tzamir. "Multidimensional Evaluation of Regional Plans Serving Multiple Objectives." *Papers of the Regional Science Association,* vol. 29 (1972), pp. 139–165.

Hill, Morris. "Planning for Multiple Objectives." Monograph Series, No. 5. Philadelphia: Regional Science Research Institute, 1973.

Hill, Morris, and Rachelle Alterman. "Power Plant Site Evaluation: The Case of the Sharon Plant in Israel." *Journal of Environmental Management,* vol. 2 (April 1974), pp. 179–196.

Hill, Morris, and Elia Werczberger. "Goal Programming and the Goals-Achievement Matrix." *International Regional Science Review,* vol. 3 (1978).

Rotham, Richard. "Access Versus Environment." *Traffic Quarterly,* vol. 27 (January 1973), pp. 111–132.

10
ENERGY ANALYSIS

10.1 INTRODUCTION

The basic idea of energy analysis (EA) is to determine the energy implications of actions so that alternatives can be compared in terms of their energy consequences. Since many impacts can be interpreted in energy terms, and since measurements can be made in uniform energy units, the method might be viewed as a grand index approach to evaluation. However, EA is not a unified technique. Different analysts approach it in different ways, and many do not adhere to the view that it is a comprehensive evaluation method.

The term "energy analysis" was adopted in the early 1970s by an international group to refer to work previously called energy accounting, energy budgeting, energy costing and energy systems analysis.[1] Interest in unifying the approaches to EA is recent, but scientific and industrial studies of this type have been conducted for decades; several origins include engineering studies of energy efficiency in man-made systems, theoretical analysis of energy phenomena in physical systems, and ecological studies of energy flows in natural systems.

There appear to be three views of the role EA can play in evaluation, although the distinctions are not well articulated in the literature: the first and broadest in scope is that EA is a completely comprehensive method which should be used instead of CBA for evaluating public actions, particularly those having significant environmental consequences. The second is that EA should be used as a comprehensive method to evaluate alternative plans for energy conservation and development. The third sees EA more modestly as an evaluation tool for assessing the energy resource implications of energy conservation and development programs and projects.

The key difference is whether energy units should be used as a rating measure for calculating a grand index, as in the first two views, or as simply a measure for computing the strict energy impacts of alternatives, as in the third. Thus the three positions can be reduced to EA as a comprehensive evaluation method versus EA as a tool for measuring a limited set of impacts. The difference interpreted in evaluation terms is obviously enormous. Advocates of the former advance, implicitly if not explicitly, a new theory of social value—an energy theory of value—which carries EA well beyond the realms of objectivity and science; advocates of the latter do not see EA entering the subjective realm at all.

10.2 ENERGY ANALYSIS AS A COMPREHENSIVE METHODOLOGY

The importance of energy as a measure of value is underscored by the view that energy is the most fundamental limiting factor on all human action.[2] Nothing can happen without energy; all work requires it as the driving force. This is true in nature, and it is true in human societies and in man-made industrial systems. As Odum put it,

In the affairs of forests, seas, cities and human beings, the potential energy sources that are available flow through each process, doing and driving useful work ... The availability of power sources determines the amount of work activity that can exist, and control of these power flows determines the power in man's affairs and in his relative influence on nature. That any and every process and activity on earth is an energy manifestation measurable in energy units is a fact of existence.[3]

Man's ability to harness concentrated energy resources has been responsible for the surge in the material standard of living in many countries during the current century. Especially significant have been the fossil fuels: coal, natural gas, and, particularly, petroleum. If the remaining reserves of these nonrenewable energy resources were huge relative to demand, energy analysis might not be useful. But we are now aware of the fact that our reserves are being rapidly depleted, particularly petroleum and natural gas. This not only threatens our ability to make further gains in the material standard of living but raises serious questions as to whether the existing level can be sustained in future generations.

Energy is viewed by some analysts as an evaluation measure more fundamental than money; it is also considered to be a more pervasive unit of measure. Wherever money flows in an economic system, the flow of resources in the opposite direction can be interpreted in terms of energy. For example, when a monetary compensation is paid for land, labor, and materials used in production, the exchange of these resources has an energy interpretation: land is the base upon which terrestrial plants fix solar energy through photosynthesis, labor requires food energy to sustain it, and materials require energy for extraction, refinement, and transportation. Each input entails an energy cost that can be calculated.

Every interaction in a natural system also has an energy interpretation. As Odum has shown, our ecological knowledge of how energy flows through natural systems permits us to draw and quantify energy diagrams that describe the environmental impacts of an action.[4] We have already seen, however, that many environmental impacts cannot be adequately monetized. Consequently, "Many kinds of public actions of sweeping importance to natural systems are justified on various kinds of cost benefit ratios based on money in such a way as to ignore the important values not part of the money economy."[5] Because energy is more fundamental and pervasive than money, Odum suggests, "Perhaps the energetic common denominator can be employed to evaluate all uses in the same terms so that planning boards can act fairly, protect the public interest, and develop patterns for the energy network that are best for man's survival."[6]

Using energy analysis as a comprehensive evaluation method, the "cost" of land for a highway can be measured by the reduced plant production (for example, in kilocalories) caused by the land transformation; the "cost" of materials can be measured by the (kilocalories of) petroleum, coal, gas, and so forth, used to extract, process, and transport the materials to the site; the labor "cost" can be represented by the food energy required to sustain the labor input.

Pollution impacts can also be "energized." A water pollution impact, such as increased turbidity or decreased dissolved oxygen, can be measured in terms of the resulting reduced energy fixation by aquatic plants. It might also include the increased petroleum consumption when recreationists have to travel past polluted rivers and lakes to reach more distant unpolluted sites for aquatic recreation. The impact of air pollution on human health can be measured by the energy lost in productive work and the energy required for medical care. Likewise, the cost of pollution control can include the energy required to produce and operate a regenerative technology, such as an advanced wastewater treatment facility. In the case of auto emission control devices, the extra fuel consumption would also be included.

One of the key concepts in EA is that the indirect energy consequences should be counted as well as the direct. For example, in analyzing the energy requirements of auto transportation, the energy utilized in making cars and in making the machines that produce the cars (and the machines that make the machines, and so forth) is counted as well as the petroleum directly consumed by the cars.

To sum the diverse energy consequences of an action, all impacts must be transformed into a uniform measure. The analyst can select from a long list of alternatives: tons of coal, barrels or kilocalories of petroleum, gallons of gasoline, kilowatt hours of electricity, and many others. A basic concept in measuring the energy content of a source is the calorific value, which is the maximum energy that can be extracted. It can be measured in units such as kilocalories, kilowatt hours, or joules (the last being the chosen international measure). However, choosing a single unit, such as kilocalories, to unify the measurement of energy content is only one step in computing the total. A kilocalorie of one fuel, say coal, is not equivalent to a kilocalorie of another, say petroleum. There are differences in "quality" among energy forms, in the sense that a unit of each is not capable of doing the same amount of work. The reason is that the full calorific value of a fuel cannot be extracted, and the portion that can be extracted varies among the fuels (and technologies as well). Consequently, a calorie of electricity is 3.5 times more powerful (in its ability to do work) than a calorie of petroleum, a calorie of petroleum is 20 times more powerful than a calorie of photosynthetic energy in plants, and a calorie of plant energy is 100 times more powerful than a calorie of the sun's energy.[7] Thus a form of energy as well as a unit must be chosen as the uniform measure; for example, kilocalories of petroleum or kilowatt hours of electricity. Once chosen, the diverse energy measures are translated in terms of it, using conversion factors. For example, to measure electricity in kilocalories of petroleum, the kilowatt hours of electricity would be converted to kilocalories and then multiplied by 3.5. Or, to measure plant energy in kilocalories of petroleum, each kilocalorie of plant energy would be divided by 20.

Let's consider how energy analysis would be used as a comprehensive evaluation method to assess a water project. Using the hypothetical example from chapter 5 (see table 5.1), the desirable impacts are electricity generation, water supply, flood protection, lake recreation, and aquatic life; the undesirable impacts are the scarce resources that must be allocated to building and operating the project, including the lost wild river for recreation, lost terrestrial life, and lost sand supply to beaches. The magnitude of each impact would be estimated and an attempt made to interpret each in energy terms. Totals would be computed for the beneficial impacts and the adverse impacts, and, presumably, these would be compared to reach a decision.

The electricity generated by the project is measured directly in energy terms, so no translation is necessary here. Kilowatt hours of electricity would be a good uniform measure for computing all the other energy consequences. Now, what is the energy implication of the water supply? This is a very difficult question if the water is for municipal supply. One possibility is that the best alternative water supply would require more energy to transport it to the city; in this case the extra energy requirement would be a savings that could be counted as energy gained. Water used by industry might save energy for production, which could be counted. Water for agriculture can increase food production, which could be counted (as photosynthetic energy), but there may be a problem here because the extra petroleum used for the food production may exceed the energy content of the additional food.

The energy implications of flood protection include the energy saved by not having to rebuild devastated buildings, the energy saved by protecting crops and the energy gained (or perhaps lost) by opening new land for agricultural production. What is the energy saved by protecting people? It could include the energy saved in medical treatment. But how do we give credit in energy terms for saving human lives? Another very difficult task is to energize recreation: Is there a positive energy interpretation of providing recreation opportunities? If the new recreation site were located closer to some people than existing equivalent facilities, then an energy savings in transportation would be achieved. But what if the new facility is farther away, inducing recreationists to travel longer distances? Would this be counted as a loss? The literature provides no answer.

On the unfavorable side of the balance, the materials for constructing the dam (such as concrete, and steel) would be measured by the energy required to extract raw materials from the ground, process them, and transport them to the site. The labor could be measured by the calories of food needed to support it—or, going even further, by all the needed energy for food, housing, clothing, transportation, and other subsistence. The energy required for on-site construction would also be calculated. The indirect energy requirements for materials and construction would be traced back as far as is practical. The energy requirement of the lost opportunity for a recreation facility is as problematical as before. If the loss of the wild river causes wild river enthusiasts to travel farther to other sites, the additional energy for transportation could be counted. But what if the loss causes them to discontinue this form of recreation altogether? Again, there is no answer. The standard method of counting terrestrial life is to measure the calorie content of the lost primary production. This would apply to the inundated land and to forested land under transmission lines which is usually cleared of the growth. Unfortunately, though, this does not include animals. Like humans, most animals do not produce energy, they merely consume that produced by plants, so animals that die as a result of lost habitat would not register in energy units. Finally, the lost sand supply to beaches could be measured by the energy required to replace it.

10.3 CRITIQUE OF EA AS AN EVALUATION METHODOLOGY

The arguments supporting EA have a great deal of force, but, as a comprehensive evaluation method, it is more an idea than a developed methodology at this point. The example of the water project illustrated a few of its basic problems. Some of its strongest advocates favor it for environmental reasons, but even on these grounds it seems to have serious flaws. For example, people may prefer preserving a particular rare plant as opposed to a common tree, but the tree might score much higher in energy production. The preservation of endangered animals is of grave concern, but most animals score zero on energy production.

People often abhor polluting a clear, deep (oligotrophic) lake, but polluting one usually increases its energy production. Man-created erosion on a mountainside would be scored as a negative energy impact measured by the loss in plant production, yet over the very long term erosion has created our fertile valleys and plains and carved the spectacular natural landscapes we all enjoy. Obviously, this statement is not made to support man-induced erosion, but only to point out another basic dilemma in using energy as a comprehensive measure of value.

Another problem with EA concerns the accept-reject criterion. Take the case of the water project again: should the project be accepted if the energy produced (that is, gained) exceeds the energy required (lost)? If so, then any but the most ill-conceived hydroelectric project would be built; the energy required is typically a minute fraction of the energy produced. Aside from energy projects, most other construction projects cause net energy losses. For example, except in rare cases, new housing projects cause a net energy loss. Does this mean we should discontinue them altogether?

These problems should make it clear that EA cannot be considered as a comprehensive evaluation method. Thus we are left with the two remaining views initially identified: EA as a method for evaluating energy conservation and development option, and EA as a tool for estimating energy impacts. The problems already uncovered should make it clear that EA should not be viewed as a comprehensive evaluation method, even for energy projects, programs, or policies. All the consequences of an action should be taken into account in reaching a decision, not just the energy implications. We have shown here that EA is not equipped to treat properly certain environmental impacts. And no analyst has indicated how it would be used to measure social impacts such as poverty, crime, drug addiction, education, mental health, alienation, or sense of community.

The ability of EA to measure economic impacts is also totally inadequate. Although it is true that many money flows in an economy have corresponding energy flows, there is no theory suggesting they are proportionate; rather overwhelming evidence indicates they are not. A few examples will be sufficient to illustrate the point. In energy terms the labor input to industrial processes is minuscule by comparison to the fuel required to run the machines; yet labor-saving machinery continues to be preferred because it is more economical. The energy input of a top manager is no greater than that of an unskilled laborer, perhaps less, yet a top manager receives more pay. Also, consider the fact that the energy content of fuels does not change over time, yet the economic value does. Finally, the economic value of art bears no necessary relationship to the energy required to create it. A sketch that took Leonardo only a few minutes to draw could be worth more than the life works of an amateur artist. The fact is that energy is only one of many characteristics that gives things economic value. Furthermore, why do we need energy analysis to measure economic value?—we already have economics.

In sum EA seems totally inadequate as a comprehensive methodology. But as a tool for estimating energy impacts it is extremely important. As our nonrenewable energy supplies dwindle we must give increasing attention to the energy consequences of alternative actions. Energy analysis provides the procedures for calculating the energy impacts.

10.4 EA AS AN EVALUATION TOOL FOR ESTIMATING AND REPRESENTING ENERGY IMPACTS

Although many researchers doing energy analysis seemed to view it as a comprehensive method in the early 1970s, most see it today as a tool for calculating energy requirements. If in its current form EA were used to estimate energy consequences in their many diverse forms, then no further discussion would be necessary here, but most applications continue to include the step of converting the diverse impacts into a common measure and computing a total. The total might be considered an index involving value weights. Although no value weights are used explicitly in the conversion process, they are implied by the unstated assumption that each converted unit is equally valued to every other unit. Before considering whether this is a reasonable assumption, more should be said about EA as it is being applied to energy policy.

Applications of EA to public policy can be distinguished according to energy conservation and energy development studies. Energy conservation studies seek to determine the energy required for different production technologies, materials, products, and services so that people could reduce their energy-intensive and energy-wasting actions and develop energy-conserving ways of living. EA can answer questions such as the following: When alternative technologies can be used to produce the same material or product, which requires the least energy per unit of output? When alternative materials can be used in making a product, which requires the least energy per unit of the product? When alternative products and services meet the same consumer interests, which requires the least energy to create and the least to maintain?

We have already learned a great deal from EA studies of this sort. For example, there is a great difference in the energy requirements of alternative steel-refining technologies. Modern mechanized agriculture uses huge quantities of energy by comparison to earlier labor-intensive methods. Indeed the calories of petroleum required in mechanized farming often exceed the calories of food harvested. Aluminum requires a great deal more energy than copper to extract and refine; yet it has made large inroads into copper markets for electrical applications. Plastics require more energy than wood or glass, yet have replaced them in many products. Less energy is required to recycle metals and glass than to extract and process virgin materials. The huge differences in fuel efficiencies of automobiles is now widely known. Refrigerators and televisions with fancy appointments require far more energy to operate than simpler models. Insulation can save a great deal of energy used for space heating. Solar energy can help save on space and water heating. These are just a few of the facts important to energy policy that have been revealed by EA.

Where EA is applied to energy development alternatives, it is now commonly referred to as net energy analysis (NEA). The purpose of NEA is to compute the energy requirements of development options and compare them to the energy gains. The difference between the energy gained and the energy required to secure it is called "net energy."

The U.S. Non-Nuclear Energy Research and Development Act of 1974 (Public Law 93-577) requires that for all new energy development ideas "the potential for production of net energy by the proposed technology at the stage of commercial application shall be analyzed and considered in evaluating proposals." As a result NEA has been applied to many energy development options, such as various geothermal schemes, shale oil extraction, converting coal to gas using different types of processes and deposits, converting coal to methanol, strip mining, solar energy technologies, and nuclear power generation as well.

The concept applies to some conservation measures as well as development options. For example, in analyzing the advisability of home insulation, we want to compare the energy saved to the energy required to produce, transport, and install the insulation. Obviously, it is only the difference, the net energy, that is really saved by insulation.

In calculating energy requirements for any of these conservation and development options, analysts typically do not include labor or land as described earlier. The reason for this convention is not given in the literature, but it probably stems from a prime concern with nonrenewable energy and its major substitutes for maintaining our current level of mechanized production.

Again it should be stressed that tracing out the indirect energy requirements is a key feature of EA. In doing this, analysts discover how interconnected our modern economies are, and how many different sources and forms of energy are used in producing a material, good, service, or fuel. This gets us back to the issue of creating an index.

Computing an index of energy requirements entails converting different energy forms to a common measure. The question is whether the conversion really puts different forms on an equal basis. Stated in other words, are we indifferent to each unit of energy so converted for decision-making purposes? Although the question is best answered when it is directed to a particular application, the general response has to be negative for two reasons: first, and most important, is the fact that certain energy forms are not readily interchangeable for doing certain types of work, and if they are for specific jobs, the general conversion factors do not reflect the degree of substitution. The central problem is that conversion factors are based on a general theoretical concept of work, not on a specific type of work. Since we place different values on different types of work we cannot be indifferent to the various partially nonsubstitutable energy resources. The best example to illustrate this point is the special character of petroleum for supporting our flexible transportation system based on automobiles and trucks, so central to the way we live and the way we produce goods and services. There are substitutes for petroleum but even with current technologies, there aren't any good ones—coal is not, and nuclear certainly is not. While either of these fuels can be used to generate electricity, electric cars still face the unsolved battery problem. Thus electricity is nowhere close to 3.5 times as powerful as petroleum for transportation work, as the general conversion factor would suggest. Another example is that for homes and industry equipped to use natural gas, nuclear fuel and electricity are not good substitutes. And for fossil fuel power plants in cities plagued with air pollution, coal and high-sulphur oil are not good substitutes for natural gas and low-sulphur oil. Many more examples could be given, but the general principle should be clear. It is the ability to do specific kinds of work that determines how we value a fuel; the generalized ability to do work is only a crude indicator of this value.

A second reason why we are not indifferent to the various fuels concerns their scarcity: the remaining reserves of some fuels are much shorter than others. For example, natural gas and petroleum reserves may not last another generation, but coal should be available for over a century. Although we might not place a high value on the work done by a fuel in short supply, we might want to conserve it if there are no good substitutes for it.

Economists will be quick to note that the two parts of the argument here concerning the differential value of fuels correspond to demand and supply.

When the demand and supply of imperfectly substitutable fuels differ, people will not be indifferent to generalized units of them for use or for conservation. However, just because economic theory can be used to explain a serious weakness in the generalized energy index does not mean that economics can solve the problem. The weaknesses of market prices or, more generally, CBA in evaluation processes have already been amply demonstrated. In the context of energy problems a serious weakness is that economic values are quite insensitive to impacts on future generations due to time discounting. More specifically, the market prices of fuels do not adequately reflect our concern to conserve them for future use. Thus money is no more acceptable as a general measure of value than energy.

10.5 CONCLUSIONS

EA has been sharply criticized because, while it has been advanced as an important decision tool for energy policy, it has failed to recognize the problems created by a generalized energy index.[8] There is scarcely any doubt on this point: EA is not a comprehensive evaluation methodology. But, EA is far from useless.

EA has a crucial role to play in evaluation, as a tool for estimating the energy impacts of alternative actions. This role is obviously a leading one for assessing energy conservation and development measures, but it doesn't end here. EA should be applied to any proposed public action that might have significant energy consequences. Impacts should be estimated separately for every energy form.[9] Whether or not these are transformed into one or more indices must be decided in each case. Where the energy consequences are not the prime concern, a generalized index of energy impacts might be adequate. When one form of energy constitutes the major energy impact, an index may be unnecessary. In cases where energy is central to an action and several forms of energy are significantly affected, a single index may be more a hindrance than a help, and disaggregated impact information may help clarify the trade-offs.

10.6 BIBLIOGRAPHY ON ENERGY ANALYSIS

Bravard, J. C., et al. "Energy Expenditures Associated with the Production and Recycle of Metals." Oak Ridge National Laboratory, Oak Ridge, Tenn., 1972.

Chapman, P. F. "1. Energy Costs: A Review of Methods." *Energy Policy,* vol. 2 (June 1974), pp. 91-103.

Chapman, P. F., G. Leach, and M. Slesser. "2. The Energy Cost of Fuels." *Energy Policy,* vol. 2 (June 1974), pp. 231-243.

Chapman, P. F. "4. The Energy Costs of Materials." *Energy Policy,* vol. 3 (March 1975), pp. 47-57.

Chapman, Peter F. "Energy Analysis of Nuclear Power Stations." *Energy Policy,* vol. 3 (December 1975), pp. 285-298.

Common, M. "The Economics of Energy Analysis Reconsidered." *Energy Policy,* vol. 4 (June 1976), pp. 158-165.

Gerrard, Michael. "Disclosure of Hidden Energy Demands: A New Challenge for NEPA." *Environmental Affairs,* vol. 4 (1975), pp. 661-706.

Gilliland, Martha W. "Energy Analysis and Public Policy." *Science,* vol. 189 (September 26, 1975), pp. 1051-1056.

Hirst, E. "The Energy Cost of Pollution Control." *Environment,* vol. 15 (October 1973), pp. 37-44.

Leach, Gerald. "Net Energy Analysis—Is It Any Use?" *Energy Policy,* vol. 3 (December 1975), pp. 332-344.

Odum, Howard T. *Energy, Power and Society.* New York: John Wiley, 1971.

Odum, Howard. "Use of Energy Diagrams for Environmental Impact Statements." In *Tools for Coastal Zone Management.* Proceedings of Conference, February 14-15, 1972, Marine Technology Society, Washington, D.C., 1972.

Odum, H. T. In *Ambio,* vol. 2, (1973), p. 220.

Pimentel, D., et al. "Food Production and the Energy Crisis." *Science,* vol. 182 (November 2, 1973), pp. 443-449.

Webb, Michael, and David Pearce. "The Economics of Energy Analysis." *Energy Policy,* vol. 3 (March 1975), pp. 318-331.

Webb, Michael, and David Pearce. "The Economics of Energy Analysis Revisited" (with comments by Michael S. Common and Peter F. Chapman). *Energy Policy,* vol. 5 (June 1977), pp. 158-161.

Wright, David J. "3. Goods and Services: An Input-Output Analysis." *Energy Policy,* vol. 2 (December 1974), pp. 307-315.

11

LAND-SUITABILITY ANALYSIS AND LANDSCAPE ASSESSMENT AS EXPERT JUDGMENT METHODS

11.1 INTRODUCTION

One of the central problems in any evaluation can be characterized by what I have referred to as the "evaluation dilemma," in which the force for detail and the force for holism oppose one another. We use the analytical technique of dividing the consequences of a plan into many manageable components that can be independently studied in order to acquire a complete and accurate understanding of how a plan would affect society. On the other hand we seek a means of synthesizing the impacts, that is, of acquiring an integrated view of a plan's implications, so that we can judge the wisdom of adopting it. However, in the process we often feel overwhelmed by the flood of analytically derived details.

There are two general ways of approaching the dilemma: one informal, the other formal. The informal approach tends to be qualitative and holistic; using this approach the individual simply studies the detailed impact information until a holistic view emerges in the mind. The formal approach is quantitative and additive; it seeks to solve the dilemma by use of an equation that can transform the many bits of information into a single score that presumably measures how the welfare of society would be affected by a plan.

Planners and other analysts with a quantitative background tend to favor the formal approach. The objective impacts are transformed into subjective ratings through some sort of weighting scheme and are added to form a grand index. CBA is one such method. By converting all impacts into their estimated dollar equivalents, a total score of net benefits can be derived. If the net benefits are positive, indicating that benefits exceed costs, the action is supported; if the net benefits are negative, it is not. In choosing from several alternatives that pass the net benefit criterion, the one with the highest benefit-cost ratio is typically favored.

PBS backs away to some extent from the formal, grand index approach, on the recognition that (1) many impacts cannot be monetized and (2) equity effects must be considered. The evaluator plays a role in synthesis by summing up for each impact category the favored plan, but affected citizens and decision-makers must judge for themselves the tradeoffs in reaching their conclusions. Thus PBS tends to rely on the informal approach to synthesis.

GAM is also based on the view that nonmonetary and equity effects must be considered. It takes the formal approach, presuming that these factors can be accommodated in a nonmonetary rating scheme. The value weights are measured in nominal units that have no meaning in themselves; they simply represent an attempt to capture human values on a numerical scale. Unfortunately, no procedure is advocated for calculating the weights, and intangibles are left out of the computations.

EA, when viewed as a comprehensive evaluation method, also takes the formal approach to impact synthesis. Impacts are converted into their energy implications, which are added to derive a total energy score. When the method is applied to energy conservation or development schemes, the grand index of net energy is analogous to the net benefit score of CBA.

Each grand index method attempts to be comprehensive, but falls far short of this ideal. Some analysts have attempted to overcome the difficulties by prescribing a strong dose of expert judgment.

Expert judgment methods of evaluation are distinguished here from all others by the fact that their ratings are based on the value judgments of experts. The type of rating procedure they use spans the spectrum from simple ratings to rescaled impacts. In most cases the ratings are numerical, but in one case shadings of gray or a color are used instead.

Another feature of some of these methods is the use of expert judgments rather than scientific procedures for estimating impacts. The substitution is made not to dismiss science but to recognize that limitations of data, budgets, and scientific knowledge often prevent following scientific procedures.

Four expert judgment methods are covered—land-suitability analysis (LSA) and landscape assessment (LA) are presented in the present chapter, and the environmental evaluation system (EES) and judgmental impact matrix (JIM) in the following chapter. Neither LSA nor LA are single methodologies; each represents a group of related methods focusing on a particular kind of evaluation problem. LSA was developed as an in-design evaluation method for preparing land-use plans and making land-use decisions that emphasize environmental concerns. LA has the more limited purpose of rating landscapes according to their aesthetic value. EES was designed to evaluate the environmental impacts of water projects. JIM was developed as an in-design evaluation procedure for analyzing the complex consequences of large-scale projects, specifically regional wastewater treatment and disposal systems.

11.2 LAND-SUITABILITY ANALYSIS

LSA represents a class of techniques for evaluating public actions affecting land-use that focuses particular attention on the natural characteristics of alternative sites.[1] The earliest variations of the method were developed by ecologists seeking means of classifying rural land according to natural features that would be useful for evaluating alternative land-uses such as cropland, forestry, range land, mineral extraction, wildlife habitat, and outdoor recreation.[2] Others, particularly landscape architects, have subsequently refined and developed the method for numerous applications, including the particularly challenging problem of land-use planning in urbanizing regions. LSA is widely used today for land-use planning in the United States and Canada, and certain variations are used for land management in many developing countries.

Typically, LSA serves as an in-design evaluation tool for planning areas that retain important natural environmental features. It can be used to evaluate alternative sites for a particular use such as a highway, power plant, or regional recreation facility. Or it can be used as an aid in preparing a complete land-use plan for a region or subregion, by evaluating the suitability of each site for each of several land-use options. Most variations of the method are designed to assure that land-use evaluations give adequate attention to the environmental impacts of land conversions. However, impacts are not made explicit by the method; rather they are implied by scientific data on land characteristics, such as topography, soils, geology, hydrology, vegetation, and wildlife. Expert judgments by planners and natural scientists play a central role in the method. Important decisions are made in selecting the categories and measures of land characteristics, estimating impacts of land conversion, and assigning ratings or priorities for land suitability.

Many of the highly controversial land-use issues today arise in urbanizing regions, where open land for agriculture, forestry, recreation, wildlife, landscape aesthetics, and so on, is threatened by urban conversion. Among the most notable applications of LSA to these situations is found in the work of Ian McHarg and his associates, reported in McHarg's colorful and compelling book, *Design with Nature*.[3] McHarg's work will be emphasized here because it focuses on some of the most difficult land-use issues, it is sophisticated, it exemplifies the two major variations of LSA, and it is supported by a well-articulated philosophy.

McHarg's work clearly is guided by environmental philosophy. He believes that man and nature should not be viewed as separate, but rather as joined together—that man is dependent upon nature and should preserve the essential elements of nature for his own survival and well-being. It goes without saying that man's survival depends on nature for clear and adequate supplies of air, water, food, fiber, and other natural resources. But equally important to McHarg is the view that nature is a source of health and restoration, meaning and order, peace and tranquility, vast beauty, equanimity, dignity, self-respect, and a lifting of the spirits; in sum, nature provides the "indispensible ingredients of a humane environment."[4] By contrast McHarg describes the typical industrial-age city as despondent, dreary, grimy, gritty, squalid, enduringly ugly, and dispiriting, exercising "the inalienable right to create ugliness and disorder for private greed."[5]

McHarg's ideal is a city of man in nature, not cities of men separated from nature. He does not place country over city. Some cities to him are fine places to live, but few of these have been born since the industrial revolution. He wants to join country and city: "We need nature as much in the city as in the countryside."[6] The beauty of nature is only one reason and not the most important:

Clearly the problem of man and nature is not one of providing a decorative background for the human play, or even ameliorating the grim city: it is the necessity of sustaining nature as source of life, milieu, teacher, sanctum, challenge and, most of all, of rediscovering nature's corollary of the unknown in the self, the source of meaning.[7]

The heart of our difficulties in properly preserving nature, according to McHarg, is the prevailing set of values in society. The most serious obstacle is the religious view, dominant in the western world for many centuries, that nature is inferior to man and exists solely to be subdued by man. This has made possible the development in more recent times of economic value systems that exclude from accounting most of nature's benefit to man:

Among us it is widely believed that the world consists solely of a dialogue between men, or men and God, while nature is a faintly decorative backdrop to the human play. If nature receives attention, then it is only for the purpose of conquest or even better, exploitation—for the latter not only accomplishes the first objective but provides a financial reward for the conqueror. . . . We have built but one explicit model of the world and that is built upon economics. The present face of the land of the free is its clearest testimony, even as the Gross National Product is the proof of its success. Money is our measure, convenience is its cohort, the short term its span, and the devil may take the hindmost is the morality. . . .

. . . Neither love nor comparison, health nor beauty, dignity nor freedom, grace nor delight are important unless they can be priced. If they are non-price benefits or costs they are relegated to inconsequence. The economic model proceeds inexorably towards its self-fulfillment of more and more despoilation, uglification and inhibition to life, all in the name of progress—yet, paradoxically, the components which the model excludes are the most important human ambitions and accomplishments and the requirements of survival.[8]

These values were not particularly dangerous in earlier centuries because the power of mankind to destroy nature, either by the sheer force of numbers or technologies, did not exist. But today the situation has changed; the growth of human population and technologies has enabled man to damage seriously the natural environment. Unfortunately, man's narrow, anthropocentric attitude toward nature has changed only slightly.

McHarg exhorts society to drop its economic view of the world and adopt the more realistic, ecological view:

Surely the minimum requirement today for any attitude to man-nature is that it approximate reality. One could reasonably expect that if such a view prevailed, not only would it affect the value system, but also the expressions accomplished by this society.

Where else can we turn for an accurate model of the world and ourselves but to science? We can accept that scientific knowledge is incomplete and will forever be so, but it is the best we have and it has that great merit, which religions lack, of being self-correcting. Moreover, if we wish to understand the phenomenal world, then we will reasonably direct our questions to those scientists who are concerned with this realm—the natural scientists. More precisely, when our preoccupation is with the interaction of organisms and environment—and I can think of no better description for our concern—then we must turn to ecologists, for that is their competence.[9]

McHarg's philosophy explains the main characteristics of LSA: expert judgment based on scientific knowledge of natural environmental features.

Most variations of LSA take either of two approaches: one I will refer to as the "quantitative" approach, the other "qualitative." The approaches differ in the manner that information is organized to derive a statement of land suitability. The quantitative approach uses the conventional method of assigning ratings and calculating a grand index—in this case of land suitability. The qualitative approach classifies land into ecological types to which land-use principles are applied for determining suitability. But both approaches start with the same types of basic information. For every proposed land-use the planner identifies with the help of certain specialists land characteristics that relate to the suitability of land parcels for the particular use. Some land characteristics are relevant because they make the site desirable or undesirable for the use. Other characteristics are important because they indicate that desirable or undesirable side effects would result from the contemplated land conversion. For example, in selecting a highway alignment, the slope of the land, soil drainage, and soil foundation will affect the cost of constructing the highway: low slopes, good drainage, and stable soils are less costly to build upon than high slopes, poor drainage, and unstable soils. The possibility of adverse side effects from highway development are indicated by land characteristics such as historic monuments, major recreation resources, and wildlife habitats—all of which would be destroyed if the land containing them were converted for highway use.

Description of the Quantitative Approach to LSA

The quantitative approach to LSA is one in which implicit or explicit numerical ratings are assigned to subclasses of each land characteristic and aggregated for each land parcel into a grand index of land suitability for a particular use.[10] McHarg uses a map overlay method in which the quantitative nature of the ratings is not explicit. The ratings are expressed in the form of shades of gray (or a color), assigned to each of the several subclasses of a land characteristic: the darker the shade, the less suitable the subclass for the proposed land-use (or the reverse). For example, in evaluating alternative sites for a highway, slopes exceeding 10 percent may be assigned a dark gray shade, slopes between 2.5 and 10 percent a light gray shade, and slopes under 2.5 percent clear (or white).

A map of each land characteristic is prepared on clear plastic overlays, using the color shadings to indicate the variations in the characteristic throughout the study area. The plastic sheets are placed one over the other and viewed with the assistance of a back-lighted map table. The composite picture that emerges is a pattern of light and dark shades indicating the estimated aggregate suitability of each land parcel in the study area for the particular land use: the lighter the shade, the more suitable the use (or the reverse). If the suitability for several land-uses is being evaluated, the procedure is repeated for each.

Although the map overlay technique is not explicitly quantitative, it is implicitly, because the optical process of adding shades can be reduced to a mathematical equation. That is, whenever two or more shades of different strengths are added together using plastic overlays, the strength of the composite shade can be predicted mathematically.

A good illustration of the map overlay technique is McHarg's analysis of a controversial five-mile linkage in the Richmond Parkway, New York.[11] A total of sixteen land characteristics were selected for the evaluation. Variations in the cost of construction among alternative sites were indicated by information on slope, surface drainage, soil drainage, bedrock foundation, soil foundation, susceptibility to erosion, and land values. Danger to life and property was indicated by information on tidal inundation. Areas of high priority natural and social features were revealed by information on historic values, scenic values, recreation values, water values, forest values, wildlife values, residential values and institutional values. Three subclasses were established for each characteristic, utilizing the criteria shown in table 11.1, and each was assigned a shade of gray.

A separate map of the study area was prepared for each land characteristic, such as shown in figures 11.1 and 11.2. The separate maps were overlaid yielding the composite map in figure 11.3, which shows the aggregate shades of light and dark gray for all sixteen land characteristics. From a careful analysis of the composite map, two alternatives (shown in figure 11.4) were identified as being minimum-social-cost alignments.[12]

On the issue of whether the composite map should be interpreted as a grand index, McHarg is equivocal but other analysts are not. Most other quantitative approaches to LSA reflect the unmistakable intention to calculate a grand index using numerical ratings for each subclass of a land characteristic. For example, if land characteristics are grouped in three classes, they may be assigned the ratings, 1, 2, 3, from most to least suitable.

Table 11.1
Land characteristics and their subclasses utilized in McHarg's Richmond Parkway evaluation

Slope
Zone 1:
areas with slopes in excess of 10 percent
Zone 2:
areas with slopes less than 10 percent but in excess of 2.5 percent
Zone 3:
areas with slopes less than 2.5 percent

Surface drainage
Zone 1:
surface water features—streams, lakes, and ponds
Zone 2:
natural drainage channels and areas of constricted drainage
Zone 3:
absence of surface water or pronounced drainage channels

Soil drainage
Zone 1:
salt marshes, brackish marshes, swamps, and other low-lying areas with poor drainage
Zone 2:
areas with high water table
Zone 3:
areas with good internal drainage

Bedrock foundation
Zone 1:
areas identified as marshlands are the most obstructive to the highway; they have an extremely low compressive strength
Zone 2:
the Cretaceous sediments, sands, clays, gravels, and shale

Zone 3:
the most suitable foundation conditions are available on crystalline rocks—serpentine and diabase

Soil foundation
Zone 1:
silts and clays are a major obstruction to the highway; they have poor stability and low compressive strength
Zone 2:
sandy loams and gravelly sandy to fine sandy loams
Zone 3:
gravelly sand or silt loams and gravelly to stony sandy loams

Susceptibility to erosion
Zone 1:
all slopes in excess of 10 percent and gravelly sandy to fine sandy loam soils
Zone 2:
gravelly sand or silt loam soils and areas with slopes in excess of 2.5 percent on gravelly to stony sandy loams
Zone 3:
other soils with finer texture and flat topography

Land values
Zone 1:
$3.50 a square foot and over
Zone 2:
$2.50–$3.50 a square foot
Zone 3:
less than $2.50 a square foot

Table 11.1 (continued)

Tidal inundation
Zone 1:
inundation during 1962 hurricane
Zone 2:
area of hurricane surge
Zone 3:
areas above flood line

Historic values
Zone 1:
Richmondtown historic area
Zone 2:
historic landmarks
Zone 3:
absence of historic sites

Scenic values
Zone 1:
scenic elements
Zone 2:
open areas of high scenic value
Zone 3:
urbanized areas with low scenic value

Recreation values
Zone 1:
public open space and institutions
Zone 2:
nonurbanized areas with high potential
Zone 3:
area with low recreation potential

Water values
Zone 1:
lakes, ponds, streams, and marshes
Zone 2:
major aquifer and watersheds of important streams

Zone 3:
secondary aquifers and urbanized streams

Forest values
Zone 1:
forests and marshes of high quality
Zone 2:
all other existing forests and marshes
Zone 3:
unforested lands

Wildlife values
Zone 1:
best quality habitats
Zone 2:
second quality habitats
Zone 3:
poor habitat areas

Residential values
Zone 1:
market value over $50,000
Zone 2:
market value $25,000–$50,000
Zone 3:
market value less than $25,000

Institutional values
Zone 1:
highest value
Zone 2:
intermediate value
Zone 3:
least value

Source: Ian L. McHarg, *Design with Nature* (Garden City, N.Y.: Natural History Press, 1969), pp. 37–38.

Note: In this table subclasses are referred to as "zones."

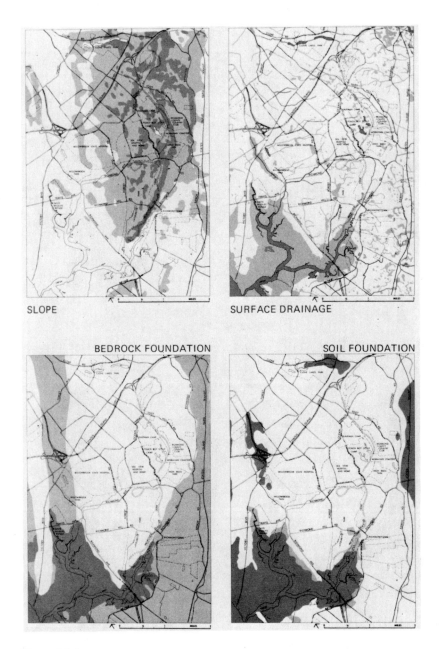

SLOPE

SURFACE DRAINAGE

BEDROCK FOUNDATION

SOIL FOUNDATION

Figure 11.1
Illustrative maps of characteristics affecting the cost of highway construction (From *Design with Nature* by Ian McHarg, p. 36. Copyright © 1969 by Ian McHarg. Used by permission of Doubleday & Company, Inc.)

SCENIC VALUES

RECREATION VALUES

FOREST VALUES

WILDLIFE VALUES

Figure 11.2
Illustrative maps of characteristics indicating areas of high priority natural and social features (From *Design with Nature* by Ian McHarg, p. 39.)

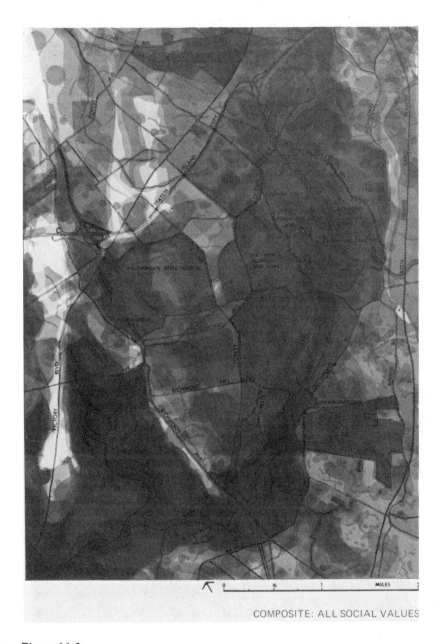

COMPOSITE: ALL SOCIAL VALUES

Figure 11.3
Composite map showing aggregate shading of all sixteen land characteristics
(From *Design with Nature* by Ian McHarg, p. 40.)

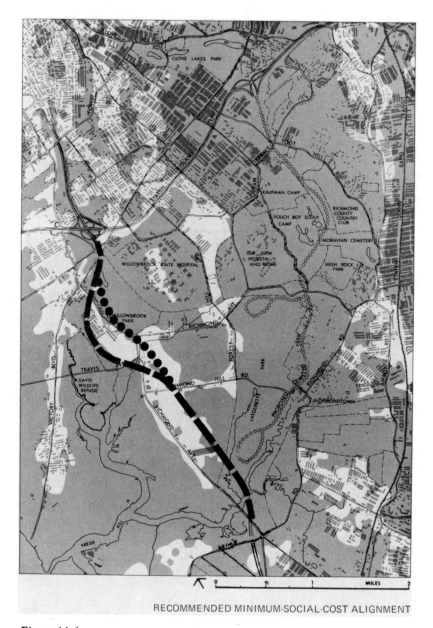

RECOMMENDED MINIMUM-SOCIAL-COST ALIGNMENT

Figure 11.4
Two minimum-social-cost alignments (From *Design with Nature* by Ian McHarg, p. 41.)

In assessing slopes for urban suitability, the following ratings might be assigned: slopes over 10 percent, 3; slopes from 2.5 to 10 percent, 2; and slopes under 2.5 percent, 1. Naturally, the subclass rated 3 should be three times less suitable for the subject use than the subclass rated 1, so the distinctions between subclasses as well as the assigned ratings are important to the usefulness of the results.

In addition to the subclass ratings, each land characteristic is assigned a special numerical value, sometimes referred to as a "multiplier," which reflects the relative importance of that characteristic in determining overall suitability. Returning to the urban suitability example, soil type may be assigned a multiplier of 2, and slope a multiplier of 5. If a particular parcel of land has a soil subclass rated 3 and a slope subclass rated 1, its suitability score would be 11 (that is, $2 \times 3 + 5 \times 1$), assuming that soil and slope are the only two characteristics used in the determination.

The use of explicit numerical ratings has the obvious advantage of revealing the precise values used in the analysis. Who can look at two shadings and determine accurately the magnitude by which one exceeds the other? But numerical ratings have the disadvantage of revealing the difficulty of accurately estimating the values. Who can support the view that slopes over 10 percent are precisely 3 times less suitable for urban development than slopes under 2.5 percent; why not 2.8 times or 3.1 times? In sum, whether implicit or explicit, the approach uses ratings to calculate a grand index. Certainly it is better to have those ratings down numerically and to be aware of the difficulty of estimating them precisely.

Description of the Qualitative Approach to LSA
The quantitative approach to LSA follows a specific pattern, but the qualitative approach does not. It tends to be open-ended, using methods and procedures judged by the planners to be appropriate to the purposes of the particular planning exercise and to the ecological features of the study area. It utilizes the same basic information on land characteristics as that by the quantitative approach, but here is where the similarities end. Most characteristics are divided into subclasses indicated by color shadings. However, the shadings do not represent ratings; they merely serve the purpose of identifying each subclass of a characteristic on a map. The maps for each land characteristic aid the planner in preparing a composite map of land

characteristics. The composite map does not contain aggregate shadings; rather it delineates the major ecological zones and other key features of the study area that are pertinent to land-use decisions. The suitability of each land parcel for a particular use is determined by applying to the map a set of land-use principles, relating suitability to ecological zones and features. The principles represent the judgments of planners and scientists on the importance of retaining different types of undeveloped land in its natural state, the importance of retaining resource land in its current use such as agriculture or forestry, and the capability of the land for accommodating the proposed use.[13]

A simple example is provided by McHarg's study of urban and open space suitability in the Philadelphia metropolitan area.[14] A set of land-use principles was prepared prioritizing land types for open space preservation. Surface water, such as rivers and lakes, was assigned highest priority, followed in consecutive order by marshes, floodplains, aquifers, aquifer recharge areas, prime agricultural lands, steep lands, forests and woodlands, and, lastly, flat (nonprime agricultural) lands. The reverse order constitutes the priority ordering for urban suitability. A description of each land type covers the factors important in setting the priority rating. It includes a discussion of the value of preserving the land in its natural state, and the suitability of the land for urban uses. The recommended uses for each type of land are summarized in table 11.2. These land-use principles are applied to a composite map of the area, locating each land type. McHarg stresses that these constitute merely an approximate hierarchy of suitability, and that much more information is needed for a more refined evaluation.

An example of a somewhat more detailed qualitative evaluation is provided by McHarg's "Plan for the Valleys," which assesses open space and urban suitability for a 70 square mile rural valley within the growth orbit of Baltimore, Maryland.[15] The land characteristics that were most important in establishing the land-use principles were hydrology, soils, topography, vegetation, and landscape aesthetics. Before being finalized, a tentative set of principles was tested against the population projections for the study area to be sure that the expected growth could be accommodated by land rated suitable for urban use. In addition to the suitability analysis and demand projections, the evaluation included economic and institutional feasibility studies.

The land-use principles for the study are shown in table 11.3. They help

Table 11.2
A simple priority ordering of land type for open space and urban suitability
analysis

Open space priority and recommended land uses (read from top to bottom
of list)
Surface water and riparian lands:
ports, harbors, marinas, water treatment plants, water-related industry, open
space for institutional and housing use, agriculture, forestry, and recreation

Marshes:
recreation

Fifty-year floodplain:
same as for surface water

Aquifers:
agriculture, forestry, recreation, industries that do not produce toxic or of-
fensive effluents; all land uses within limits set by percolation

Aquifer recharge areas:
same as for aquifers

Prime agricultural lands:
agriculture, forestry, recreation, open space for institutions, housing at one
house per twenty-five acres

Steep lands:
forestry, recreation, housing at maximum density of one house per three
acres, where wooded

Forests and woodlands:
forestry, recreation, housing at densities not higher than one house per acre

Flat (nonprime agricultural) lands:
high density urban uses are acceptable

Urban suitability priority (read from bottom to top of list)

Source: Adapted from McHarg, *Design with Nature,* pp. 57–62.

Table 11.3

Select conservation and development principles for valley plans

Valley floor:
should be prohibited to development save by such land uses as are compatible with the present pastoral scene. These would include agriculture, large estates, low-intensity use, institutional open space, parks, and recreation.

Cockeysville marble acquifers:
should be prohibited to development

Fifty-year floodplains:
should be exempted from all development save agriculture, institutional open space, and recreation

Surface water courses:
should be reatined in their natural condition to a width of not less than 200 feet on each side of the stream

Forested valley walls:
exclusive of slopes over 25 percent, should be developed in such a manner as to perpetuate their present wooded aspect. The maximum density permitted for development should be one house per three acres.

Unforested valley walls:
should be prohibited to development and should be planted to forest cover. When they are covered with the appropriate distribution of mixed hardwoods to an average height of 25 feet, they may be considered as above.

Valley walls and slopes over 25 percent:
should be prohibited to development and planted to forest cover

Forested plateau:
can be developed to densities not in excess of one house per acre

Unforested plateau:
can receive the largest concentration of development

Promontory sites:
in wooded locations can be developed for tower apartments with low land coverage

Source: McHarg, *Design with Nature*, pp. 86–87.

Table 11.4
Analysis of urban suitability for combinations of forestation and slope
characteristics

	Slope	
	Less than 10 percent	10 to 25 percent
Forested	Forested plateau: light development	Forested walls: light development
Unforested	Unforested plateau: heavy development	Unforested walls: no development

reveal a basic difference between the quantitative and qualitative approaches
to LSA. The quantitative approach is additive: it assumes that the contribution of a land characteristic to the suitability of a particular use can be determined independent of other characteristics. By contrast, the qualitative
approach considers combinations of characteristics; it holds open the possibility that the contribution of one characteristic depends upon the others
with which it is joined. An extreme example of the effect of combinations
can be seen in the urban development prescriptions for slope and forestation
characteristics. These are extracted from table 11.3 and organized in table
11.4. Note that the urban suitability of unforested, in contrast to forested,
lands is reversed by the slope. Unforested lands with medium slopes have a
lower suitability, whereas unforested lands with low slopes have a higher
suitability. No additive equation or map overlay of shadings could yield this
result.

Perhaps the most important feature of the qualitative approach to LSA is
that it provides planners and scientists more flexibility in judging suitability,
enabling them to use deeper knowledge of the unique ecology of the study
area and how it would be affected by land-use alterations.

Critique of LSA

LSA is not a comprehensive evaluation methodology, rather it is limited to
evaluating alternative sites within a specified study area for a particular land-
use or for a set of land-uses. It does not attempt to examine all considerations
but focuses primary attention on those revealed by the natural characteristics
of the land. Impacts are implied but not explicitly reported. Expert judgment
based on scientifice knowledge controls the outcome of the evaluation.

Despite these common characteristics, there are variations in the work of different authors. Thus it would be a mistake to critique LSA methods as a class. This critique therefore focuses on the work of McHarg.

The basic characteristics of LSA follow directly and logically from McHarg's philosophy. McHarg is concerned with designs that integrate city and country and preserve the important features of nature for man's survival and well-being. He apparently does not trust the majority of people to form wise judgments concerning the use of nature because their values are too much influenced by the prevailing religious and economic views in the western world, although certainly he must be encouraged by the strength of the recent environmental movement. Furthermore, the public does not have the specialized knowledge of the natural sciences, particularly ecology, necessary to recognize those elements of nature that should be preserved. This is the domain of the scientists, so their judgments and those of the planners working with them, he places at the center of the evaluation process.

The primary evaluative information provided by LSA are the land characteristics in the study area and the land-use priorities or ratings determined by expert judgment. The priorities and ratings by their very nature combine objective and subjective considerations, although one can easily get the impression from McHarg's discussion that they can be determined by scientific knowledge alone. The LSA method provides no guidelines for evaluators in setting priorities or ratings. Thus the evaluators are free to use their own values or the values they think the public should hold, which violates an important criterion established in chapter 3.

It might be argued that there is no doubt about the importance of human survival, and that the judgments of ecologists may be critical in heading off long-term disasters. However, the value judgments exercized in LSA deal with more than survival; they include such factors as the cost of construction, aesthetics, recreation, and the like, which indeed are very important but fall far short of being life-and-death matters. Why are scientists needed to judge the importance of these items? Furthermore, if human survival is at stake in a land-use decision, is there no faith that citizens and their elected representatives will give it due weight in their deliberations?

In a democratic society the values of the people are supposed to guide governmental actions. If the instrumental values of the public fail to take into account new scientific facts, it is the responsibility of scientists and, more importantly, the government, to communicate these facts to the public; that is, to *educate* the public. It is not appropriate for experts to take control of decision tools such as evaluation methods, or decision making.

The quantitative approach to LSA may appear much less subjective than the qualitative approach, but this is not the case. The personal judgments of the evaluator can greatly affect the outcome of the assessment. The shading assigned each subclass of a characteristic has an obvious affect on the grand index. If an evaluator feels that a particular characteristic deserves high priority for preservation, he or she can assign it a very dark shade, virtually assuring that land containing the characteristic will receive a high grand index score for preservation.

Not so obvious is the effect on the outcome of selecting characteristics to be included in the analyses. Because there is a tendency with the map overlay method to give each class of characteristic equal weight in the rating process, the detail by which the evaluator classifies characteristics is quite important. For example, if the evaluator, in assessing wildlife impacts of a proposed urban use, prepares separate maps for each specie rather than a single map for all, areas containing many species would receive much higher aggregate scores for preservation. Similarly, in examining the recreation impacts of urban use, if maps are prepared for each of the characteristics that help determine the recreation potential of land, such as water, vegetation, wildlife, topography, aesthetics, and accessibility, areas with high recreation potential would receive a much higher score for preservation than otherwise. Because of the subtle manner by which the map overlay method "computes" the grand index, the effects of the evaluators' judgments are not easily discerned by the layman. The use of explicit, numerical ratings can help to overcome this problem.

Among the key facts that should be contained in an evaluation report are the impacts estimated to result from each of the alternative actions. Unfortunately, these are not made explicit by LSA. Presumably, in using the method, evaluators would secure estimates of impacts in order to assign ratings (as in the quantitative approach) or prepare land-use principles (as in the qualitative approach), but these are not displayed. Only the land characteristics of a piece of land indicate the impacts that would occur if it were converted to a particular use. Some types of impacts are obvious to any layman; if prime agricultural land, a unique recreation site, or a wildlife habitat were converted to a residential use, there would be a reduction in agricultural production, recreation activity, or wildlife populations.

Other types of impacts are not so obvious, requiring specialized knowledge to be interpreted. Expert knowledge is required to determine when sloping land would be more expensive to build on than flat land. It is also needed to determine the soil, vegetative, and topographical conditions under which residential development would increase soil erosion and siltation of water bodies.

Whether or not expert knowledge is required to determine the types of impacts from maps on land characteristics, it is necessary to estimate the magnitudes of the impacts. Even though a layman can spot an agricultural, recreational, or wildlife impact with the appropriate map, usually he is not able to ascertain the magnitude. This requires more detailed information than maps usually provide.

The maps used in LSA are extremely effective tools for communicating evaluative information to citizens and decision-makers. However, they don't convey some of the most important information, so additional maps as well as text should be provided that report as precisely as possible the estimated impacts which would occur from converting each parcel of land to a particular use.

It is also important to recognize that land characteristics fail to reveal many important impacts of land-use, particularly those that are not location specific. These typically are excluded from LSA. For example, the pattern of urban development (that is, dispersed or concentrated) affects transportation cost, air and noise pollution from vehicles, and energy consumption. The magnitude of urban development in a region affects air and noise pollution, ground water withdrawals, water runoff from precipitation, and water quality. The bulk of construction costs for most projects is relatively invariant with locations in a region. Also, the demand for land-use (an indicator of benefit) is not reflected by land characteristics. So, for example, an LSA may suggest that 20 percent of a study area be converted to urban use, whereas the demand may be for 90 percent. Finally, equity considerations are ignored. In sum, many important impacts that should be considered in making land-use decisions are not included in the typical LSA. These limitations are well known to McHarg. In directing professional planning studies, he augments LSA with studies of other factors to fill out the picture.

There are several advantages to computerizing LSA.[16] First, it facilitates the handling of large quantities of data on land characteristics, which increasingly are being geocoded and stored in computer-readable form. It also enables evaluators to test quickly and inexpensively a large number of alternative assumptions about suitability ratings or principles, and observe on computer-produced maps their implications for land use. For example, if one were uncertain about selecting the quantity to represent the maximum permissible slope for urban development, he could conduct a sensitivity test simply by changing a single number in the computer program and preparing alternative composite maps of urban suitability. Similarly, if one is uncertain about a rating or multiplier, he can easily conduct a sensitivity test by using a range of quantities to observe the effect on the suitability index. In order to do this with map overlays, new maps must be prepared by hand, involving a great deal of time and expense. In addition, the computerized version greatly facilitates the calculation of land areas in each land category and changes in land area due to different suitability assumptions.

As indicated earlier LSA does not consider the demand for land-use, so frequently the results of an application must be adjusted. This is very easy to do using a computerized version of the method. For example, if the amount of land rated suitable for urban use must be increased, the restrictiveness of certain assumptions can be relaxed and a new composite map prepared in a matter of minutes.

Another advantage of computerization is in preparing alternative suitability maps on the basis of different values. Just as the planning study in Britain used GAM to generate alternative land-use plans using the values of different planners and interest groups, so could a computerized LSA be utilized to generate alternative plans during an early design stage using the suitability values of different people. This application helps get away from the assumption that there is one and only one set of correct values.

One team of researchers attempted to develop a computerized version of LSA, going beyond the land characteristics, to compute the *impacts* that would occur by placing a given land-use on a piece of land.[17] Their work represents an heroic attempt to carry LSA to its logical conclusion but reveals the limitations of our current knowledge about the operations of natural environmental systems. While some environmental impacts can be estimated with computer-programmable models, many cannot, requiring at this time to be estimated by expert judgment rather than scientific procedures.

An important shortcoming of most LSA techniques is a failure to establish any systematic procedure for securing expert judgment, which clearly will be necessary in estimating impacts for some time to come. The other expert judgment methods discussed in this and the next chapter provide examples of how this might be done.

LSA has several advantages over CBA:

1. It is especially designed to give full consideration to issues of nature preservation such as the preservation of wildlife habitats, unique vegetation and ecosystems, landscape aesthetics, and prime agricultural land which are seldom included in CBA.
2. It is capable of incorporating unmonetized impacts, including intangibles, in its grand index of land suitability.
3. LSA makes full use of effective graphical methods for communicating evaluative information to citizens and decision-makers. Because of this, an LSA report can be understood by a layman much more quickly and fully than a CBA report.

On the other hand, LSA has the following disadvantages as compared to CBA:

1. Important economic impacts are not included by the method.
2. Because it ignores impacts that are invariant with location, it cannot be used to make accept-reject decisions, whereas in principle CBA can be used for such decisions.
3. No guidelines are established in LSA for setting ratings. Thus there are no assurances that the values of the public will be reflected in the results. The evaluator is free, and as an expert even encouraged, to use his own values in setting ratings. The evaluator using CBA does not have this freedom.
4. Impacts do not have to be estimated to complete a land-suitability study, whereas they are necessary in CBA. This could cause LSA evaluators to be sloppy in their work.
5. LSA is limited to evaluating land-use alternatives, whereas CBA has broader applications.

Conclusions

LSA is an excellent evaluation tool for identifying, organizing, and representing certain factors important in land-use decisions. It is especially effective for communicating the considerations that vary across the landscape, including certain social and economic as well as environmental factors, but it is not capable of dealing with aspects of a plan that are spatially invariant. And even the graphical representations of some factors should be augmented with other descriptions to clarify their characters and magnitudes. Thus LSA cannot be considered a comprehensive evaluation method. Although its expert judgment approach to calculating a grand index fares poorly on democratic criteria, this could be modified so that ratings are determined by a more democratic process.

The greatest usefulness of LSA arises in the early design stages of land-use planning where a large number of alternative spatial patterns must be screened in order to narrow down the list to the few most promising options. As the design work progresses toward the detailed definition and assessment of a few alternatives, generalized mappable information becomes less important and more precise evaluative information, including that gained from special field studies, becomes more crucial.

11.3 LANDSCAPE ASSESSMENT

LA methods serve a variety of purposes, including the preparation of landscape preservations plans, the preparation and evaluation of general land-use plans, and the measurement of aesthetic impacts. The methods make no attempt to measure factors other than aesthetics, so in a sense a discussion of them is out of place in this survey of methods purporting to be comprehensive. Nevertheless, the discussion is included, for several reasons. First, the treatment of intangibles is an especially tricky problem in evaluations, and aesthetics is the textbook example of an intangible. It is helpful to know how those who have devoted the most time to it have decided to deal with it. Second, the subject offers a good opportunity for contrasting holistic approaches to evaluation with analytic approaches. Finally, a particular method of landscape assessment, the East Sussex method, is of special interest because of its novel use of a subjective measurement scale that helps to systematize its procedures without being analytical.

Overview of LA Methods

A variety of methods for LA are used for planning purposes, ranging from simple rating procedures utilizing no guidelines to sophisticated constant value weight schemes. In recent years major efforts have been made to get away from emotional responses to aesthetics and develop quantified scores in as systematic and objective a way as possible. It is widely believed that, if quantified, landscape values would receive more weight in decision making.

The traditional method of assessment was to obtain the judgment of a person trained in landscape design, following no specific procedures. The method was quick and inexpensive to administer, but the results sometimes were attacked as being unscientific. Today most research is devoted to analytical approaches. The methods vary but the pattern is similar: (1) elements of landscapes are identified that contribute most to their beauty, (2) the elements are scored, and (3) the raw scores are either added or multiplied by a set of value weights to obtain a total landscape value. Thus the approaches are not fundamentally different from the more comprehensive evaluation methods. Elements are analogous to impacts, which are rated, sometimes using value weights, and a grand score is computed.

With some analytical approaches the element scores can be objectively measured. For example, Leopold's uniqueness score is derived by counting the number of landscapes that have similar characteristics for each of many elements.[18] The inverse of this number for an element represents the rating of that element. The fundamental idea is that the more unique a landscape, the higher should be its score. In his studies of landscape preferences judged from photographs, Shafer used surface measurements of water, vegetation, and nonvegetated areas.[19] Hopkinson tested the notion of measuring the solid angular subtense of objects as an indicator of visual intrusion.[20] In these cases the values enter into the results through the selection of the element categories and measures, and, when used, the selection of value weights.

Other approaches require that the elements be scored (or rated) subjectively. Linton and Wright used similar methods in which ratings are assigned separately to factors such as permanent features (for example, mountains, plains, and hills), temporary features (forest, houses, pasture), and transitory features (wildlife, clouds).[21] In these cases all aspects of the rating procedure are subjective.

The judgment of design experts is commonly used to provide the subjective information, although a mild controversy appears in the literature over the issue of whose judgments should be used. It appears that the majority of researchers favor the use of experts rather than lay citizens, as might be expected. However, quite a few studies have been done that take citizen preferences of landscapes as the base and attempt to develop formulas that can replicate these from measured landscape elements.

Statistical studies indicate that the preferences of different people are very similar in selecting the *most beautiful* and the *ugliest* landscapes from a long list of alternatives.[22] The variations in aesthetic tastes appear in the middle range. Studies also suggest that the rankings of scenes by design experts and citizens are very similar, but that expert ratings show more sensitivity to subtle aesthetic differences.[23] One researcher has very cautiously concluded from this that "the role of the designer when evaluating alternative landscape settings can be that of the articulate and skilled spokesman representing at least some publics beyond his own profession within our pluralistic society."[24]

An important issue rarely raised in the literature that has a crucial bearing on the selection of a landscape assessment methodology is whether the whole is equal to the sum of the parts, or, to be more specific, whether the beauty of a landscape is equal to the sum of the beauty of its elements. The analytical method assumes that it is. Yet many designers claim that the visual impression created by a design results from a complex interaction of the parts, the contribution of each depending on the precise character of the others. If this is so, and certainly personal reflection will suggest that it is to some degree, then the linear, additive formulas of analytic procedures will not accurately reflect holistic impressions.

An interesting study of landscape preferences sheds some light on this issue.[25] Shafer and others at the Northeastern Forest Experiment Station at Syracuse, New York, gathered information on natural landscape preferences by asking 250 different campers to rank a series of photographs. Then adding the rankings for each of 100 photos, a total landscape score was derived representing group opinion. In addition, the landscape of each photograph was measured for 46 elements, which were reduced to 6 independent elements (using factor analysis) including measures of water area, vegetation, and nonvegetation.

These steps were necessary to establish a data bank prior to conducting a regression analysis to predict landscape scores from the landscape elements. In order to take account of simple nonlinearities, a polynomial expansion of the 6 elements generated a fuller set of predictive variables. The most accurate predictive equation explained 66 percent of the variation in landscape preference scores, which is a respectable level of accuracy for research work but well below that with which one can forecast with confidence. Ten predictive variables were statistically significant in the equation; of these, two were squared terms, six were cross products and *only two were linear.* Later, Shafer conducted a follow-up study in Scotland and obtained nearly identical results.[26] The research indicates that a simple linear, additive formula is not likely to be accurate in predicting landscape ratings (and even a two-degree polynomial is not sufficient for many purposes). The research supports the view that the whole is *not* equal to the sum of the parts; it is much more complex.

An alternative to the analytical approach is the holistic approach. The idea is simple: one merely looks at the landscape to be rated, observing the various elements and the holistic impression that their special combination creates, and assigns a score. In its simplest form it is equivalent to the traditional approach to LA, which researchers have been trying to get away from. Yet it is interesting that when researchers seek to validate an analytic method, they obtain holistic judgments of landscape values as the base for comparison. Since this is so, why not simply use the holistic judgments themselves rather than some analytic formula that attempts to mimic them? The reason is that simple holistic ratings are not especially replicable; that is, the scores assigned by different evaluators are often quite different. Consequently, they are considered to be weak evidence in planning debates—just one person's opinion. One way of overcoming this problem is to have a committee of people do the evaluating. An interesting variation of this idea is offered by the East Sussex landscape assessment method.[27]

The East Sussex Method
The central feature of the East Sussex method is a general scale of landscape values, established to guide the work of field evaluators. In developing the scale, a representative sample of 45 persons was selected and each asked to rate the beauty of twenty carefully chosen color photographs depicting a wide range of landscape and townscape scenes. The numerical scores were

compared for different subgroups of people to determine if sex or design training and experience affected the ratings. It was determined that the rankings of the photographs was unaffected by sex or design background; however, the range of scores for the experienced designers was greater. The ratings by the *designers* were used to construct a general scale of landscape values, shown in figure 11.5. Two reasons are given: "first, such people are most likely to seek and obtain the greatest enjoyment from landscape; secondly, the extended scale of values associated with this group approximates to an absolute scale which, it is hoped, may eventually represent the experience of the majority as the standard education and amount of leisure time increases."[28]

The scale ranges from 0 to 32, and is divided into six descriptive categories: unsightly (0–0.9), undistinguished (1.0–1.9), pleasant (2.0–3.9), distinguished (4.0–7.9), superb (8.0–15.9), and spectacular (16.0–32.0). The types of views rated most spectacular are "great mountains, canyons, and waterfalls," followed by "classic towns" (such as Florence and Venice). The most unsightly types of views are "slums and derelict areas" followed by "countryside spoiled by excessive litter," "modern industrial and commercial areas," and "modern suburbia." The highest normal score for Great Britain is 18.0 and for East Sussex, 12.0.

The scale and the photographs used to depict the numerical values represent a set of guideposts prescribed by a panel of experts that can facilitate the judgments of field evaluators and improve the replicability of ratings. The assessment method is easy to apply. The landscape value of each land tract in a region is rated by a field surveyor, trained in a design discipline, following a prescribed procedure. Each tract is observed from a variety of viewpoints. The score for each view is judged holistically, rather than determined analytically. The holistic judgment is guided by the general scale of landscape values and illustrative photographs. The descriptive category of each view is usually decided first (for example, superb, distinguished, or pleasant), setting bounds for the rating, then the precise score is determined. The overall score for a tract is formed from the various view scores, giving more weight to full than to partial views.

The planning department has used the methodology for several years in setting open space priorities and assessing the landscape impacts of urban developments. The measurement of development impacts is made possible by

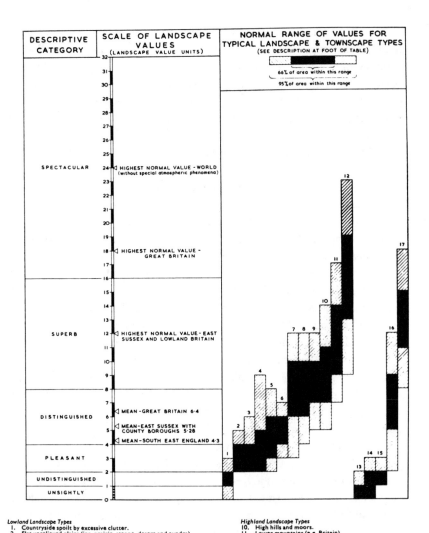

Figure 11.5

East Sussex scale of landscape values (*Source:* K. D. Fines, "Landscape Evaluation: A Research Project in East Sussex," *Regional Studies,* vol. 2, 1968.)

the fact that the general scale of values is sensitive to the presence and type of man-made elements. A method was devised for assessing the impact of power transmission lines on the landscape beauty of an area. Basically it involves the computation of a formula in which the ratio of the height of the towers to the square of distance is summed over the observable towers. In cases where potential recreation use is a consideration, landscape scores are adjusted by a population accessibility factor common in gravity models that raises the score of tracts near populated centers.

A research group at the Middlesex Polytechnic in Britain compared the East Sussex method to two others: a simple rating procedure devoid of guidelines and an analytical method.[29] Each technique was used to rate a group of landscapes through a series of field surveys. It was concluded that the East Sussex method is the easiest to use and the analytical the most difficult. The East Sussex method was also judged the most replicable; even better than the analytical method. However, the researchers felt that the method was too heavily influenced by two factors, topography and the presence of urban development, and not sufficiently sensitive to other important qualitative differences.

The general conclusion from the comparative study was that LA research and practice should emphasize improved analytical methods—a conclusion that could probably have been predicted in advance due to the typical analytical orientation of university researchers.

Conclusions

Most researchers in the field of landscape assessment today are using the same general analytical techniques to deal with the intangible, aesthetics, as those used in the more comprehensive evaluation methods. The techniques make the results appear more scientific, but they are no less subjective. Replicability of the results is an important characteristic that analytical methods are able to achieve, but the East Sussex method demonstrates that a well-designed holistic approach can achieve it also. The holistic approach has the advantage over analytic procedures of being potentially able to consider the complex interrelations of elements affecting the value of the whole.

The idea of creating a subjective scale for systematizing the measurement of intangibles has merit, but the use of expert judgment for calibrating it must be questioned. Landscape preservation is a general governmental function that should serve the interests of all people, not just one small group (such as design professionals). Thus, if a subjective scale is used to guide the work of field evaluators, it would seem more appropriate to base it on citizen judgments instead.

A final note is that there is a danger in carrying too far the objectification of something inherently subjective.[30] Replicability has advantages, but it is not the only criterion to strive for in designing evaluation procedures. Whenever human values are involved, there will be variability. Replicating the average value may be acceptable when the subject is only moderately important or the variation in values is small, but when the subject has high priority and values vary widely, a perfectly replicable average is not worth much; it serves few people particularly well. If evaluations and decisions are to be sensitive to the variety of interests, they must find out what that variety is. Neither analytical methods nor holistic methods generating unitary answers provide it.

11.4 BIBLIOGRAPHY FOR LAND-SUITABILITY ANALYSIS

Christian, C. S. "The Concept of Land Units and Land Systems." In *Proceedings of the Ninth Pacific Science Congress,* vol. 20 (1958), pp. 74–81.

Hills, G. Angus. "The Ecological Basis for Land-Use Planning." Research report no. 46. Ontario Department of Land and Forest, Toronto, 1961.

Kamnitzer, Peter, and Stan Hoffman. "Intuval: An Interactive Computer Graphic Aid for Design and Decision Making in Urban Planning." *Proceedings of the Environmental Design Research Association* (1971), pp. 383–390.

Lewis, Philip H. "Quality Corridors for Wisconsin." *Landscape Architecture Quarterly,* (January 1974), pp. 100–107.

Lewis, Philip H. "Regional Design for Human Impact." Prepared for the U.S. Department of the Interior, National Park Service, Northeast Region, Madison, Wisc., 1967.

Lyle, J., and M. von Wodtke. "An Information System for Environmental Planning." *Journal of the American Institute of Planners,* vol. 40 (November 1974), pp. 394–413.

McHarg, Ian. *Design with Nature.* New York: Natural History Press, 1969.

Steinitz, Carl, et al., "A Comparative Study of Resource Analysis Methods." Department of Landscape Architecture, Harvard University, Cambridge, Mass., 1969.

Yafie, S., and C. A. Miller. "Toward a Regional Power Plant Siting Method: AEC-Maryland Regional Siting Factors Study." Oak Ridge National Laboratory, Oak Ridge, Tenn., 1974.

11.5 BIBLIOGRAPHY FOR LANDSCAPE ASSESSMENT

Brancher, D. M. "Critique of K. D. Fines' Landscape Evaluation." *Regional Studies,* vol. 3 (April 1969), pp. 91–92.

Burnham, J. B., et al. "A Technique for Environmental Decision Making Using Quantified Social and Aesthetic Values." Prepared for the Atomic Energy Commission, Battelle Pacific Northwest Laboratories, Richland, Wash., 1974.

Fines, K. D. "Landscape Evaluation: A Research Project in East Sussex." *Regional Studies,* vol. 2 (September 1968), pp. 41–55.

Gauger, Stephen E., and J. B. Wyckoff. "Aesthetic Preference for Water Resource Projects: An Application of Q Methodology." *Water Resources Bulletin,* vol. 9 (June 1973), pp. 522–528.

Hopkinson, R. G. "The Quantitative Assessment of Visual Intrusion." *Journal of the Royal Town Planning Institute,* vol. 57 (December 1971), pp. 445–449.

Klein, David R. "Cultural Influences on Landscape Aesthetics: Some Comparisons Between Scandinavia and Northwestern North America." *Environmental Affairs,* vol. 2 (1975), pp. 80–89.

Leopold, L. B. *Quantitative Comparison of Some Aesthetic Factors Among Rivers.* U.S. Geological Survey, Circular 670. Washington, D.C.: Government Printing Office, 1969.

Linton, David L. "The Assessment of Scenery as a Natural Resource." *Scottish Geographic Magazine,* vol. 84 (December 1968), pp. 219–238.

Litton, R. Burton. "Forest Landscape Description and Inventories—A Basis for Land Planning and Design." USDA Forest Service research paper, 1968.

Lynch, Kevin. *The Image of the City.* Cambridge, Mass.: MIT Press, 1960.

Melhorn, W. N., and E. A. Keller. "Landscape Aesthetics Numerically Determined: Applications to Highway Corridor Selection." *Highway Research Record,* no. 452 (1973), pp. 1–9.

Penning-Rowsell, E. C., and D. I. Hardy. "Landscape Evaluation and Planning Policy: A Comparative Survey in the Wye Valley Area of Outstanding Natural Beauty." *Regional Studies,* vol. 7 (June 1973), pp. 153–160.

Peterson, George L., and Edward S. Neumann. "Modelling and Predicting Human Response to the Visual Recreation Environment." *Journal of Leisure Research,* vol. 1 (Summer, 1969), pp. 219–237.

Shafer, Elwood L., Jr., John F. Hamilton, Jr., and Elizabeth A. Schmidt. "Natural Landscape Preferences: A Predictive Model." *Journal of Leisure Research,* vol. 1 (Winter, 1969), pp. 1–19.

Shafer, Elwood L., and Michael Tooby. "Landscape Preferences: An International Replication." *Journal of Leisure Research,* vol. 5 (Spring, 1973), pp. 60–65.

Weddle, A. E. "Techniques in Landscape Planning: Landscape Evaluation." *Town Planning Institute Journal,* vol. 55 (November 1969), pp. 387–389.

Wright, G. McK. "Landscape Quality: A Method of Appraisal." *Royal Australian Planning Institute Journal,* vol. 11 (October 1973), pp. 122–130.

Zube, Ervin H. "Rating Everyday Rural Landscapes of the Northeastern U.S." *Landscape Architecture,* vol. 63 (July 1973), pp. 370–375.

12
ENVIRONMENTAL EVALUATION SYSTEM AND JUDGMENTAL IMPACT MATRIX AS EXPERT JUDGMENT METHODS

12.1 INTRODUCTION

The environmental evaluation system (EES) and the judgmental impact matrix (JIM) are distinguished from those in the previous chapter by their more quantitative orientation and by the fact that they each use a procedure called "Delphi" for systematically obtaining and processing expert judgments. Before describing the evaluation methods, it will be useful to summarize the Delphi procedure. It was originally developed for estimating objective phenomena, so it is particularly applicable to impact estimation, but it has also been used for subjective judgments including value weight quantification.

We don't give nearly enough credit these days to the enormous powers and subtle qualities of the human mind. Science has a central, irreplaceable role to play in the evaluation process, but we must recognize that it often is not capable of providing the answers we seek. During the in-design phase of evaluation, when a long list of alternatives must be screened, data and budget limits permit few scientifically prepared impact estimates. And even after the alternatives have been narrowed down to a few (or one), some impacts will continue to resist scientific estimation. Human judgments are the alternative. We recognize that the human mind is often able to make quite accurate judgmental estimates due to its marvelous ability to store and process huge quantities of information. People who have devoted much study to the functioning of a particular system (for example, ecological, economic, or social) are in a special position to judge the magnitude of impacts it might generate. Expert judgment has been the common means for solving the age-old problem of incomplete information and will no doubt continue to be in the future. Delphi represents a procedure for obtaining and processing expert judgments for the purpose of maximizing the accuracy of the resulting estimates.

It is obvious that the rationale for an expert judgment is accuracy, so normally we would not ask a microbiologist to judge a wildlife impact nor a banker to judge property tax impacts. Also, considering that two heads are better than one, we should ask several experts for their judgment, when possible, rather than one. And when the opinions of several experts are quite similar, we can be more confident in using the average opinion than if they are quite different.

Not so obvious is how the *process* of acquiring judgments from a group of people affects the accuracy of the outcome. The Delphi researchers at the Rand Corporation have studied a variety of group decision-making situations with interesting results. For example, they have demonstrated that the median of judgments made independently is more accurate than a consensus arrived at in a face-to-face meeting. Apparently, the most vociferous person at a meeting strongly influences the group consensus, but loudness is a poor indicator of expertise. In addition, they have shown that if the median and range of the independent judgments are reported to the participants for reconsideration, the judgments of a subsequent round will converge somewhat. More often than not the convergence is toward the correct answer, and it will continue for several iterations, though diminishing with each round. These results explain the essential features of Delphi. Many variations are possible, but the basic steps are as follows:

1. Each expert is asked for an independent opinion on one or several carefully prepared questions without consulting the other experts.
2. The median and range of the opinions are calculated and fed back to the experts for their consideration in another round of estimates.
3. The process of gathering opinions and feeding back results is continued for one or more rounds.
4. The median of the final round is calculated as the best estimate.

The most obvious application of Delphi in evaluation problems is to estimate impacts. However, the originators feel that it can also be useful in securing value judgments. Research has shown that value judgments also narrow during the iteration process, though obviously the correctness of the judgments cannot be verified.[2]

Although the accuracy of expert judgments can be increased using Delphi, experience indicates that the added cost in money and time over less formalized procedures is not insignificant, especially when the iteration process is repeated several times. Consequently, the use of only one or two iterations is common. EES uses Delphi for setting value weights, and JIM uses it both for estimating impacts and assigning value weights.

12.2 ENVIRONMENTAL EVALUATION SYSTEM

Description of the Method
EES was developed for the U.S. Bureau of Reclamation by researchers at the Battelle Columbus Laboratories in Ohio.[3] It is an in-design and post-design method for assessing environmental and certain social impacts of water projects including intangibles. The method is intended to be *comprehensive* in its coverage of all the important environmental, but not economic, considerations, *systematic* in generating replicable answers, and *interdisciplinary* in its use of experts from a variety of fields.

Impact categories are preset by the EES method to be used in all applications, and the impacts are estimated by scientific procedures where possible. The rating system calculates a composite score of environmental impacts by rescaling the impacts and multiplying them by a set of constant value weights based on expert judgment. A positive net score—obtained by subtracting the adverse from the beneficial impacts—reflects favorably on the project, whereas a negative score reflects unfavorably.

The environmental factors are organized in four levels, as shown in figure 12.1. The two most telling levels are environmental *categories* and environmental *parameters*. There are four categories—ecology, pollution, aesthetics, and human interest—for classifying seventy-eight parameters. Figure 12.2 gives the parameters along with further breakdowns: included are ecology parameters of population, species, habitats, and communities; pollution parameters of water, air, land, and noise indicators; aesthetics parameters of land, air, water, biota, man-made objects, and composition; and human interest parameters of educational or scientific excavations, historical trends, cultural heritages, mood or atmosphere, and life patterns. The lowest level in the hierarchy, termed "environmental *measurements*," constitutes the data used to measure the parameters.

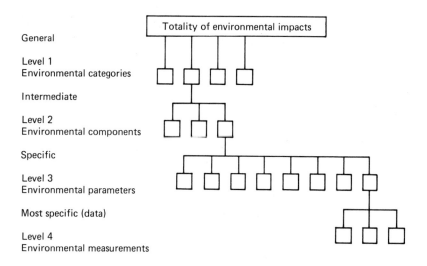

Figure 12.1
The four levels of EES (Source: Norbert Dee, "An Environmental Evaluation System for Water Resource Planning," *Water Resources Research.* vol. 9, June 1973, pp. 523–535.)

The process of calculating the composite score has three steps. First, impact estimates are made by forecasting parameter levels with and without the subject project. For example, forecasts are prepared—with and without the project—for terrestrial browsers and grazers, pest species, water losses, dissolved oxygen, appearance of water, man-made objects, and the life patterns of people residing in the area.

The second step begins converting these parameter estimates from diverse units to commensurate units. In this step each parameter measurement is transformed by a "value function" into a measurement on an "environmental quality scale" ranging from 0 to 1, where 0 represents "extremely bad quality". and 1, "very good quality."[4] The value functions were developed by the interdisciplinary research team using scientific information where possible but clearly incorporating value judgments as well. Many of the functions are nonlinear as shown in figure 12.3, reflecting the fact that each unit change in an environmental parameter is not equally valued to every other unit change in that parameter. There are two reasons for this: first, as the natural conditions of an environment are altered, such as by an air or water pollutant, each

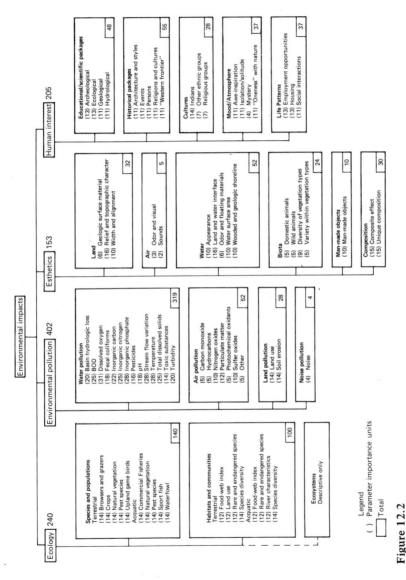

Figure 12.2
Environmental parameters. Value weights are in parentheses (Source: Dee, "An Environmental Evaluation System," 1973.)

Environmental quality

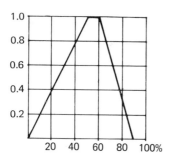

Carrying capacity based on
annual units

Environmental quality

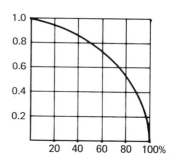

$$\text{Ratio} = \frac{\text{man-made losses}}{\text{annual natural discharge}}$$

Environmental quality

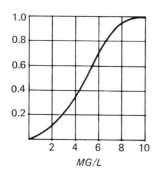

MG/L

Environmental quality

Quality of construction and design
(consonance with nature)

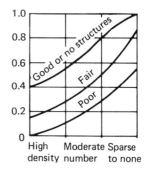

Density of man-made structures

Figure 12.3
Examples of value functions (Source: Dee, "An Environmental Evaluation
System," 1973.)
a. Browsers and grazers
b. Water loss
c. Dissolved oxygen
d. Man-made objects

successive increment of alteration (up to a point) has more serious consequences for the life that depends on that environment. Beyond a certain point
most of the damage has been done, so further alterations are less serious.
Second, the law of diminishing marginal utility suggests that the more we have
of something desired, the less we value each additional increment. Implied by
this is the law of increasing marginal disutility, that the more we have of
something not desired, the more we value avoiding each additional increment.

Figure 12.3a shows how environmental quality (on the 0 to 1 scale) varies
with browsers and grazers, measured by the number of animals as a percent
of the maximum number sustainable by the land, that is, the carrying capacity. The maximum environmental quality score (1.0) is attained when
the number of browsers and grazers are between 50 and 60 percent of carrying capacity; the minimum score (0) is reached when either the percent is
0 or between 90 and 100. The function delineates the value that some animals are better for a fully functioning ecological system than none, but
that a large number would be ecologically damaging. If a project caused
browsers and grazers to drop from 60 to 40 percent of carrying capacity, the
environmental quality scale would drop from 1.0 to 0.8 (or minus 0.2). In
step two, all seventy-eight parameters would be similarly assessed in terms
of their scores on the environmental quality scale, with and without the
proposed project.

It should be noted that the environmental quality scale is used for measuring intangible as well as quantifiable parameters. The method of quantifying an aesthetic impact, such as caused by a man-made object, could
utilize the East Sussex landscape assessment procedures.

The third and last step in deriving the composite score is to multiply each
environmental quality score by the value weight (called "parameter importance units") assigned to the corresponding parameter, and then total the
products. The value weights are predetermined based on the expert judgment
of the research team using the Delphi procedure. It is their view that the
weights should be fixed for all projects. As they explain, "... if weights
were allowed to vary from project to project, the assignment of weights
would be the responsibility of the investigating team. Essentially, each team
would have their own special weights depending on their views and background; thus results would be produced that would be extremely difficult to
replicate."[5] A total of 1,000 points was distributed among the seventy-eight

parameters; the assigned weight for each is shown in parentheses to the left of each parameter in figure 12.2.

Mathematically, the computation of the composite score is represented by the following equation:

$$E = \sum_{i=1}^{78} (V_{1i} - V_{2i})w_i,$$

where

E = composite score of environmental and social impacts,
V_{1i} = value, in environmental quality units, of parameter i *with* the project,
V_{2i} = value, in environmental quality units, of parameter i *without* the project,
w_i = the value weight (or parameter importance unit) assigned to parameter i.

In addition to the composite score, EES identifies potential problem areas by placing red flags on parameters estimated to be seriously affected by the project. For the ecology parameters, minor flags are assigned to negative changes between 5 and 10 percent and major flags to changes above 10 percent. For parameters in the other three categories, minor flags are assigned to negative changes between 10 and 30 percent and major flags to changes above 30 percent. These rules were determined by the research team from field tests of the sensitivity of parameters to change and the significance of the change. "The broad nature of the ecology category is the primary reason for the differentiation in the red flag rules. Field tests indicate that a small change in the ecological parameters was comparable in impact to larger changes in all other parameters."[6] The adoption of the warning system can be interpreted as a recognition that the whole is not equal to the sum of the parts, that the large adverse impacts are not adequately reflected by the points they add to the grand score and therefore should be identified for special consideration.

Critique of EES
EES is a thoughtfully devised method for calculating a composite score. Its ability to incorporate unmonetized impacts including intangibles in its index is a feature that distinguishes it from most other evaluation methodolo-

gies. Although designed for evaluating the environmental and certain social impacts of water projects, in principle its procedures could be adapted to any evaluation task and could be expanded to incorporate all types of impacts, much like GAM. Its method of rescaling impacts solves (theoretically, at least) the problem with the constant value weight procedure that impact increments usually are not equally valued. The warning flags are a useful supplement to the composite score, calling attention to adverse impacts that deserve special consideration in project design and decision making. The fact that EES is especially sensitive to preserving ecological systems means that it is well tailored to represent the environmental interests of future generations.

EES in its present form, however, is not without weaknesses. Its impact categories are fixed, as if the same set of issues will recur for all proposed water projects, which is highly unlikely. Impact categories should be flexible, so that they can be adapted to the special conditions of each evaluation problem.[7] Some of the impacts are defined and measured in technical terms that few citizens and decision-makers can understand, such as a food-web index (of habitats), the coliform count (of water), and particulate concentrations (in air). These are technical measurements of means, and they don't indicate by themselves the nature and magnitudes of the ends to which they are linked. Without information on the ends it is not possible to judge adequately the tradeoffs between these impacts. For example, how can one assess the tradeoff between coliform count and particulate matter without determining their implications for human health? Presumably, the research team made such determinations both in rescaling the impacts and assigning the value weights. This is important information that should be reported rather than remain hidden in the files of the evaluation team. If the means-ends linkages are uncertain, as many are, this too should be reported; when it is not, the evaluators are not being honest about the limits of our technical knowledge.

Another weakness in EES is that the values utilized in the procedure for selecting the parameters, determining the value functions, and assigning the value weights provide no assurance that the interests of the broader public will be adequately considered.[8] The researchers state that the weight they assigned each parameter "is an indicator of the degree to which water resource projects may disturb or enhance the dynamic stability of man's relationship with the natural and social environment. . . ."[9] But the researchers' position is terribly abstract and offers no evidence to citizens that their concerns have been incorporated into the value weights. Another weakness of the method is that it ignores equity effects.

Finally, one must question the usefulness of the EES composite score, measured in nominal units that have no particular meaning. Presumably, in making an accept-reject judgment, one would compare the net score (for environmental impacts) to the net benefits (for economic impacts). Suppose that a proposed dam scores −50 using EES (the minus sign indicating a net adverse effect on environmental parameters) and yields $10 million in estimated net benefits. How can one judge the tradeoff between the fifty-point loss and the $10-million gain? Since the fifty points have no special significance, there is no basis for making the comparison; we can compare two or more things only when each has a particular meaning to us. Yes, one could conduct studies that would provide some meaning to the points. For example, EES could be applied to past actions to derive the average dollar value of a point implied by past decisions. But applying this value to future decisions carries the dubious assumptions that (1) we are satisfied with past decisions, (2) the values of society are not changing over time, and (3) the *average* value is an adequate indicator of the variety of values that come to bear on decisions. Other approaches also could be suggested, but none really solves the problem. Returning to the example, it would be natural in judging the tradeoff posed by the dam decision to ignore the composite score and compare the net economic benefits to the more detailed information on environmental and social impacts to which meaning can be attached (such as lost wildlife, loss of a rare ecosystem, aesthetic damage, and disruption of social ties).

Rather than stressing comprehensiveness in its design, EES might have been developed for the more limited objective of creating an index measuring the viability of aquatic ecosystems. In this case parameters unrelated to the functioning of aquatic ecosystems, such as housing, employment, and aesthetics, would be excluded from the index computation. The parameter importance units would not represent *value* weights; instead they would be judgmental estimates of objective weights indicating the relative importance of each parameter to the overall health of an aquatic environment. Significance could be attached to points along this new scale by indicating how prominent ecosystems such as Lake Tahoe and Lake Erie (or, more pertinent, prominent river stretches) score on the index, analogous to the East Sussex Landscape Assessment Index.

In comparing EES to CBA, the main advantage of EES is its ability with simple adjustments to take account of all the important environmental consequences of an action, including those to future generations. Not only is it able, like GAM, to reflect the quantified but monetizeable impacts, but unlike GAM it also is able to consider intangibles.[10] CBA only considers monetized impacts.

But EES has disadvantages to CBA also:

1. Many of its impacts are technical and therefore not understandable to most citizens and decision-makers.
2. It does not consider economic impacts (by design).
3. Its composite score is measured in units that have no meaning, whereas the dollar units of CBA obviously do.

12.3 THE JUDGMENTAL IMPACT MATRIX

Description of the Method

Extensive use of expert judgment is made by JIM developed by researchers at Northwestern University.[11] The method was created for the U.S. Army Corps of Engineers to assess alternative wastewater management systems for Chicago and the south end of Lake Michigan. Its procedures are especially suited for in-design evaluations of complex systems, where a large number of alternatives must be screened on the basis of their many diverse impacts. Expert judgment is used both to estimate impacts and assign value weights, but the originators don't consider the grand index of social welfare computed by the procedure as a necessary feature.

The unique contribution of JIM is the way it subdivides the impact estimation problem into a large number of needed bits of information that, once obtained, can be hooked-up by a computational procedure. There are two general stages to impact estimation, as shown in figure 12.4. First, the impacts of the project or "system" on the environment are estimated; then the consequences of the environmental impacts for things of more direct concern to society are estimated. An additional step, beyond impact estimation,

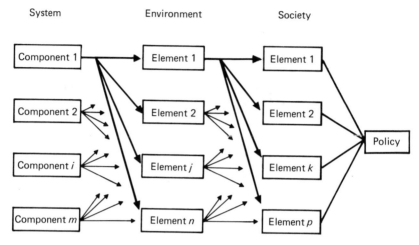

Figure 12.4
A diagram of the JIM model (Source: George L Peterson, Robert S. Gremmell, and Joseph L. Schofer, "Assessment of Environmental Impacts: Multi-disciplinary Judgments of Large-Scale Projects," *Ekistics*, vol. 218 January 1974, pp. 23–30.)

converts the societal impacts into a grand index of social welfare change using a set of constant value weights. JIM estimates environmental impacts differently than other methods. The usual procedure is to estimate the impacts generated by all the components of a project or system combined, but JIM estimates the impacts of each component separately. The advantage is that, since a component might be used in several alternative designs, its impacts can be estimated only once and used for each alternative in which it appears.

The application of JIM in the Chicago wastewater management study illustrates what is meant by "system," "environmental," and "societal" elements. The system components included alternative means of: (1) collecting, transporting and storing sewage (ranging from centralized to decentralized facilities); (2) managing sludge (ranging from advanced treatment to land disposal); and (3) effluent treatment (ranging from advanced treatment for municipal water supply to land disposal). Environmental impacts included elements such as surface water quality and quan-

229
Environmental Evaluation System and Judgmental Impact Matrix

tity, ground water quality and quantity, air quality, sensory quality (appearance, noise, odor, and so on), residential land-use, recreation and open space land, soil quality, energy, and unique or rare things or species. Societal impacts included elements of more direct human concern such as industrial production, food production, the supply and cost of public services, population density, health and safety, employment, income, recreation, and aesthetics.

Each linkage in the impact generation process corresponds to a needed bit of impact information: the impact of each system component on each environmental element and the impact of each environmental element on each societal element. Naturally some of the impacts are zero. All of these bits of information fit into a linear computational procedure, shown in the following matrix equation:

$V = SABW,$

where

V = a scalar index of the estimated social welfare change due to a particular system design,

S = a vector (with m columns) containing zeroes and ones, the ones corresponding to the set of alternative system components forming the project being evaluated,

A = a matrix (with m rows and n columns) each element of which represents the impact of system component i on environmental element j,

B = a matrix (with n rows and p columns) each element of which represents the change in societal element k resulting from each one-unit increase in environmental element j,

W = a vector of value weights (with p rows), each weight representing the relative importance of the societal element to which it is assigned for the social welfare.

If the grand index is not wanted, one can simply drop the vector of value weights (W) from the equation and obtain from the remaining matrix product (SAB) a set of societal impacts. The means of measuring impacts is not spelled out by JIM; only that semantic differentials with numerically defined scales are used. Although not mentioned, it is presumed that intangibles and tangibles are measured in the same way.

The JIM procedure uses expert judgments of a multidisciplinary team, following a variant of Delphi, to (1) determine the specific environmental and societal elements to be used in the evaluation, (2) estimate the magnitude of each impact linkage, and (3) assign the value weights. The originators are careful to point out the many problems in obtaining and using judgmental information. First is the problem of communicating the alternatives to the judges. The manner in which they are described can influence judgments. Sketchy, uneven, or excessively detailed descriptions should be avoided; a balance must be struck between thoroughness and brevity. Second is the problem of aggregating individual judgments into a single number. Because experts have different backgrounds, some are more qualified than others to judge certain impacts. One solution to this problem is to have each person assign a numerical score representing his confidence in making each estimate and use these scores to compute weighted averages. Alternatively, it could be reasoned that the discipline of each expert gives him or her special insights into impacts not known to others, so a total view can be amalgamated from partial views. If it can be assumed that an opinion is as likely to be high as low, the nonrandom errors might cancel each other out. Accordingly, simple averages would be sufficient, provided the panel of experts is carefully selected to represent all the relevant disciplines.

A third problem of using expert judgment is explaining the results. Each impact estimate is the average of many judgmental estimates, so each expert can only offer a partial explanation of why a group estimate is particularly large or small. To solve this problem it is suggested that each expert be asked to record the reasons for each estimate so that they can be pulled together into a composite explanation. The researchers conclude that the difficulties with expert judgment can be minimized through "(1) skilled use of the best available measurement techniques, (2) careful selection of panel members, (3) careful and patient education of the judges regarding the systems and their environment, (4) attention to the verbal comments and recommendations of the judges, and (5) cautious use of the numerical results as aids to decision making, not as determinants of it.[12]

Critique of JIM

JIM provides a well-defined procedure for obtaining and organizing impact information. It is especially suited for the difficult in-design evaluation problem of screening a long list of alternatives, where limited resources and knowledge can prevent scientific estimation of impacts. By distinguishing each of the linkages in the cause-effect chain of impact generation, it helps clarify the role of different types of expertise in judging impacts, and demonstrates the importance of coordinating this expertise so that the judgmental information connects together.

The JIM method helps reveal the proper position of technical environmental impacts in impact estimating. Technical impacts are only an intermediate step used to estimate the impacts of more direct human concern. Thus JIM overcomes the false assumption in several other methods that technical impacts can be treated as ends, directly amenable to tradeoff assessment. However, the method seems to imply that no environmental elements are valued in themselves, which of course is false; a case in point is rare and endangered wildlife species. The problem is easily rectified, though, by repeating such items in the list of societal elements.

The gain in clarity of the impact generation process is not achieved without a cost in oversimplifying it. The researchers are careful to identify certain weaknesses in the JIM model:

Obviously, the real impact process is far more complex. There may be interactions among elements within stages and there may be channels of impact from system elements directly into human elements, bypassing the environment. There may also be reverse flows. Finally, the temporal rates at which channels operate may vary from channel to channel. However, with a limited budget, a judgment of steady-state primary impacts [provided by the model] is certainly a good first step.[13]

However, in some applications these weaknesses may be serious. Evaluators should not let neat mathematical frameworks divert their attention from the more important goal of estimating all the important impacts. A model may be clean and symmetrical, but if it leaves out important factors, it should be amended.

It is worth noting that the model oversimplifies the real world with its built-in assumptions of additivity and linearity. It assumes that the impacts generated by a system component can be determined independently of the other components with which it is combined. But sometimes impacts spring from particular combinations. Also, JIM assumes that the impacts of the environment on societal elements is linear which is clearly inaccurate. The use of many nonlinear value functions in the EES method reflects this fact. Walter Isard and others at the Regional Science Research Institute in Philadelphia also attempted to use matrix methods to estimate environmental and societal impacts. Following an input-output format, they found that the many nonlinearities were extremely difficult to manage.[14] The existence of these difficulties serves more to underscore the general problems of impact estimation than the weaknesses of JIM.

Like other expert judgment methods, JIM does not delineate where the role of experts should end in evaluations and the role of citizens and decision-makers should begin. The experts select the impact categories and prepare the impact estimates. They might even set value weights for computing a grand index; however the originators minimize the importance of a single index, noting that politically valid weights might be difficult to obtain. Like many other methods, JIM ignores equity considerations and does not specify how time should be treated.

Although JIM was developed to utilize expert judgment, it is not limited to this application. Scientific estimates of impacts can also be inserted into the matrix framework. The emphasis on judgmental procedures seems to overlook this point. More importantly, JIM might be interpreted as favoring judgmental estimates, which would be a mistake. Even at the in-design phase of evaluation, some impacts can be easily estimated using scientific procedures, and these estimates should be favored. Impact estimation should not be used to supply estimates that cannot be made by scientific procedures. The role that a framework like JIM can play is to organize all impact estimates and direct judgmental procedures toward filling the missing information from scientific work. However, evaluators should not let the framework diffuse their attention from the key issues. It may be far better to devote extra time to estimating the really important impacts and comparitively little to unimportant ones.

Comparing JIM to CBA, JIM shares the advantage with other expert judgment methods that nonmonetized as well as monetized impacts are included in the analysis. Also, by using judgmental rather than scientific procedures, it can reduce the cost of preparing impact estimates, though the cost of judgmental estimates is not small. But by comparison, CBA can be very expensive to apply because it emphasizes the use of scientific procedures for estimating monetary impacts. The cost of using a full-blown CBA for in-design screening would be prohibitive in most situations.

On the other hand, JIM is not a fully developed evaluation method like CBA is. Perhaps its major disadvantage is ambiguity in how the results should be used for assessing alternatives. If the grand index is not used for comparing alternatives—which seems to be the attitude of the originators—the remaining option is to compare the alternatives on the basis of the impacts. However, the impacts are apparently measured on nominal scales rather than in measurement units that have particular significance. Thus irrespective of whether experts, decision-makers, or affected citizens make the comparison, it would be an abstract exercise. It could be argued that the experts serving as judges for the impact estimates would be in a good position to compare the alternatives on the basis of real rather than abstract impacts, because of their extensive exposure to the project information. But relying on experts to make public choices raises the same old problem of technocratic versus democratic decision making. We can be reasonably certain that experts are not representative of the values of all the people who will be affected by the decision.

12.4 CONCLUSIONS

The usefulness of the environmental evaluation system seems to rest on the acceptability of the formal mathematical approach to solving the evaluation dilemma. It is a well-designed, expert-oriented grand index methodology, but its designers do not offer any evidence to support the premises that expert values and a grand index are necessary or useful characteristics of an evaluation method.

Although JIM is also a grand index method, the originators do not consider its rating system a necessary feature. Indeed, its main contribution to the evaluation field lies in the framework it establishes for organizing and processing impact information. Although reality is seldom as neat as the matrix mathematics implies, the method helps to cut through a great deal of complexity in representing impact linkages, and the limiting assumptions can be overcome with appropriate adjustments. The fact that JIM is explicitly formulated to deal with in-design evaluations using expert judgments for impact estimation makes it especially suited to the current requirements for project assessments.

12.5 BIBLIOGRAPHY FOR THE ENVIRONMENTAL EVALUATION SYSTEM

Dee, Norbert, et al. "An Environmental Evaluation System for Water Resource Planning." *Water Resources Research,* vol. 9 (June 1973), pp. 523–535.

Dee, Norbert, et al. "Environmental Evaluation System for Water Resources Planning." Battelle Laboratories, Columbus, Ohio, 1972.

Whitman, Ira L. "Design of an Environmental Evaluation System." Battelle Laboratories, Columbus, Ohio, 1971.

12.6 BIBLIOGRAPHY FOR JUDGMENTAL IMPACT MATRIX

Peterson, George L., Robert S. Gemmel, and Joseph L. Schofer. "Assessment of Environmental Impacts: Multidisciplinary Judgments of Large-Scale Projects." *Ekistics,* vol. 37 (January 1974), pp. 23–30.

Wachs, Martin, and Joseph L. Schofer. "Structuring a Participatory Decision Framework for Public Systems." Paper presented at the Speciality Conference on Human Factors in Civil Engineering Planning, at the State University of New York, Buffalo, June 18–20, 1975. Sponsored by the American Society of Civil Engineers.

13
CITIZEN PARTICIPATION IN PLANNING AS CITIZEN JUDGMENT

13.1 CITIZEN JUDGMENT AS AN EVALUATION TOOL

No formal evaluation procedure, different from those discussed in prior chapters, has been advanced establishing a "citizen judgment" methodology. Nevertheless, the contrast between citizen judgment and expert judgment is worth making, because in principle any of the expert judgment methods could be applied using citizen inputs exclusively. For example, a group of citizens who would be affected by a plan could be asked to fill in the cells of the judgmental impact matrix, as indeed Wachs and Schofer have suggested.[1]

Asking citizens to determine impacts and assign value weights has the obvious disadvantage that they may not be qualified to judge those impacts that are best approached from a solid background of scientific knowledge. Although it is true that, in general, the citizenry includes all of our experts, there is no assurance that experts would step forward to do the work. More importantly, if they did, the process could easily revert to an expert judgment method, with the experts dominating the effort. Because it is our purpose here to contrast citizen judgment with that of experts, this possibility should be excluded temporarily from our definition of what constitutes a citizen judgment method.

We should recognize that the lack of specialized knowledge for judging certain impacts is a less serious disadvantage in relatively less technical areas, such as recreation planning. But it can be a major disadvantage in highly technical areas, such as energy planning and wastewater management. In the absence of sound and widely respected information on the consequences of alternatives, planning debates can easily break down into purely rhetorical contests in which the side that can talk the loudest and longest has the most influence.

Another disadvantage is that establishing and maintaining a citizen judgment process is less convenient. An expert judgment evaluation can often be conducted with people inside the planning organization, people who already know and can easily communicate with each other. Meetings are easier to schedule and can be conveniently located at the planning office. And the participants can be expected to attend meetings regularly, even if the work is conducted over a prolonged period of time. Scheduling meetings for citizen groups faces difficult timing and location conflicts. If the task is time consuming and prolonged, the size of the group may erode away. If the planning effort involves important technical considerations, the citizens may require a crash course or two before they can even begin to approach their task. And the job of organizing and managing a citizen group requires skills that planners have not traditionally nurtured.

On the positive side of the balance sheet, citizens are not disadvantaged in judging impacts of all kinds. Some impacts, particularly the most subtle social and psychological ones, are less susceptible to scientific determination. The nature and severity of these impacts might be best judged by citizens potentially affected by the planning action, drawing on their personal knowledge rather than the more formalized types of processed knowledge. Contrary to the view in some circles that only the quantifiable impacts are worth considering, sometimes the unmeasurable impacts on people are the most significant of all.

Finally, among the criteria for assessing evaluation methods established in this book were (1) that evaluators should not assume that their values are a good indicator of the values held by the people they serve, (2) that technical experts, in general have no special claim to superior values, and (3) that evaluations should reflect the values of all the people potentially affected by a proposed action, not just some of the people. These criteria underscore the key advantage of a citizen judgment approach to evaluation—that direct citizen input has a far greater potential of accurately reflecting the full range of values held by the multiple publics. By contrast, we can be quite confident in stating that planners engaged in design and evaluation tasks are seldom able to represent the full range of public views.

Perhaps the most obvious application of citizen values is in weighing the impacts of alternatives to reach a judgment regarding the preferred choice. But values enter the in-design and post-design evaluation process in several other important ways. The goals and issues, hopes, and concerns of the planning exercise shape the initial choice of alternatives. The selection of feasibility criteria determines which alternatives survive the early screening process. And the selection of impact categories and measures establishes the scope of the impact analysis. The planners may think that their selections will adequately mirror public sentiments, but more than likely they won't if the citizens are not consulted in some way. Citizen judgment provides a direct means for making all of these important value-based choices.

The representative character of citizen input, however, should not be overstated, because it obviously is not automatic; it must be built into the way that a citizen group is selected and organized. Full representation often requires a special outreach program to include specifically people who are not inclined toward active participation, especially the various disadvantaged members of society. Meetings should not be held during working hours, because low-income wage earners can least afford to take time off from their jobs. And if the planning effort is serving a large territory, the meetings should be held at decentralized locations, so that people are not excluded by the time and expense of long-distance travel. With adequate attention to details such as these, a reasonably representative group of citizens can usually be assembled.

13.2 COMBINING CITIZENS AND EXPERTS IN THE EVALUATION PROCESS

This brief critique of citizen judgment reveals an important complementarity between citizen input and expert skills. All of the evaluation methods we have reviewed that don't explicitly include citizen inputs score poorly on human value and democratic criteria. On the other hand, exclusive use of (nonexpert) citizen judgment has the serious weakness of lacking scientific rigor in estimating certain types of impacts. Therefore it seems reasonable to design evaluation processes that include both citizens and experts. Citizen participation in planning is the obvious vehicle for acquiring citizen inputs, so an overview of the subject will be useful.

13.3 CITIZEN PARTICIPATION

It has long been argued that active citizen involvement in public affairs is essential for maintaining a truly democratic government. But achieving effective and acceptable citizen participation in government seems much more difficult today than it was two hundred, one hundred, or even fifty years ago. The kind of grass roots democracy that Toqueville praised of early nineteenth-century America does not seem possible. Rather than being the predominantly rural and small town people that entered the twentieth century, we have become not only urbanized but metropolitanized. As residents of populous cities and counties, we have little opportunity individually to influence the actions of our municipal governments. For the vast majority, town meetings and town councils are only interesting historical relics.

The alienation and deterioration of self-sufficiency and self-determination wrought by the growing scale of organizations in other dimensions of living have been paralleled in political affairs. Corresponding with and related to the rise in urbanization has been the growth in governments at all levels. Governments now exert a considerably greater influence over our lives. Much of this growth has occurred in the governments that are least accessible to the people: state and federal. Thus not only has the fountainhead of participatory democracy become clogged, its center has shifted to new locations that have never been able to claim effective participation. Thus citizen participation in democracy has simultaneously been rendered less available due to greater governmental centralization, yet more urgent due to greater governmental power.

Unfortunately, attempts to establish active citizen involvement in planning are often met with resistance. Citizen participation means citizen power. But to give power to citizens requires that those who have it give some of it up, which elected officials, agency heads, organizational representatives, and other leaders are not in the habit of doing.

The important advances in citizen participation have not come without a great deal of struggle. Most politicians in office seek to exercise their authority, not share it. Large agencies seek to meet their mandate in accustomed ways and are very good at protecting their bureaucratic turf. And organized interest groups having well-established channels of influence resist measures that would dilute it. Where the resistance is overcome, there is always the threat that the participatory process will be manipulated by the power structure to engineer support for its views.

Also, as governments have grown, they have become staffed with growing numbers of technical experts needed to advise decision-makers on the rising number of complex problems. The evolution in the role of these experts has further hampered participation. Among some, the attitude has been that the problems are technical, requiring technical solutions. Accordingly, decisions can be made on the basis of technical considerations alone, free of values. Others have believed that experts are better qualified than citizens to judge what is in citizens' interests. These attitudes have spawned a technocratic approach to planning and decision making that increasingly is being rejected as unacceptable in a democracy.

Citizen involvement in planning also must face some contradictions. Elected representatives historically have been given broad powers to make many day-to-day decisions on behalf of the electorate. The call for participation challenges these long established powers without specifying how they are to be amended. Also, planning staffs have historically regarded certain public officials as their clients, not citizens, and this remains common. Under these circumstances the entry of citizens into the planning process confuses the traditional lines of authority and allegiance.

To achieve genuine citizen participation in the face of the many forms of resistance and contradictions entails more than principled statements of democratic ideals; it requires among other things clear legal mandates identifying citizens' rights, and access to legal counsel to gain enforcement of the laws through court action, if necessary. And as Rousseau long ago pointed out, it also requires a persistently keen commitment to active participation among citizens.[2]

The role of citizen involvement in the federally funded local programs of earlier decades was small, but more recently, certain federal programs have led the way requiring far more participation than would otherwise have been adopted by many of the local governments administering them. A key event in the recent citizen participation movement was the requirement for "maximum feasible participation" in the Economic Opportunity Act of 1964, which attempted to expand economic opportunities for low-income people. To permit impoverished people to play a major role in planning and managing programs to aid themselves was unheard of—revolutionary. Partly as a result, the program had a stormy existence. Edgar and Jean Cahn have assessed the results as follows:

There are three general propositions which sum-up the experience which has been generated by (though not confined to) citizen participation under the poverty program.

First, citizen participation is fraught with dangers and risks. Even at its best, and when most fully realized, it is precarious, fragile, vulnerable and easily destroyed or perverted. It is threatening, likely to invite retaliation, and likely to generate highly explosive and controversial situations.

Second, citizen participation in all its varied aspects and dimensions has demonstrated that it can make major and unique contributions.

Third, and finally, the values of citizen participation are such that they out-weigh the liabilities, the risks and dangers. The evidence is compelling that as a society we have no choice but to accept the risks and costs of an expanded democratic ideal, if we are to achieve the goals we have set for ourselves as a nation.[3]

The support for citizen participation among Washington decision-makers is reflected in the fact that since 1964, model cities, transportation, urban renewal, education, health, environmental, and most other programs require it in their planning and management.

The classical arguments emphasizing the importance of active citizen participation in a democracy remain fundamental. Accordingly, through citizen participation, the tendency for people to misuse power—given the opportunity—will be checked, and citizens will become more informed about public affairs and thereby make wiser choices at the ballot box. To these have been added a few others of more recent thought and experience. First, as governments have grown, decision-makers and planners have had less contact with citizens and consequently have oftentimes been poorly informed on public attitudes. Citizen participation provides a valuable channel for com-municating these attitudes. Planning should serve the interests of the public, which is difficult to do when the public interests are not known! In the past innumerable plans prepared at great expense have been abandoned as unim-plementable for lack of public support. And there are more than a few cases where major projects (such as freeways and water projects) have been per-manently halted in mid-construction, standing as painful (and costly) symbols of communication failures. Citizen participation, beginning in the earliest stages of planning, can help avoid these problems.

Second, as the government's influence over our lives has risen, citizens have demanded a stronger voice in decision making, not simply to select decision-makers every four or so years but to have the opportunity to actively participate in discussing major issues and developing programs for addressing them. Without this opportunity, people feel more powerless, more alienated, less self-reliant, and less important than in the past: more like pawns pushed around for the benefit of others. Thus, as the size of government has grown over the decades, so, too, has the importance of expanding opportunities for active citizen involvement.

Third, it is believed by some observers that the process of citizen participation, if properly organized, can help promote conflict resolution. As the power of government has grown and society has become divided into large, well-organized interest groups, public decisions seem to create greater conflicts among citizens. It is widely advocated that people having interpersonal conflicts ought to talk over their problems. The same principle of communication applied to public issues suggests that the process of citizen participation should include opportunities for individuals and representatives of opposing interest groups to discuss with each other their views, interests, concerns, and positions, as well as provide the opportunity to explore possible compromise solutions.

Finally, it is becoming recognized that the citizenry represents a huge pool of valuable knowledge that should be tapped in the problem-solving process. The general educational level has steadily risen over the decades. And, by definition, the "citizens" include all of our experts, only a small fraction of whom officially assume this role in each public planning action. Some of the remainder would willingly provide their expert knowledge as citizen participants, though often in the role of advocates. Also, as discussed earlier, scientific knowledge is incomplete, and some of the personal consequences of public actions can be best predicted and described by the citizens who are the potential recipients.

In sum, active citizen participation in the planning process is both essential and useful for a variety of reasons: to check the possible misuse of power, for a more informed and wiser electorate, to communicate citizen attitudes to planners and decision-makers, to help recapture a sense of self-determination, for conflict resolution and to tap the expertise in each person.

13.4 CASE STUDIES OF CITIZEN PARTICIPATION IN ENVIRONMENTAL PLANNING

The traditional approach to planning was for the planning team to conduct its work in relative isolation from citizens and then present the final results for adoption at a meeting of public officials, which citizens were allowed to attend. Many planning endeavors have changed a great deal from this old style, using a number of tools for improving communications between planners and citizens (or their elected representatives). The brief case studies that follow illustrate a variety of approaches to participation today, ranging from passive to active. They do not constitute a representative sample of citizen participation programs; that would be extremely difficult to achieve. The cases reported here are fresh examples of recent efforts at citizen participation. The first three deal with the preparation of community land-use plans; the final four address regional issues of land-use, sludge management, water quality, and recreation.

Venice Community Land-Use Plan[4]

Venice is a small, early-settled coastal community in the city of Los Angeles, with many modest old homes and duplexes, and a water canal system, long since fallen into disrepair and disuse. The area is a mixture of poor to upper-middle income blacks, Chicanos, and whites with a sizable community of counter-culturists, artisans, and simple living collectives. It has recently come under pressure for private redevelopment from the demand generated by a large boat marina adjacent to it.

The preparation of the Venice Community Plan is an interesting example of a major reversal in planning procedures. In 1970 the Los Angeles City Council adopted a general plan, including a plan for the Venice community that called for major redevelopment with high-density residential structures. The plan was prepared in the city planning department with no effort to obtain significant community input to the process. Public hearings were held, both by the city council planning committee and the city council, itself, but no effort was made to communicate the staff's plan to the community or to inform the citizens about the hearings. As one close observer analysed the situation,

The attitude of both the Planning Department and the City Council at this time seems to have been that the Planning Department contained an eminently competent pool of planning expertise and that City Council approval provided all the necessary guarantees that the people's interests were adequately addressed. The only flaw in this logic was the fact that the plan was thoroughly unacceptable to the majority of Venice residents . . . [5]

When the residents of the community learned of the new plan, they protested vigorously to their city councilwoman; they liked the existing community atmosphere and wanted it preserved, not changed. The councilwoman was able to obtain authorization from the council to form a "citizens advisory committee," which in fact functioned as a citizen planning committee. The 23 members of the committee were selected to provide an adequate representation of all interests in the Venice community. The committee met regularly for thirty-two months to draft a proposed new community plan. Present at all meetings were members of the local councilwoman's staff and two or more members of the city-planning staff to provide technical advice when requested. Attendance at the meetings waned as time passed; only 8 members were present to approve the proposed plan at the final meeting in early 1977. Copies of the proposal were distributed in the community, and the proposed plan received strong support at community-wide public meetings where it was reviewed. As of mid-1978 the proposal has not been approved by the city. At issue is whether or not a new regional traffic artery will be extended into the area. The community is against it, but city transportation planners feel it is a necessary facility. The planning department will have to decide how it will attempt to resolve the matter in the proposed plan it will submit to the planning commission. Presumably this plan will in all other respects coincide with the community-supported proposal. The planning commission will conduct public hearings before making its recommendation to the city council.

Revision of the Community Plan for Del Mar[6]

Del Mar is a small, middle-income coastal community in Southern California that recently revised its community land-use plan. Because the city budget for planning was small and extensive citizen participation was desired, the planning commission and city council decided to form citizen-planning committees to do most of the work. Requests for citizen volunteers were well publicized in local newspapers, and 140 offered their services. Four committees were formed, one for each of the plan elements to be revised: commercial development, residential development, open space, and circulation. In addition, a steering group was organized with two members elected from each of the four committees. With the professional assistance of planning staff and consultants, the committees tackled two tasks: first, to prepare a set of goals and objectives to guide their work; second, to revise the plan elements consistent with the goals and objectives.

Drafts of the goals were circulated among the planning commission and city council for comments, and revised in final form. The emphasis was on preserving the small town, single-family atmosphere and the open space of the community. The proposed plan revisions took about a year to complete and were officially endorsed by the citizen-planning committee members. The planning commission and city council conducted public hearings on the proposed revisions. Some strongly voiced opposition to the revisions suggested that the work of the committees had not reflected all interests in the community. The main issues were over proposed denial of duplex developments and extensive open space acquisitions. Attempted compromises were not accepted by either side, so a task force of public officials representing both sides of the issues was appointed to prepare a ballot for a nonbinding plebiscite. The ballot, mailed to every registered voter in the city, enabled each citizen to record his or her position on the controversial issues. Two-thirds of the ballots were returned. The planning commission and city council drafted a revised plan based on the results. The new proposed plan was submitted to the voters for their acceptance or rejection at the next regular election. In this case the preservationists were successful.

Pier Renovation in Santa Monica[7]

Sometimes power is not so much given to citizens as taken by them. A good example is the case of the municipal pier in Santa Monica, California. Santa Monica is a coastal community of over 100,000 people, adjacent to Los Angeles. The community is quite heterogeneous, economically, racially, and in most other respects.

The city has a municipal pier serving several million visitors every year, particularly elderly and low-income youths, with many recreation opportunities and snacks at modest prices. But the structure had been deteriorating, and in the early 1970s it became clear that something would have to be done about it. The city manager, supported by pro-development city councilmen, announced a proposal for major upgrading of the pier and connecting it to a thirty-five-acre island to be built in the bay, both to accommodate a host of new commercial facilities. The services of the pier would become limited to higher income people. A new city election was approaching and the anti-development forces jumped into action. A ballot measure was qualified requiring that any new structure, pier, or island built in the bay must first be approved by the majority of Santa Monica residents. Also, a slate of anti-development candidates was placed against the three pro-development councilman up for re-election. The results of the election were that the ballot measure won by a 78 percent vote, the pro-development councilmen were thrown out of office, and the city manager was fired.

In a subsequent election, the preservationists sought to further reinforce their position on the pier issue by qualifying a ballot measure making it unlawful to destroy or demolish the pier. It too was approved, by 64 percent of the voters. Thus the citizens of Santa Monica selected the plan of their choice by using ballot measures to make the alternatives illegal without their formal approval.

North Los Angeles County Land-Use[8]

North Los Angeles County is an inland area comprising 2,500 square miles of semi-arid mountains and desert. Primarily undeveloped, the population numbers over 130,000. A new regional airport is planned for the area, but the Federal Aviation Administration announced it would not provide support until a master plan is prepared for the region. Such a plan is also required by the state, so the planning wheels were set in motion in 1971. After the institutional and financial details were settled, the planning process was designed. It called for extensive citizen participation, including a door-to-door survey of needs and attitudes covering 1,000 households, a questionnaire survey of the business community, the establishment of field offices in several communities staffed by members of the planning team, a monthly newsletter reporting the status of the project mailed to the residents of the region and other interested citizens, presentations of the planning work to chambers of commerce and other community groups, and the usual public hearings. The most committed element of the program was the establishment of a 35-member, paid citizen work group selected by the county supervisor representing the region follow-ing demographic guidelines for composition established by the department of regional planning. Officially called a "citizen-planning council," its func-tioning lay somewhere between a workshop and a citizen-planning com-mittee. The council met regularly with members of the planning team for two years and participated in three planning tasks: the identification of issues to be addressed in the planning effort, the design of alternative solutions, and the evaluation of the alternatives. In each task the planning team played the major role in dealing with regionwide considerations (such as aggregate population growth and regional transportation systems) because of its greater knowledge on these subjects. The council played a more active role in local considerations, particularly with respect to future land-uses in and around communities, for the obvious reason that the members were intimately familiar with local conditions.

The planning team and council decided to identify planning *issues* rather than *goals* in order to avoid the possibility of spending a great deal of time producing nothing more than a set of general "motherhood" statements that would be of little value in guiding the subsequent planning tasks. Each issue identified a component of the plan around which alternatives were to be designed.

The design phase was the most time consuming for the council. It was divided into three groups, each to prepare a set of alternative land-use plans for a designated area of the region. Prior to the design work the planning team conducted a series of seminars to educate the council members on the general factors land-use planners must consider in conducting their work. A LSA was prepared, based on environmental data assembled by the planning team. For each land-use, the council prioritized the environmental characteristics according to the perceived suitability to accommodate that land-use, and a land-suitability map was prepared. The suitability maps, combined with maps of existing land-uses in the region, provided the game board on which a land-use game was played The game was a "design-in" that involved each of the three council groups in designing alternative land-use development patterns for its assigned area, using chips representing residential, commercial, and industrial development of designated densities. A group would assemble a collection of chips on the map until it had arrived at a land-use pattern it felt represented a reasonable solution to the issues. The result was recorded, the chips removed, and another round of designing begun. Throughout the design process, the planners acted as educators and mediators. The planning team, working independently, also prepared its own version of a land-use plan for the region.

In evaluating the alternatives the planning team estimated the regionwide impacts of the alternatives. The land-use patterns were evaluated by identi-

fying the common and conflicting features of the alternatives developed by
the citizen-planning council. The common features were checked against the
teams' plan, and agreements were recorded as plan "fixes," which included
existing land-uses not likely to change, consensus land-use conversions, and
areas of environmental sensitivity and hazards requiring specialized planning
attention. The team discussed the conflicting features of the alternative plans
with the council and then prepared a first draft of the proposed regional plan.
A series of public hearings was held in the area on the draft proposal, which
was subsequently modified. The county board of supervisors has approved
the final draft proposal as it applies to one section of the region. But as of
mid-1978, approval of the balance has been delayed due to a city incorpora-
tion within the area and the preparation of revisions to the countywide
general plan.

Los Angeles-Orange County Metropolitan Area Sludge Management[9]
A regional planning effort was launched in 1977, "to develop a long-term
plan, including an implementation strategy, to use or dispose of residual
solids resulting from industrial and municipal wastewater treatment in the
Los Angeles-Orange County Metropolitan Area in an environmentally,
economically and socially acceptable manner."[10] Although the work plan
does not call for extensive citizen participation throughout the effort, it
identifies several participation tools to be used, including public hearings to
obtain citizen input on draft plans prepared at various phases of the work;
special on-site public meetings to obtain citizen views on site-specific reuse or
disposal alternatives (such as evaporation ponds in the low desert or agricultural application in the high desert); information dissemination on work in
progress through brochure and report mailings, news releases, media coverage
and slide presentations; and public comment reports summarizing citizen
input received at public hearings and otherwise, and descriptions of how the
planning team responded to them.
    As of mid-1978 a number of workshops and semi-formal meetings have
been held for agency personnel and elected officials to present the alternatives the planning team is thinking about and to get feedback. These meetings
have been well attended. In addition two day-long public meetings have been
held, one in each of the counties, to present to citizens the planning alternatives, but the turnout was extremely disappointing. No more than 50 people

attended each meeting, and to make matters worse, the nontechnical participants were intimidated by others who were technically competant on the
subject of sludge management.

In the future there are plans (1) to make educational presentations on
sludge management to city councils and community groups, (2) to prepare
media shorts on sludge management to raise the level of public knowledge,
and (3) to hold neighborhood meetings among residents adjacent to potential
sludge disposal sites.

The general prospects for more active citizen participation in this planning
effort seem poor. Many of the issues are technical and not particularly interesting to the average person. So far the planning effort has dealt principally
with broad regional issues, so citizens have difficulty interpreting the implications for them personally. And many other planning programs in the region
call for active citizen involvement, therefore competing with the sludge
management effort for the attention of that fraction of the citizenry inclined
toward active involvement in public affairs.

No doubt the upcoming neighborhood meetings to review proposals for
specific sludge disposal sites will be well attended by the adjacent residents.
Citizen involvement in the siting of locally unwanted regional facilities is
useful, but it poses a difficult planning problem because typically the local
opposition is well represented by it whereas the regionwide support for the
beneficial services of the facility (assuming that they are beneficial) is not.

Southern California (208) Water Quality Planning[11]

As a component of a larger program for improving water quality—"to make
our rivers and lakes and oceans swimmable and fishable by 1983"—208
planning calls for comprehensive areawide planning and management focusing
on nonpoint sources of water pollution, coordinated with land-use and air
quality planning in the region. The Southern California Association of
Governments (SCAG) was designated to lead the 208 planning effort in its
region, which covers Los Angeles, Orange, Riverside, San Bernardino, and
Ventura Counties, thus 10 million people. SCAG's work plan calls for citizen
participation throughout the two-year period, eighteen months of which have
passed as of this reporting.

The designated steps in this planning effort are: prepare a work plan;
identify goals, policies and standards; collect data, conduct preliminary

analyses and prepare forecasts; design alternative regional plans; evaluate the alternatives; select a plan and refine it; adopt a plan and implement it. The citizen participation, occurring in each step of the process, has four major components: public information, public meetings, a citizen advisory committee, and an ongoing assessment of the citizen participation program.

The public information component, by itself, is extensive. A 208 information brochure has been prepared to acquaint the public with issues in water quality planning, and SCAG's role. It has been passed out at public meetings, and mailed to interested citizens and community groups as well as public officials. A quarterly series of 208 newsletters has been published and distributed to citizens and officials, reporting progress on the planning effort. Feature articles have been prepared for publication in a variety of journals, periodicals, and local agency newsletters as well as SCAG's bimonthly publication. Press releases have been prepared for use by community newspapers. SCAG attempts to encourage the broadcast media to make public service announcements and offer documentary programs on water quality issues and 208 planning. A speakers bureau was established in which planners, public officials, and others interested in speaking on water quality matters conduct SCAG-prepared presentations to various community groups. Finally, reports have been produced summarizing the work of major planning tasks for distribution to interested parties.

Three workshops and three public hearings have been held as of mid-1978 to review milestone and early-action reports. The meetings have been well attended by personnel from the various public agencies in the region that will be affected by the plan. But attendance by the citizens at large has been disappointingly meagre.

In addition to several committees composed of public officials representing participating agencies, a citizen advisory committee was formed. The members were invited as representatives of commercial, civic, and environmental organizations in the region as well as unaffiliated interests. The advisory committee meets once a month to supply the planning staff with criticisms and suggestions. Although 50 people accepted appointments to the committee, the average attendance at meetings is only 25. The committee has been very frustrated by the feeling that it doesn't have any influence over the planning process. The many complex technical, institutional, and legal constraints that the planning team must face may make the demands of the citizen advisory committee seem unimportant. In addition, the legitimacy of the advisory committee to represent the interests of all the people in the region probably appears very weak to the planners compared to the other SCAG committees which contain elected officials.

Yosemite National Park Master Plan[12]

The preparation of the master plan for Yosemite National Park offers another example of a major reversal in the planning process. In 1968 the National Park Service planners, advised by a citizen advisory committee and the park concessioner, began work on a draft master plan that was completed three years later and presented for public review. The only citizen input to the plan was the committee, an 18-member group appointed by the Secretary of the Interior. Formally designated the Western Regional Advisory Committee, its general purpose was to advise the regional director of the National Park Service on park policy issues.

At the public hearing strong opposition was voiced, particularly over the transportation policy for the valley, so the need for additional analysis was clear. Subsequently, a large public corporation purchased the concession rights and apparently was able to obtain substantial influence over the planning. By mid-1974 a revised plan was completed for review, but news reports appeared exposing the nature of the planning process. Members of Congress, the Department of the Interior, and the National Park Service were flooded with letters from angry citizens protesting the commercial influence on the planning of a national park. Although $750,000 had been spent on the planning to this point, everything was scrapped, and a fresh planning effort initiated, this time in full public view.

The new work plan was prepared by the planning team after they had received some special training in citizen participation methods. It called for substantial citizen input in identifying the issues, designing alternative plans, evaluating the alternatives, and responding to a final draft of the one proposed for adoption.

The first step, initiated early in 1975, was to hold a series of workshops in California and other states. Announcements were made in the media, and 10,000 letters were mailed to people who had made previous requests for a copy of Yosemite draft plan. To help insure that the citizen input would be effective, the announcements asked the people to come ready to talk about park issues and problems, the kinds of opportunities that ought to be available and the way the park should be managed in the future.

The workshops were well attended, about 5,600 people in all. The time at each session was spent mostly in small-group discussions to give each person sufficient opportunity to contribute his or her ideas. The ideas were recorded, reproduced, and mailed to the participants for their review and added suggestions.

In addition, a visitor use survey was conducted at the park in the summer and fall of 1975. A sample of visitors was asked to fill out a questionnaire on how they had spent their time in the park and what their opinions were of the recreation experience. Some 3,100 were returned.

The information gained from the workshops and user survey established the full range and details of thinking on the possible futures for Yosemite. What was needed now was to organize these into a limited number of alternative plans that could be evaluated. The planning staff didn't want to formulate the alternatives entirely on their own; they wanted citizen input on this task. This gave rise to the innovative idea of creating a workbook that would enable each citizen to prepare his or her own master plan for Yosemite; a sort of do-it-yourself master plan kit. The workbook was well publicized and mailed to every person requesting a copy. The requests were far beyond expectations, requiring four printings of the material.

I won't go into the details of the workbook here, except to say it was designed in a most professional manner. It was well written, it was comprehensive, and it forced the respondent to be realistic in assembling components of a plan into a workable whole. The planning team was so overwhelmed with returned workbooks that they were unable to tabulate them all on their computer. The response was close to 50 percent, which is remarkable given that a meticulous person could spend several days to complete the workbook.

The team analyzed the results of the workbook and derived two composite plans from them that encapsulate a high proportion of the ideas they contained. To these, three other alternatives are being added: the concessioner's preferred plan, the no-action alternative, and the planning team's proposed plan. Summary reports describing and evaluating these alternatives will be distributed to the public in mid-summer, 1978. Detailed reports will be available for public purchase and placed in the main branch of each public library system in California and at other locations in the country. After public review of the draft plan and feedback, the planning team will reconsider its proposed plan and make whatever changes it feels are appropriate. The revised plan will be made available for public review before the western regional director of the National Park Service makes the final decision.

13.5 CONCLUDING OBSERVATIONS

Fully active and direct citizen input to the evaluation process is a useful goal, but it is more like an ideal to strive toward than a standard that we can be expected to achieve regularly. Active citizen involvement throughout the in-design and post-design evaluation process seems reachable mainly in situations where the problem being addressed by planning is relatively nontechnical and the affected population is not too large. To the degree that the planning problem is highly technical and the affected population is very large, active forms of participation are more difficult to implement and passive forms are more likely. The average citizen feels less qualified and tends to be less interested in actively pursuing technical issues. And active involvement from a sizable populace yields very large groups, which can pose serious management problems. Small committees can work effectively, but large ones usually cannot. This is a prime reason we have a representative democracy, not a pure democracy. Also, larger populations mean more elected officials, with a stronger claim to representing the masses than any limited group of nonelected citizens.

Nevertheless, even in the least favorable situations, passive techniques of citizen participation can be used to yield essential evaluative information. Citizen attitude surveys can be conducted at an early stage of design to gain citizen reactions to the initial ideas of the planning team regarding alternatives and their possible consequences. Progress reports can be released to the news media to keep the public informed and enable citizens to react to the planning effort if they have strong feelings about the directions it is taking. Summary reports can be distributed to the public at a later design stage describing and evaluating the major alternatives. Citizens and public officials can be invited to react to these by writing to the planning team as well as by presenting testimony at public hearings for this purpose. And the planning team can follow an established schedule of presenting their work-in-progress to elected officials for feedback. It must be admitted that these inactive and indirect forms of citizen input leave out some of the most effective ways of obtaining citizens' views, and they fall far short of fully addressing some of the key purposes of citizen participation in a democracy. Nevertheless, the information obtainable by them can place the evaluation process on a much stronger footing than without them.

Sometimes when the planning problem is technical or the affected population large, the use of a task force or an advisory committee can be particularly helpful. The work of a special task force for air quality planning in the Los Angeles area illustrates a few last points I would like to make before closing this chapter.

A complex task that had to be performed a couple of years ago for air quality maintenance planning in the south coast region was to review roughly one hundred alternative tactics and strategies for reducing air pollution and then select a limited number for immediate implementation and another small group as promising options deserving further study. A task force composed of public officials and citizens representing various interest groups was charged with the job.

The task force was supplied with information on the effectiveness (of reducing emissions) and the financial cost of the alternatives by a consulting firm. In addition, it identified ten other impact areas it considered important to the evaluation, including energy, employment, special populations, and safety. Then the work of the group proceeded by the following set of ordered tasks, performed mainly at weekly meetings during a two-month period:

1. The group reviewed the 100 alternatives to be sure they had a clear idea of what each one represented.
2. In the absence of formal impact estimates for the 10 additional impact items, each person formed a judgment of what he or she thought they would be and assigned ratings to the 10 impacts for each of the 100 alternatives. The ratings were based on the following ordinal scale:

Rating	Meaning
++	very favorable impact
+	favorable impact
0	impact is inconsequential or unlikely
−	unfavorable impact
− −	very unfavorable impact

Each person was supplied with a large tabular sheet for recording his or her ratings, the rows representing the options and the columns, the impacts. (Extra columns on the right side of the table were provided for recording overall ratings and rankings.)

3. Each committee member then assigned an *overall* rating to each of the 100 alternatives using the same ordinal scale.

4. The group discussed their ideas on the impacts, so that the knowledge of each member could be shared. Then, as in the Delphi process, each member had the opportunity to revise his personal ratings.

5. On the basis of the revised ratings, each person ranked the 100 options from best to worst.

6. The members were supplied with Delphi type of information on tabulated ratings, showing for each alternative the number of people who had assigned each of the ratings (+ +, +, 0, —, and — —), and were given the opportunity to revise their personal rankings.

7. Then each member was provided the information on effectiveness and costs, and was asked on the basis of this information and their previous rankings to vote on each alternative, either to accept early implementation of the strategy or not.

8. The votes were tabulated, and a list of the alternatives was prepared ordering them according to the votes they received. The group reviewed the votes for early implementation and decided on a cutoff point democratically.

9. The alternatives not chosen for early implementation were the subject of another round of voting to select those that deserved further study in the planning process.

The task force concluded that this evaluation procedure was very helpful to them in addressing this especially complex task.[13]

This case illustrates a few points that are quite important. First, it shows that a group of nontechnical people are quite capable of tackling a complex, technical evaluation task, even when only a bare minimum of impact information is provided them. Second, it supports the view that a personal-rating procedure can help individuals in comparing a large number of alternatives. Of course, it does not suggest that the use of ratings is necessary. People face complex decisions every week of their lives and are able to make choices. If rating procedures were essential in complex situations people would use them in their personal lives, but outside the economic realm, I suspect the practice is rare, although I have never seen statistics on it.[14] Nevertheless, in extremely complex situations, such as the one the task force confronted, ratings can be helpful.

Third, it is useful to observe that the process of rating each impact often helps to sharpen one's understanding of alternatives beyond what can be achieved by simply reviewing the impacts. After rating each impact of an alternative, one is able to assign, holistically, an overall rating with some confidence. That is, an overall score does not have to be derived mathematically from the separate impact ratings. This is not meant to imply that numerical ratings and computations should be rejected, only to indicate that even in complex cases they are not absolutely necessary. A final note is that the task force reached its decisions democratically rather than on the basis of an aggregated grand index.

13.6 BIBLIOGRAPHY FOR CITIZEN PARTICIPATION

Arnstein, Sherry R. "A Ladder of Citizen Participation." *Journal of the American Institute of Planners,* vol. 35 (January 1969), pp. 216–224.

Arnstein, S., and E. Metcalf. "Effective Citizen Participation in Transportation Planning: Volume II, A Catalogue of Techniques." U.S. Department of Transportation, Federal Highway Administration, Washington, D.C., 1976.

Bleiker, Hans. "Augmentation and the Meta-Process: A strategy for Responsive and Responsible Decision Making by Public Agencies." Ph. D. dissertation, Massachusetts Institute of Technology, Cambridge, September, 1971.

Borton, Thomas E., and Katharine P. Warner. "Involving Citizens in Water Resources Planning: The Communication-Participation Experiment in the Susquehanna River Basin." *Environment and Behavior,* vol. 3 (September 1971), pp. 284–306.

Bowen, Mignon. "A Visit to the Front Lines." *Cry California,* vol. 13 (Spring, 1978), pp. 13–17.

Buck, J. Vincent, and Barbara S. Stone. "Yosemite Park Planning." *Cry California,* vol. 13 (Spring, 1978), pp. 18–21.

Cahn, Edgar S., and Barry A. Passett. *Citizen Participation: Effecting Community Change.* New York: Praeger Publishers, 1971.

Clark, Roger N., and George H. Stanky. "Analyzing Public Input to Resource Decisions: Criteria, Principles and Case Examples of the Codinvolve System." *Natural Resources Journal,* vol. 16 (January 1976), pp. 211–236.

Cole, Richard L. *Citizen Participation and the Urban Policy Process.* Lexington, Mass.: D. C. Heath, 1973.

Grant, Richard A., Jr. "208: A Vision Few Can See." *Cry California,* vol. 13 (Spring, 1978), pp. 22–24.

Grigsby, J. E., III, and B. Campbell. "A New Role for Planners: Working with Community Residents in Formulating Alternative Plans for Street Patterns." *Transportation,* vol. 1 (1972), pp. 125–150.

Hamson, Daniel M. "The Yosemite National Park Planning Process: A Study in Citizen Participation." University of California, Los Angeles, 1977.

Los Angeles County Regional Planning Commision, "North Los Angeles County General Plan Study Design." Regional Planning Commission, Los Angeles, 1971.

Manheim, Marvin L., et al. "Community Values in Highway Location and Design: A Procedural Guide." Report no. 71-4, final report of National Cooperative Highway Research Program Project 8-8 (3). Urban Systems Laboratory, MIT, Cambridge, Mass., 1971.

Marris, Peter, and Martin Rein. *Dilemmas of Social Reform.* Middlesex, England: Penguin Books, 1972.

Martz, Marjorie, and Carolyn Thomas. "The Public Participation Elemnets of the Southern California Association of Governments' AQMP and 208 Plans." University of California, Los Angeles, 1977.

McKay, Floyd. "How to Abuse a Valuable Resource." *Cry California,* vol. 13 (Spring, 1978), pp. 2–5.

O'Riordan, Jon. "The Public Involvement Program in the Okanagan Basin Study." *Natural Resources Journal,* vol. 16 (January 1976), pp. 177–196.

Palmer, Francis H., Jr. "The Role of Citizen Participation in Determing the Future of the Santa Monica Pier." University of California, Los Angeles, 1977.

Quinton-Redgate, "North Los Angeles County General Plan." Regional Planning Commission, Los Angeles, 1975.

Sanderson, Philip. "Citizen Participation in the Development of the Venice Community Plan of 1977." Los Angeles: University of California, 1977.

Scofield, Rob. "An Evaluation of the Public Participation in the LA/OMA Sludge Management Project." University of California, Los Angeles, 1977.

Sloan, Allan K. *Citizen Participation in Transportation Planning: The Boston Experience.* Cambridge, Mass.: Ballinger Publishing Company, 1974.

Southern California Association of Governments. "Section 208: Areawide Wastewater Treatment Management Planning—Final Work Plan." SCAG, Los Angeles, Calif., 1976.

Spiegel, Hans B. C., (ed.). "Citizen Participation in Urban Development: Volume I, Concepts and Issues." NTL Institute for Applied Behavioral Science, Washington, D.C., 1968.

Susskind, Lawrence. "The Importance of Citizen Participation and Consensus-Building in the Land Use Planning Process." Paper prepared for the Lincoln Institute Land Use Symposium, Cambridge, Mass., October 27–29, 1977. Environmental Impact Assessment Project, Laboratory of Architecture and Planning, MIT, Cambridge, Mass., 1977.

Synergy Consultants. "Citizen Participation/Public Involvement Skills Workbook." Synergy Consultation Services, Cupertino, Calif., 1972.

Turnbull, George. "Citizen Participation in the Del Mar Community Plan Revision Process." University of California, Los Angeles, 1977.

Vaz, Mark. "A Visit to the Front Lines." *Cry California*, vol. 13 (Spring, 1978), pp. 6–12.

Wachs, Martin, Barclay M. Hudson, and Joseph L. Schofer. "Integrating Localized and Systemwide Objectives in Transportation Planning." *Traffic Quarterly*, vol. 28 (April 1974), pp. 159–184.

Wachs, Martin, and Joseph L. Schofer. "Structuring a Participatory Decision Framework for Public Systems." Paper presented at the Speciality Conference on Human Factors in Civil Engineering Planning, at the State University of New York, Buffalo, June 18–20, 1975. Sponsored by the American Society of Civil Engineers, 1975.

Wengert, Norman. "Citizen Participation: Practice in Search of a Theory." *Natural Resources Journal*, vol. 16 (January 1976) pp. 23–40.

Wilkinson, Paul. "Public Participation in Environmental Management: A Case Study." *Natural Resources Journal*, vol. 16 (January 1976), pp. 117–135.

Williams, Curtis. "Citizen Participation in North Los Angeles County." University of California, Los Angeles, 1977.

Yukubousky, Richard. "Community Interaction in Transportation Systems and Project Development: A Framework for Application." State Department of Transportation, New York, 1973.

See also the bibliography for chapter 4 on Democratic Philosophy.

III
CONCLUSIONS

14
TOWARD A MORE REFINED VIEW OF EVALUATION

14.1 INTRODUCTION

No evaluation methodology we have reviewed is truly comprehensive. And no method is clearly superior. Each has its strengths and weaknesses. But the methods do not have to be used in their totality. Evaluators can draw on the strong features of each in conducting their work, leaving out the less desirable characteristics. Cost-benefit analysis can be used for estimating and reporting the strictly economic impacts of plans without trying to force dollar signs on everything, and modifying its treatment of equity and time. Energy analysis is useful for dealing with the energy consequences of public actions, excluding from the calculus elements that are not usable as energy by humans. The planning balance sheet and goals-achievement matrix provide useful ideas for the treatment of equity and intangibles. The concept of organizing impacts around goals promoted by GAM can be used without computing a goals-achievement index. Land-suitability analysis offers valuable ideas for obtaining, organizing, and reporting information on the spatial implications of alternatives, which can be applied without computing land-suitability scores. The East Sussex landscape assessment index might be used for representing landscape impacts, and its concepts could be used to modify the environmental evaluation system as a procedure for measuring the viability of aquatic ecosystems. The judgmental impact matrix provides ideas for approaching the difficult task of in-design evaluation systematically. And certainly there are valuable ideas contained in other methods not reviewed in this book that can be added to the evaluator's kit.

The methodologies deserve a great deal of praise for improving the evaluation of plans. Assessments today are much more systematic and technically competent than they would have been otherwise. But if further improvements are to be made we must devote our attention to some of the remaining weaknesses.

CBA has dominated the field of evaluation for too long, as if it were a comprehensive methodology. Its one-dollar-one-vote criterion establishes a "dollar democracy" in public decision making that contradicts the fundamental democratic value of equality. Not only does it fail to represent equally all people of the present generation, it almost totally ignores the interests of future generations. And it has been proven quite inadequate in representing social and political values as well as environmental values like clean air, clean water, the conservation of natural resources, and the preservation of nature.

The weaknesses of CBA have been recognized for some time, and this has led to the development of other evaluation methods. Like cost-benefit, most of these methods seek to place public decisions on a more solid factual footing than existed in previous periods. And many of them have made important new contributions to the field. But nearly all of them suffer from a common set of weaknesses that derive from their overly narrow approach.

Evaluation in environmental planning is a process more than a method, a process that begins at the earliest stage of design and continues to the point that a final decision is taken. Throughout this process major value-based choices are made by the planners. Nearly all of the methodologies promote the attitude that these choices can be made on the basis of technical computations and expert judgments without the planners ever needing to consult the people for whom the plans are being prepared. The methods take a technocratic approach to planning that carries science well beyond the bounds of its ability to advance the wisdom of public decisions, an approach that moreover is increasingly being challenged as untenable in a democracy. The methods assume that the appropriate values to be attached to impacts can be derived on the basis of expert knowledge alone. Many of them seem to assume that either the values of experts are superior to those of citizens or are an adequate expression of them. And most of them assume that the "optimal solution" for society can be derived by scientific procedures, as if the welfare of society were so well understood that it could actually be measured by a numerical index.

14.2 ON THE GRAND INDEX

Despite its advantages, it is argued here that the use of a grand index in evaluations should be abandoned. True, it does represent a neat technical solution to the age-old evaluation dilemma of making trade-offs between the many, diverse impacts of complex public actions. Rather than wading through a mass of information on the consequences of alternatives, decision-makers, so it is argued, have only to look at the grand index for each alternative to see which should be selected.

The use of ratings to calculate a grand index is also supported by the argument that, because decisions imply the application of values to impacts, the values should be made explicit, so they can be discussed and debated rather than remain hidden. In some cases ratings can be used in the early design stages of planning to help identify alternatives worthy of further exploration and possible elaboration. Those keen on mathematical optimization find the use of ratings absolutely essential for deriving their "optimal" solutions. And to the extent that values are uncertain, it is argued that sensitivity testing can be used to determine the effect of different value assumptions on the "optimum."

Although these arguments appear strong, closer examination reveals their weaknesses. First, our knowledge of what determines the welfare of society is entirely too weak to reduce it to a mathematical equation, which all grand index methods imply can be done. Thus all mathematical rating formulas must be seen for what they are: simplified approximations that yield highly questionable results. If it were otherwise, we could pursue the solution of all public issues with dogmatic certainty, which clearly we cannot. No amount of sophisticated mathematics or statistics can alter this fact. Although the extensive use of numbers and equations can make an effort appear very scientific and precise, if the end result is a grand index, it is neither. The unqualified use of the terms "optimal" and "best" is so misleading that it should be avoided in the evaluation literature.

The argument that values, in the form of numerical ratings or weights, ought to be explicit so they can be debated is also weak. Many ratings are measured in meaningless units, so arguments about them will be equally meaningless. For example an argument that a particular impact should be rated 40 points rather than 30 can get nowhere; it is directed at too abstract a level. Solid arguments must deal directly with the facts, namely, the impacts in the context of a particular situation, and their perceived significance to society.

Of course a few rating methods use units that have real meaning, such as dollars in CBA and calories (or, even better, gallons of gasoline) in EA. Discussions of ratings in these units are not too abstract, but it is well established that many important considerations cannot be represented adequately in money or energy units. Thus debates confined to these values, while useful for some purposes, would be unable to span the full range of issues surrounding a public action. So again, we reach the conclusion that arguments should be directed at the impacts, described or measured in whatever terms impart the most meaning.

As for the idea of applying sensitivity tests to ratings, we must ask why we need to use computers to tell us what is readily observable? If a proposed public action with well-publicized impacts is controversial, by definition the values of different people or interest groups lead to different conclusions. If a proposal is unopposed, then the solution is insensitive to differing values. Evaluators can learn far more about the value basis of alternative actions by talking to citizens and their elected representatives than by making computer runs.

A major reason against the use of grand index schemes is that they short-circuit the citizen participation process. They contain the built-in assumption that there is no need to consult the affected citizenry about the planning effort because everything important to the selection of alternatives is included in the index computations. The assumption is that we can plan *for* people without needing to plan *with* people. And by suppressing the variation in public attitudes, they exclude information that is essential for pursuing compromise solutions. Furthermore, reports of grand index evaluations such as cost-benefit studies are technically oriented and therefore very difficult to understand. Although their purpose is to simplify complexity, more often they confuse instead. Thus citizens and elected officials are often forced either to accept the results on blind faith or to ignore them.

In principle, citizen participation could be used to obtain a set of value weights for computing grand index scores for alternatives. This approach might seem to meet citizen participation goals while retaining a grand index methodology. But would it be useful? I don't think so. Imagine being called to a public hearing on a proposed plan of great consequence to you—a new community land-use plan, the siting of a nuclear power plant in your area, the alignment of a new freeway. You have some strong views on the matter, and you have come to the meeting to express them. After you and the others have settled into your seats, questionnaires are distributed requesting each person to rate, on a scale from 0 to 10, factors such as noise, cost of construction, employment, air pollution, community disruption, and so forth. This is the limit of the response being requested of you. How would you react? Would your numerical responses be a meaningful representation of your attitudes? Would the information thus obtained be truly helpful to planners?

The emptiness of such an approach is apparent to anyone who has attended a well-organized planning workshop or public hearing. As an opportunity for citizen participation, it would be less than meaningless; it would be frustrating and demeaning. As a means of acquiring information for planning, it would be like communicating in monosyllable words.

A table of impact figures comes to life when citizens are given the opportunity to express their reactions to a proposed plan. The consequences of a plan become elaborated in all the richness and detail that words, tones of voice, and gestures can convey. One can study a plan for a long time and not learn as much about its implications as from going to a single, well-attended public hearing on it. Planners who attend a public critique of their plan and carry the right attitude—that they have done their best in the alloted time and now desire feedback with which to make improvements—can gain a wealth of information to bring back to the drawing board. Numerical responses compared to these provide little guidance.

Thus, although grand index schemes are appealing as elegant technical solutions to the evaluation dilemma, they are neither valid nor acceptable. There is no *simple* shortcut to the time-consuming personal task of reviewing the many consequences of proposed actions until a holistic impression of their significance forms which can be used to judge the preferred action. However, many aids can be used to facilitate the process, including a major alternative to the grand index.

14.3 IMPACTS

Role of Experts

The purpose of the formal evaluation work, conducted by the evaluation experts on the planning team, should be to estimate the impacts expected to result from the alternatives, and to report these in a form that makes them readily understandable to citizens and decision-makers. Obviously, impacts should be estimated by the most accurate means permissible within the budget. Established scientific procedures should be used whenever possible, but expert judgments should be allowed. Insufficient scientific knowledge, data, time, and budgets are common reasons for resorting to judgmental estimations. Formal procedures should be followed in obtaining judgmental estimates, and two or more independent judgments should be secured for each relevant item.

In most cases experts should play the main role in preparing impact estimates. Their scientific training in the nature of the various physical, biolological, social, political, and economic systems through which impacts are transmitted as well as their knowledge of the tools for tracing and measuring the magnitudes of impacts clearly dictate this role. Although their training usually emphasizes the importance of being objective in doing this kind of analysis, we know that it is difficult for anyone to prevent personal views from creeping into his or her professional work. The possibility, however, that peers could spot an error and thereby discredit an expert's work can serve to minimize this problem, particularly when the work is routinely circulated for peer-group review. The procedures and calculations used to estimate impacts should be reported (at least in a technical appendix) to aid the process of validation. Naturally, this kind of check on power and accuracy is limited to objective information, which underscores the worth of clearly separating objective information from value judgments.

Not to be overlooked, however, is the role that citizens can play. People potentially affected by a plan can also be valuable sources of impact information. The strength of our scientific knowledge is greatest in the realm of physical systems, and it narrows as we approach the more intangible aspects of human linkages and perceptions. The knowledge that the average person accumulates through life experiences enables him to offer descriptive judgments on how he and others would be affected by a proposal, sometimes well beyond the capability of scientists to predict it. Evaluators should seek opportunities to obtain this type of information from citizens first hand.

Selecting Categories and Measures

The first rule in selecting impact categories is the obvious one that the most important impacts should receive the most attention. With a limited budget only a small subset of all the potential impacts can be analyzed. The evaluators should not assume that their personal judgments in the matter are adequate. These are value judgments that should be tested against inputs from citizens and elected officials.

The categories and measures used to describe impacts should be selected for the purpose of communicating the information as clearly as possible to citizens and decision-makers. A useful rule to follow in this regard is to select categories and measures that are closely linked to the visible ends of human action, such as the preservation of life, health, security, and justice, rather than those representing means, such as dissolved oxygen, particulate matter, geology, and soil type, that only experts can link to ends. Evaluators must not assume that the impact categories and measures that make the most sense to them are the best to use in an evaluation. They must remember that their specialized knowledge enables them to understand and make personal sense of technical measures that the average person is unable to do. Their responsibility should be to estimate and report impacts in the forms that their clients—citizens and decision-makers—can understand.

Sometimes, however, impacts described by technical categories and measures can be estimated more accurately than the ends to which they are linked. For example, air pollution impacts (such as concentrations of carbon monoxide, particulates, nitrogen oxides, and photochemical oxidants) can be estimated more accurately than the consequent damage they do to human life and health, aesthetics and recreation opportunities, plants and animals.[1] Thus it would appear that in deciding the manner of reporting, a trade-off must be made between accuracy and understandability. But the evaluator can avoid sacrificing either by reporting *both* types of impacts, showing one as the consequence of the other and making clear the uncertainties of the estimates.

Goals

Some impact categories and measures should address directly the purposes or goals of the proposed action, as advocated by Morris Hill. Explicit goals statements can play a valuable role in the planning process, not only in evaluating alternatives but in guiding the work of the designers as well. The potential effectiveness of each alternative in terms of the main goals of the planning effort should be set out distinctly among the impact estimates.

By requiring that citizens or their elected representatives play a central role in preparing the goals statements, evaluators can be more assured that the categories and measures they select for impact estimation are understandable and address considerations important to their clients. But the exercise should not be couched in terms of defining *the* community goals. Values vary widely among people, and so will the perceived goals of a public action. Learning the variety of goals and issues, hopes and concerns among the multiple publics is far more valuable for planning than the generalized goals statements that all people can agree upon.

Quantification

The quantification of impacts is useful, but is often overemphasized. Numerical descriptions have the advantage over words and graphics of being more precise in conveying magnitudes of changes. They are also favored by the fact that the procedures for preparing scientifically based estimates are organized around measurable units. However, evaluators must recognize that quantification is not all important.

The central criterion for describing impacts should be to communicate to citizens and decision-makers as effectively as possible the consequences of proposed actions. A quantitative description that leaves out crucial information or cannot be understood is, in this sense, useless. Rather than utilize a sophisticated measure, it may be far better to provide verbal or graphical descriptions. Words and graphics have the advantage of being richer and more powerful communication mediums; they are capable of conveying certain facts and feelings with more dimensions of human meaning. We are all familiar with the notion that a picture is worth a thousand words. In the same spirit it can be said that a poem is worth a thousand numbers. Evaluators must be sensitive to these differences so that their choices of descriptors convey most fully and effectively the consequences of proposals to their clients.

Not to be overlooked, though, is the fact that technical, quantitative measures, if repeatedly exposed to the public, can come into common use. A good example of this, at least in Caifornia, is the Richter scale for measuring the severity of earthquakes. After experiencing several earthquakes, the damage they do, and their magnitudes, one begins to acquire a feel for the scale's meaning. Of course, even more familiar are the units by which we measure length, weight, volume, time, and temperature. One system of weights and measures is so deeply engrained in American thought and use that we strongly resist attempts to convert it to different scales which have proven advantages.

One way to facilitate the understanding of a technical measurement is to relate the various points on the scale to terms and descriptions people are familiar with. After repeated exposure, the scale becomes a shorthand for the fuller explanation, the repetition of which begins to fade in importance. The East Sussex scale for measuring landscape aesthetics is an example of a method that might come into common use if people were repeatedly

exposed to it in parallel with a string of photographs that depict points on the
scale. Evaluators can play a role in this process by reporting impacts both in
terms of measurement scales and fuller descriptions. First, though, they
should ask themselves the question whether the scale is worth promoting.
Will people really be saved enough time by learning the scale? Does the scale
really have the potential to replace the more complete descriptor? For
example, does the East Sussex scale have the potential to be a substitute
for photographs and drawings in describing landscape impacts? If the answer
is no, why use it?

Subindices

When impacts can be measured in the same units, they can be consolidated
into impact indices, thus simplifying the reviewer's task of comparing the
many diverse consequences of alternatives. Although it has been argued that
ratings are inappropriate for calculating a grand index, they can play a valuable,
although more limited, role in computing subindices of impacts. The application is analogous, so the same kinds of problems can occur if it is carried too
far. Subindices are desirable if they don't incorporate controversial value
judgments, don't leave out important details, and are understandable. Citizens
and decision-makers can gain from a reduction in the bits of information they
must review, but not if in the process values are forced on them they are un-
willing to accept, or important information is left out. CBA and EA are
useful tools for computing subindices if their limitations are respected.

CBA provides concepts and procedures for converting some impacts into
their direct monetary equivalents, frequently enabling the evaluator to summarize a large number of impacts in one or a few indices of economic impact.
If an impact can only be partially monetized it should be divided and redefined to reflect this fact. For example, the lost work and medical care that go
along with an adverse health impact can be monetized, but do not reflect the
attending pain and suffering. If the medical expenses and lost earnings are
included in the index of economic impact, the pain and suffering should be
recorded elsewhere in the evaluation. If the estimated monetary equivalents
of impacts are highly unreliable, they should not be described in dollars but
left in their more fundamental terms. Impacts that are best understood in
their own terms, such as human life and wildlife, should not be monetized
at all.

EA's most useful application is to impacts that can realistically be considered energy resources. The stocks and flows of energy in ecosystems not utilized by man are not usefully converted to energy units. The representation of ecological damage in calories is not particularly helpful (and might be considered a hindrance). The most obvious application of EA is to programs and projects for which energy conservation or development is a major goal.[2] But any action that has important energy consequences is a likely candidate.

A great deal of research has been devoted to the task of creating useful social indicators, and more recently environmental indicators, but little progress has been reported to date. The obstacles are similar in kind, although not in degree, to those for creating a grand index. The researchers doing this work might find it instructive to view their task from an evaluation perspective. Perhaps future advances will be made that add useful new techniques to the evaluator's repertoire. Certainly, as water budgets become tighter, evaluations analogous to EA which we could call "water analysis" will come into use.

Equity

In principle the idea of estimating and reporting the distribution of impacts as they are felt by different people or interest groups is a good one. Certainly, we are interested in the general equity question: Who pays and who benefits? Unfortunately, fully implementing the idea is, in most cases, impractical because of the large extra cost it would entail for impact estimation. But the idea should not be abandoned altogether, for it is possible to form judgments regarding the few groups that might be most inequitably affected by proposed actions and focus the equity analysis on them. At the bare minimum evaluators should estimate the impacts of plans on minority groups to consider the issue of tyranny by the majority. The disadvantaged minorities are the most obvious subjects for the analysis—call it an "equity impact analysis"—since they would be most seriously damaged by adverse impacts. If a few people stand to make large gains from an action, this too could be reported.

Future Generations

Also related to the issue of equity is the treatment of impacts on future generations. CBA offers the only explicit technique for treating the time-

dimension of evaluation. Other methods that recognize it adopt the cost-benefit procedure of discounting future impacts to their present value. But discounting is in direct conflict with the human concern for protecting the interests of future generations. Any positive discount rate applied to distant impacts yields so little present value that cost-benefit studies commonly use a cutoff point of about fifty years, beyond which all impacts are ignored. Such insensitivity to future generations in evaluations is unacceptable.

The only way to give fair treatment to the interests of our children, our children's children, and those beyond is to be specific about the consequences for them of proposed actions. Impacts affecting the current generation (covering, say, twenty-five years) might be discounted or converted to a rate-of-return measure. But impacts on future generations should not be discounted and should be reported separately.

Feasibility

Some impacts relate to public standards and regulations, such as air and water pollution. In these cases there is a tendency in impact reporting to consider the narrower question of whether or not the proposed action meets or violates the standard. This treatment assumes that people are unconcerned with levels below the standard, an assumption that has no necessary basis in facts. In the cases of both air and water pollution, human health is the main criterion for the standard, yet pollution levels below the standard can have other important consequences for aesthetics, recreation, wildlife, and ecosystems that cannot be ignored. Nevertheless, the existence of the standards indicates that higher public priority is attached to achieving these targets. In fact the priority is so high that it constitutes a sort of absolute.

Evaluation criteria that are absolutes constitute the subjects of feasibility analysis. Legal requirements and constraints form an important basis for these criteria. For example, a proposed action that does not pass legal criteria for air quality, water quality, private property rights, or rights guaranteed by the Constitution is automatically unacceptable, unless of course the laws are changed. A second level of feasibility criteria may spring from certain goals of the plan that themselves are absolutes. For example, a goal for a public plan may be the provision of a service in a way that is financially self-supporting; that is, the full cost of providing the service must be covered by a user charge, such as in the case of FHA-insured home loans or natural hazards insurance. In such a case the initial ideas for providing the service must be screened to eliminate those that would not pass the financial feasibility analysis. Only the alternatives that pass the feasibility analysis should become candidates for the post-design evaluation.

14.4 IN-DESIGN AND POST-DESIGN EVALUATIONS

The evaluation process encompasses a continuous set of activities beginning at the outset of design and ending just short of the final decision. This view is represented in the flow diagram in figure 14.1. As Lichfield, Kettle, and Whitbread have pointed out, if the formal evaluation process does not begin at the earliest phase of design, some of the potentially best designs may not be advanced or may be eliminated before being given formal consideration.[3]

Although the evaluation process should be established as an integrated flow of activities maintaining continuity from design onward, it is useful to distinguish two rather distinct phases: in-design and post-design, in which the style of the evaluation must differ. In-design evaluations must screen a large number of design ideas, filtering out the ones least likely to be successful and retaining the few that should receive detailed design and evaluation attention. Post-design evaluation has the task of assessing in depth the few major alternatives. The overall evaluation procedure can be visualized as shown in figure 14.2, in which a long list of alternatives are passed through a series of filters until only a few survive.

The major purposes and potential pitfalls of the planning effort are set forth in a group of goals and issues statements that help establish the basis for preparing the initial list of design ideas. The list is too lengthy to permit either detailed designing or in-depth evaluation of each alternative, so judgments must be used extensively. Strategies are pursued that direct attention to the factors judged to be most critical in distinguishing likely alternatives. The development of such strategies is a subject that has been almost completely overlooked in the formal evaluation literature, yet the function can be crucial. Impacts, even large ones, that are judged to be relatively invariant among the alternatives can be ignored. The impacts that are likely to be the main sources of controversy will receive extra analysis. A feasibility analysis will filter out unacceptable options, and some careful attention will obviously be given to the effectiveness of the alternatives in meeting the planning goals.

As the least likely alternatives are rejected, more attention can be given to those that remain. In the selection process designers develop a more articulated understanding of the design problems and the various design components with which they are working; they become better able to identify successful components and combinations of components, and to recognize others that create serious adverse impacts. Experiences such as this enable designers to select and merge components into new, superior design alternatives, replacing old ones, as well as to develop compromise solutions and mitigating measures.

As the evaluation continues, the few alternatives that survive the in-design phase receive detailed design attention, then are presented for the post-design evaluation. The no-action alternative is one of these, and for this reason is automatically passed through the screening. The post-design is different from the in-design phase more in degree than in kind.[4] The consequences of the major alternatives can be analyzed in much greater detail. Scientific procedures are followed wherever possible, but judgmental estimates are used where appropriate. While the evaluators will still want to focus most of their attention on the critical issues, they will have the time and resources to estimate more accurately a larger set of impacts.

14.5 CITIZEN PARTICIPATION

Plan assessments can be placed on a much sounder footing by infusing them with information on public attitudes, beginning at an early stage of design. Citizen participation is the logical vehicle. It is useful to recognize that a major portion of what we call citizen participation in planning is, more precisely, citizen participation in the *evaluation* process. Most evaluation methods overlook this fact.

There are at least three points in the evaluation process, shown in figure 14.1, where citizen input can play a crucial role. The first is concerned with establishing planning goals and issues and identifying possible solutions to the planning problem at an early stage of design. Citizen workshops might be held to obtain public opinions on these items in small group discussions. A more passive approach would have the planners prepare their initial ideas on

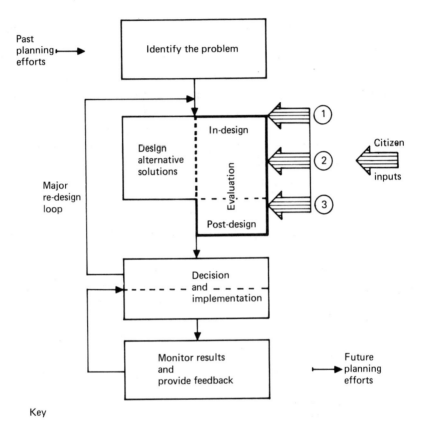

Past planning efforts

Identify the problem

In-design

Design alternative solutions

Evaluation

Post-design

Major re-design loop

Citizen inputs

① ② ③

Decision and implementation

Monitor results and provide feedback

Future planning efforts

Key

① Identify goals, issues, and possible solutions.

② Screen long list of alternatives.

③ Compare major alternatives.

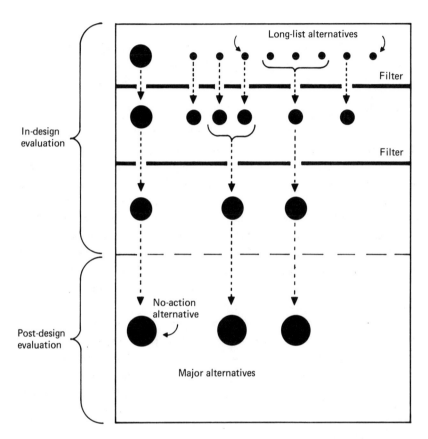

Figure 14.2
Screening and detailing the alternatives through in-design and post-design evaluations

goals and issues, potential alternatives and their impacts and write these into a brief report which would be distributed and critiqued by citizens and public officials. Armed with a set of specific public attitudes, the planners are able to be sensitive to their clients' views as they pursue their early design and evaluation tasks.

The second point lies at an intermediate stage of design, when the long list of options must be narrowed down to the few alternatives that receive major design attention. At this time the planners can prepare a report that reviews the long list of alternatives, summarizes the possible consequences of each, and explains for each option why the planning team thinks it should either be dropped or pursued further. A series of public meetings can be held to give citizens and public officials an opportunity to discuss and debate the options. Alternatively, written comments can be solicited. The inputs help shape the directions of the more detailed design and evaluation tasks. If the planning problem is especially technical or affects a very large population, a citizen advisory committee might play a valuable role in this in-design screening process.

The last point where citizen input is crucial is the post-design evaluation. It is at this stage that the major planning document is prepared, identifying and evaluating the major alternatives. Public hearings are held to receive public testimony and possibly for discussions among public officials. If there are major objections to the recommended plan, the decision-makers might direct the planners to revise their designs and hold another round of public hearings. If there are serious doubts about the views of the larger public, the decision-makers might order a public opinion survey or a non-binding plebiscite before taking action.

14.6 ALTERNATIVES TO A GRAND INDEX METHOD

The limits of grand index methods can be understood by seeing the evaluation dilemma as essentially a personal problem. It is a problem that each individual faces in attempting to synthesize diverse evaluative information. Beyond this personal dilemma, society has the task of transforming the various views of individuals into a group decision.

The two general approaches to solving the personal dilemma, discussed in chapter 1, are the informal procedure of reviewing the impacts, taking as much time as necessary for a coherent impression to emerge in the mind, and the formal procedure of assigning ratings and computing a composite impact score. It is essential to recognize that grand index methods attempt to go well beyond the formal solution to the dilemma. They represent *social rating* rather than *personal rating* procedures. They attempt to leap directly from impacts to composite *social* scores from which group decisions can supposedly be reached on the basis of predetermined decision criteria. In the process of leaping directly to social scores, they ignore the personal dilemma, as if there were no need for citizens or public officials to review the detailed impact information and reach their own personal conclusions. This leap not only carries evaluators beyond the realm of technical expertize, it also sets up a different political relationship between citizens and planning that violates basic democratic principles.

It is argued here that the central purpose of evaluations should be to help individuals—both citizens and public officials—reach personal judgments regarding the desirability of plans on the basis of the best obtainable information, not to compute grand index scores that seem to tell people what their attitudes ought to be. Transforming personal judgments into group decisions is a political problem that should remain within the realm of accepted democratic procedures.

In helping citizens and public officials synthesize a diversity of evaluative information a number of aids can be utilized. Many of these have already been discussed, but it will be useful to bring them together in one place. Evaluation reports and presentations can be prepared to maximize communication and minimize unnecessary technical jargon. Impacts can be described in terms that are most understandable to the public. Subindices for economic, energy, and perhaps other impacts can be used to help reduce the amount of impact information that must be compared.

Evaluation reports can contain summary sections utilizing arrangements and graphics that facilitate the process of comparing the advantages and disadvantages of alternatives. Space can be set aside in summary sections for reviewers to apply a personal rating procedure, if they are so inclined. The reports could even suggest a couple of rating methods that interested people might find helpful in shaping their opinions.

An idea that is simple and commonly used in legislative and judicial settings, yet not found in the formal evaluation literature, is to provide for each major alternative in evaluation reports written arguments favoring it. The arguments could be articulate, logical, and compelling factual statements. They could be prepared by supporting interest groups subject to the approval of the evaluators for factual validity.[5] Verbal statements are a major alternative to grand index measures, and might even be seen as superior, for they can crystallize the key advantages of alternatives with greater meaning and human significance. Furthermore, they can help liberate decision-making from the occasional preoccupation with numerical information, and provide an opportunity for giving qualitative expression to values that are central to planning issues. Reading the summary arguments would not be a substitute for reviewing detailed impact information, but after studying the impacts, reviewers should find the arguments helpful in crystallizing their own opinions.

Similar to written statements is the advantage of hearing spoken arguments for alternatives. Thus public hearings that give people the opportunity to hear and to participate in discussions and debates about plans can also be seen as aiding the synthesis process.

In addition to these aids, helpful to citizens and public officials alike, decision-makers can benefit from specially designed opinion polls and non-binding plebiscites.

In conclusion, helpful strategies for dealing with the evaluation dilemma are readily available. By rejecting the grand index approach, the formal solution can still be chosen by individuals voluntarily applying a personal rating procedure. Many aids can be used to help people form their opinions about complex plans, including an alternative to the grand index that has major advantages over numerical summaries.

No new evaluation methodology is proposed here. A useful set of tools is already available. The effectiveness of evaluators can be enhanced by learning a variety of methods, their strengths and their weaknesses. Evaluation is more an art than a science, an art requiring planners to approach each evaluation problem as a separate case, selecting that set of tools most suited to its particular characteristics and requirements. Outstanding evaluations will result more from the exercise of sound personal judgment than from following a rigid set of standardized procedures.

14.7 BACK-UP SUPPORT

The work of evaluators could be greatly advanced by outside support of various kinds. First, and most obvious, the budgets for conducting evaluations are meagre compared to the societal consequences of plans, and deserve more support. Second, the evaluators preparing impact estimates could use a great deal more back-up research for expanding the range of scientific procedures and improving the accuracy of estimates. Generally, this means more applied research, research aimed at the specific problems of estimating the impacts of public actions. A component of this would be to do more monitoring of implemented programs and projects. The results of this kind of research should be reported in a way that makes them readily available to all people conducting evaluations.

There are many other research questions worth pursuing. How can we improve strategies for conducting evaluations under conditions of limited budgets and data? How can we better deal with uncertainties of large losses? How can we prepare evaluation reports that more effectively communicate evaluative information to citizens and decision-makers? Would it be feasible to merge the many federal requirements for evaluations of various types, including environmental impact statements, into one unified law for evaluating all federally supported actions—evaluations that would systematically examine all the consequences of each plan and report them in a single document? What about merging requirements at the state level also?

Finally, the media could play an especially valuable role in disseminating evaluation information to the public. Newspapers could add a new dimension to their public service function by publishing the summary sections of evaluation reports for plans affecting their circulation area. Television news reports could do something similar. Public service television specials could be produced to present evaluations of critical regional and national planning issues, particularly those that can be communicated more effectively by the television medium.

14.8 A FINAL NOTE

In his 1932 book, *Ethics,* John Dewey expressed the view that the philosophical field of ethics could be of valuable assistance in addressing the critical societal issues of the day.[6] Indeed, there are many parallels between Dewey's ethics and the current field of evaluation. Evaluation can rightly be considered a branch of ethics.

Although Dewey held high hopes for the usefulness of ethical studies, he was also very careful to point out its limitations, as revealed by the following passage:

Study from ... [the social] point of view ... enforces, as nothing else can, a conclusion reached in our theoretical analysis. It discloses in a concrete fashion the limitation of moral theory and the positive office which it can perform. It shows that it is not the business of moral theory to provide a ready-made solution to moral perplexities. But it also makes it clear that while the solution has to be reached by action based on personal choice, theory can enlighten and guide choice and action by revealing alternatives, and by bringing to light what is entailed when we choose one alternative rather than another. It shows, in short, that the function of theory is not to furnish a substitute for personal reflective choice, but to be an instrument for rendering deliberation more effective and hence choice more intelligent.[7]

If Dewey were alive today, he would be both pleased and shocked by the manner in which we evaluate public actions. He would be quite pleased that increasingly we attempt to estimate the impacts of alternatives, using objective, scientific methods. This was seldom attempted in earlier decades. It is the impacts that reveal what is entailed when we choose one alternative over another.

He would be shocked by the narrow conception of social welfare that is either explicit or implicit in certain standard evaluation methodologies. He argued that "morals are personal because they spring from personal insight, judgment, and choice," and that they "must remain personal in that social problems have to be faced by individuals, and decisions reached in the forum of individual minds have to be carried into effect by individual agents, who are in turn personally responsible for the consequences of their acts."[8] By contrast some evaluation methods constitute attempts to set up a moral guide for deciding correct public actions.

Dewey also warned against the dogmatism that can follow from tightly defined conceptions of social welfare (or social morals):

There are still those who think they are in possession of codes and principles which settle finally and automatically the right and wrong of ... [societal issues, such as] divorce, the respective rights of capital and labor, the exact limits of private property, the extent to which legislative should go in deciding what individuals shall eat, drink, wear, etc. But there are also many other persons, an increasing number, who see that such questions as these cannot be settled by deduction from fixed premises, and that the attempt to decide them in that fashion is the road to the intolerant fanaticism, dogmatism, class strife, of the closed mind. Wars waged in the alleged interest of religion, or in defense of particular economic conceptions, prove the practical danger of carrying theoretical dogmatism into action.[9]

May we cast aside our shaded lenses and see the world with clear vision.

NOTES

NOTES TO CHAPTER 1

1. Of course impact estimates are often disputed before the fact, but this does not change their essentially objective nature. The key consideration is that the estimates might be verifiable against the real outcomes sometime in the future.

2. To illustrate further, using a highly simplified hypothetical example, the impacts of a rapid transit system are (a) transportation services, (b) reduced air pollution, (c) reduced energy consumption, (d) the expense of building and operating the system, and (e) the disruption it creates in the communities through which it passes. The magnitude of each impact must first be estimated, then each is assigned a rating, bearing in mind the type and severity of the impact. If the ratings in a particular case were (a) 56, (b) 22, (c) 10, (d) 85, and (e) 8, the score would be 88 for the desirable impacts (a, b, and c) and 93 for the undesirable (d and e), implying that the proposal should be rejected.

3. If several alternatives are being evaluated, and one or more pass the test, the selected alternative would be the one with the greatest differences in scores or the greatest ratio of desirable impacts over undesirable.

NOTES TO CHAPTER 2

1. Leo Tolstoy, *My Confessions,* in *The Complete Works of Count Tolstoy,* vol. 13 (Boston: Dana Estes, 1904), pp. 18–19.

2. For a discussion comparing personal knowledge to secondhand, or processed, knowledge for planning, see John Friedmann, *Retracking America: A Theory of Transactive Planning* (Garden City: Anchor/Doubleday 1973).

3. A. H. Malow, *Motivation and Personality* (New York: Harper and Row, 1954).

4. The leading proponent of this school, and originator of the notion of "ends-in-view," was John Dewey. See John Dewey, "Theory of Valuation," in *International Encyclopedia of Unified Science* (Chicago: University of Chicago Press, 1939).

5. For an overview of these see, Robert B. Zajonc, "The Concepts of Balance, Congruity, and Dissonance," *Public Opinion Quarterly,* vol. 24 (Summer, 1960) pp. 280–296.

6. F. Heider, "Attitudes and Cognitive Organization," *Journal of Psychology*, vol. 21 (January 1946), pp. 197–212.

7. C. E. Osgood and P. H. Tannenbaum, "The Principle of Congruity in the Prediction of Attitude Change," *Psychological Review*, vol. 62 (January 1955), pp. 42–55.

8. F. A. Festinger, *A Theory of Cognitive Dissonance* (New York: Harper, 1957).

9. Peter Marris, *Loss and Change* (Garden City, N.J.: Anchor/Doubleday, 1975).

10. Carter and Dale have suggested that several ancient civilizations disappeared because they depleted their soils. See Vernon Gill Carter and Tom Dale, *Soil and Civilization* (Norman, Okla.: University of Oklahoma Press, 1955).

11. Arnold Toynbee, *A Study of History*, 12 volumes (New York: Oxford University Press, 1935–1961).

NOTES TO CHAPTER 3

1. Ernest Barker, *The Politics of Aristotle* (London: Oxford University Press, 1958), pp. 111 and 114.

2. Ibid., p. 280.

3. Ibid.

4. For example, see Jay William Hudson, *Why Democracy* (New York: D. Appleton-Century Company, 1936).

5. John Locke, *Two Treatises of Government,* edited by Peter Laslett (New York: New American Library, Inc., 1965), pp. 309–412.

6. Locke's analysis clearly suggests absolute equality but some believe he did not intend this conclusion.

7. Aristotle believed that democracy fell short of absolute justice, because in his day it permitted the poor, uneducated masses to rule over the rich, better educated, minority.

8. If one were to question the applicability of Aristotle's analysis to the broader span of history, it would have to be on the grounds that his interpretation is too mild. Many would argue that absolute misuse of power has been the more common reason for sedition, rather than mere differences in the perception of rights. Excerpt from Barker, *The Politics of Aristotle*, pp. 203–205.

9. Alexis de Toqueville, *Democracy in America,* vol. 1, edited by Phillips Bradley (New York: Alfred A. Knopf, 1948), p. 166.

10. Ibid., p.6.

11. However, the majority rule is not without important limitations, as will be discussed subsequently under the heading: tyranny over the minority.

12. Baron de Montesquieu, *The Spirit of the Laws,* translated by Thomas Nugent (New York: Hafner Publishing Co., 1949), p. 154.

13. Ibid., p. 150.

14. James Madison, "The Size and Variety of the Union as a Check on Faction," No. 10 in Alexander Hamilton, James Madison, and John Jay, *The Federalist,* edited by Benjamin Fletcher Wright (Cambridge: The Belknap Press of Harvard University Press, 1961).

15. Toqueville, *Democracy in America,* vol. 1, p. 6.

16. Jean Jacques Rousseau, *The Social Contract,* translated by G. D. H. Cole (New York: E. P. Dutton and Company, Inc., 1950), pp. 93–94.

17. James Madison, "Checks and Balances," No. 51 in Hamilton et al., *The Federalist,* p. 358.

18. Tocqueville, *Democracy in America,* vol. 1., pp. 268–269.

NOTES TO CHAPTER 4

1. I regret omitting so many of the leaders of the environmental movement from the text, but some of them at least are represented in the bibliography to this chapter.

2. I wish to acknowledge my debt here to Roderick Nash, for his excellent reader on the American history of environmental thought, which was especially valuable to me in writing this section. Roderick Nash (ed.), *The American Environment* (Reading, Mass.: Addison-Wesley, 1976).

3. George Catlin, *Letters and Notes on the Manners, Customs, and Conditions of North American Indians* (New York: Dover, 1973). Volume 1 of two volumes, p. 2. Originally published in 1844.

4. Ibid., pp. 8–10.

5. Ibid., p. 7.

6. Ibid., pp. 256–257.

7. Buffalo hide had commercial value only when taken during the months that the fur was particularly thick.

8. Catlin, *Letters and Notes*, pp. 258-260.

9. Ibid., pp. 261-262.

10. Ibid., pp. 14-15.

11. Ibid., p. 260.

12. Ralph Waldo Emerson, *Nature*, in *The Selected Writings of Ralph Waldo Emerson*, edited by Brooks Atkinson (New York: The Modern Library, 1940) p. 6.

13. Ibid., pp. 7-8.

14. Ibid., p. 36.

15. Ralph Waldo Emerson, *Essays: Second Series*, in *The Selected Writings of Ralph Waldo Emerson*, edited by Brooks Atkinson (New York: The Modern Library, 1940), p. 408.

16. Ralph Waldo Emerson, *Nature*, pp. 9-10.

17. Ibid., p. 10.

18. Bradford Torrey and Francis H. Allen (eds.), *The Journal of Henry D. Thoreau* (Boston: Houghton Mifflin, 1906), vol. 2, pp. 156-157.

19. Henry David Thoreau, *Walden* (New York: Thomas Crowell, 1961), p. 118.

20. Ibid., p. 219.

21. Ibid., p. 281.

22. Ibid., p. 286.

23. Ibid., p. 17.

24. Ibid., p. 15.

25. The first quote is from Lewis Mumford, *Brown Decades* (New York: Harcourt Brace, 1931), the second from Steward L. Udall, *The Quiet Crisis* (New York: Holt, Rinehart and Winston, 1963); both as reported by David Lowenthal in his introduction to a republication of the original issue of George Perkins Marsh, edited by David Lowenthal, *Man and Nature* (Cambridge, Mass.: The Belknap Press of Harvard University Press, 1964).

26. Marsh, *Man and Nature*.

27. Marsh, *Man and Nature*, p. 36.

28. Ibid., pp. 91–92.

29. Ibid., p. 104.

30. Ibid., p. 42.

31. Ibid., pp. 201–202.

32. Ibid., pp. 258–259.

33. Ibid., pp. 278–279.

34. Ibid., pp. 279–280.

35. Frederick Law Olmsted, "The Yosemite Valley and the Mariposa Big Trees," *Landscape Architecture,* vol. 43 (October 1952), pp. 12–25.

36. Ibid., p. 21.

37. Ibid., pp. 22–23.

38. Theodore Roosevelt, "Opening Address by the President," *Proceedings of a Conference of Governors in the White House,* edited by Newton C. Blanehard (Washington, D.C.: Government Printing Office, 1909).

39. A bibliography of the literature from which this summary is derived can be found at the end of the chapter.

40. Albert Schweitzer, *Out of My Life and Thought* (New York: Henry Holt, 1949).

41. Louis Fisher, *The Life of Mahatma Gandhi* (New York: Harper and Brothers, 1950).

42. E. F. Schumacher, *Small Is Beautiful* (New York: Harper and Row, 1975).

43. Rene Dubos, *So Human an Animal* (Boston: Charles Scribner, 1968).

44. An outstanding magazine serving this movement is *Countryside* (Waterloo, Wisc.).

45. One can learn a great deal about this movement from the magazine, *Communities* (Box 426, Louisa, Va.).

46. David Morris and Karl Hess, *Neighborhood Power* (Boston: Beacon Press, 1975).

47. See for example, NEFCO Handbook Collective, *The Food Co-op Handbook* (Boston: Houghton Mifflin, 1975), and Darryl McLeod, "Urban-Rural Food Alliances: A Perspective on Recent Community Food Organizing," in *Radical Agriculture,* edited by Richard Merrill (New York: Harper and Row, 1976).

NOTES TO CHAPTER 5

1. Luna Leopold, *et al.*, "A Procedure for Evaluating Environmental Impacts," U.S. Geological Survey, Circular 645 (Washington, D.C.: Government Printing Office, 1971).

2. If this conclusion isn't apparent, here is a mathematical explanation: let some impact on characteristic i, for an alternative action, A, be measured as $s_i^{WA} - s_i^R$, where s_i^{WA} is the state of i *with* the alternative, and s_i^R is the reference state. Impact i for the no-action alternative is $s_i^{WO} - s_i^R$, where s_i^{WO} is the state of i with *no* action. The impact, comparing A to no action, is $(s_i^{WA} - s_i^R) - (s_i^{WO} - s_i^R) = s_i^{WA} - s_i^{WO}$. This result is identical to the measured impact by A, if $s_i^R = s_i^{WO}$.

3. George L. Peterson, Robert S. Gemmell, and Joseph L. Schofer, "Assessments of Environmental Impacts: Multidisciplinary Judgments of Large-Scale Projects," *Ekistics*, vol. 37 (January 1974), pp. 23–30.

4. A book that emphasizes this view is Nathaniel Lichfield, Peter Kettle, and Michael Whitbread, *Evaluation in the Planning Process* (Oxford: Pergamon Press, 1975).

NOTES TO CHAPTER 6

1. Scaled value weights represent the ideal in CBA, but in some situations, discussed later, the use of constant value weights is acceptable.

2. The reader unfamiliar with microeconomics will have to read this chapter *very* carefully, and perhaps twice. A basic knowledge of the microeconomic theory of consumption such as is contained in any introductory text on microeconomics greatly facilitates an understanding of CBA theory.

3. J. R. Hicks, *Value and Capital* (Oxford: Clarendon Press, 1939).

4. John von Neumann and Oscar Morganstern, *Theory of Games* (Princeton, N.J.: Princeton University Press, 1947).

5. For example, if we wanted to scale the changes in utility of an individual for receiving items x, y, and z, we would first ask him to rank them according to his preference for them: say that the ranking is x-y-z, x being most preferred and z least preferred. Then we would arbitrarily set the change in utility from receiving x at 1 and that of z to 0. The change in utility due to y must then be established on the scale from 0 to 1. This is accomplished through an interactive, trial-and-error questioning procedure that seeks to establish for the person the point of indifference between two options: (a) having y with certainty and (b) having x with probability p or z with probability $1 - p$. The value of p is adjusted until the point of indifference is

found. Von Neumann and Morganstern provide a mathematical proof that the value of p at the point of indifference is equal to the change in utility due to y on the 0-to-1 scale.

To illustrate the technique, assume that x is $1,000, y is $500, and z is $0. We set $U(x) = 1$, $U(z) = 0$, and seek to estimate $U(y)$ for a specific person. We ask the person which he would prefer: (a) $500 or (b) $1,000 with probability 0.5 or $0 with probability 0.5. (Note that (b) is equivalent to a game in which $1,000 can be won on the flip of a coin). If he answers (a), the value $p = 0.5$ must be too low, so we ask his preference again: (a) $500 or (b) $1,000 with probability 0.8 or $0 with probability 0.2. Assume this time that he answers (b) which means that $p = 0.8$ must be too high. The process continues until a value for p is found that makes the person indifferent between (a) and (b). If the value is, say, 0.65, then according to game theory, $U(\$500) = 0.65$ for the person questioned, when $U(\$0)$ is set at 0 and $U(\$1,000)$ at 1.

6. The perfect market is defined as a market situation in which (1) all buyers and sellers have full information about all goods and services, and their prices, (2) all consumers and all producers pay the same prices (that is, there is no price discrimination), (3) there is sufficient competition among buyers and among sellers so that no one is able to influence prices, (4) there are no externalities, which are uncompensated impacts between buyers and sellers, such as when a manufacturer imposes air pollution on the residents of an area.

7. That is, for any two goods (or services):

$$\frac{MU_{y_1}}{P_y} = \frac{MU_{x_1}}{P_x}$$

where

MU_{y_1} = the marginal (or increment in) utility of person 1 resulting from the last unit of good y,

P_y = the market price of y.

8. Mathematically it is

$$\frac{P_x}{P_y} = \frac{MU_{x_1}}{MU_{y_1}}.$$

9. Mathematically it is

$$\frac{P_x}{P_y} = \frac{MU_{x_1}}{MU_{y_1}} = \frac{MU_{x_2}}{MU_{y_2}} = \cdots = \frac{MU_{x_i}}{MU_{y_i}}.$$

10. Although Thoreau never made a statement to this effect, he had the following to say:

I should like to ask the assessors what is the value of that blue mountain in the northwest horizon to Concord, and see if they would laugh or seriously set about calculating it. How poor, comparatively, should we be without it! It would be descending to the scale of the merchant to say it is worth its weight in gold. The privilege of beholding it, as an ornament, a suggestion, a provocation, a heaven on earth. If I were one of the fathers of the town I would not sell this right which we now enjoy for all the merely material wealth and prosperity conceivable. If need were, we would rather all go down together.

See Bradford Torrey and Francis H. Allen (eds.), *The Journal of Henry D. Thoreau* (Boston: Houghton Mifflin, 1906), vol. 4, pp. 263–264. The entry was made July 27, 1852.

11. Readers interested in pursuing the theoretical aspects of CBA further are referred to the bibliography at the end of this chapter.

12. Otto Eckstein, "A Survey of the Theory of Public Expenditure Criteria," in *Public Finances: Needs, Sources, and Utilization* (Princeton, N.J.: Princeton University Press, for National Bureau of Economic Research, 1961).

13. R. N. McKean, *Efficiency in Government Through Systems Analysis* (New York: John Wiley and Sons, 1958).

NOTES TO CHAPTER 7

1. The fact that people differ in their personal time preferences is revealed by observing that, at the market rate of interest, some people buy goods on credit, whereas others save a portion of their income. Those that save are sacrificing a certain amount of present consumption in order to enjoy a sufficiently larger amount in the future. The future gain is determined, of course, by the interest earned on the savings. Thus, if a person's personal rate of interest exceeds the rate of interest paid on credit accounts, he will buy on credit; alternatively, if it is below the rate earned on savings accounts (or on investments) he will save (or invest).

2. This example, of course, is a gross simplification. Construction costs are incurred over a period of several years rather than at one point in time. Operating costs, although small by comparison to construction costs, nevertheless, are incurred over the lifetime of the project. And benefits tend to rise over time rather than remain constant.

3. Uncertainty in the discount rate is only one of many applications of sensitivity testing. It can be used in any situation in which a range of uncertainty exists regarding a quantity that may be important to the outcome of an analysis.

4. See the bibliography on discounting at the end of the chapter for citations.

5. C. A. Nash, "Future Generations and the Social Rate of Discount," *Environment and Planning,* vol. 5 (1973), pp. 611–617.

6. The 37½-year time point is chosen because it is the midpoint in the 25- to 50-year range of the next generation.

7. Some public agencies require that the benefits exceed the costs by some stated margin, such as 20 percent.

8. In practice, the internal rate of return is calculated on a computer, using a trial and error procedure.

9. Both the cost and boater day figures are discounted present value figures.

10. Paul Davidson, F. Gerard Adams, and Joseph Seneca, "The Social Value of Water Recreational Facilities Resulting from an Improvement in Water Quality: The Delaware Estuary," in *Water Research,* edited by Allen V. Kneese and Stephen C. Smith (Baltimore, Md.: Johns Hopkins University Press, 1966).

NOTES TO CHAPTER 8

1. The Clawson method is described and elaborated upon in many sources. The original presentation of the method is found in Marion Clawson, "Methods of Measuring the Demand for and Value of Outdoor Recreation," RFF reprint no. 10 (Washington, D.C.: Resources for the Future, 1959). Other methods of monetizing recreation, including questionnaire surveys of willingness-to-pay or willingness-to-travel, are reviewed in J. L. Knetsch and R. Davis, "Comparison of Methods for Recreation Evaluation," in *Water Research,* edited by Allen V. Kneese and Stephen C. Smith (Baltimore, Md.: Johns Hopkins University Press, 1966).

2. A perfect linear relationship is used here to keep the example simple, but empirical studies repeatedly show that trips decline at a decreasing rate with distance. Naturally, real data points rarely form a perfect curve; they usually scatter around the best-fit curve.

3. Presumably the site is not open to use at the time of the evaluation.

4. For example, see Leonard Merewitz, "Recreational Benefits of Water Resource Development," *Water Resources Research,* vol. 2 (1966), pp. 625–664; E. Boyd Wennergren and D. B. Nielsen, "Probability Estimates of Recreation Demands," *Journal of Leisure Research,* vol. 2 (Summer, 1970), pp. 112–122; Donald M. McAllister and Frank R. Klett, "A Modified Gravity Model of Regional Recreation Activity With an Application to Ski Trips," *Journal of Leisure Research,* vol. 8 (January 1976), pp. 21–34.

5. For example, see Arthur H. Darling, "Measuring Benefits Generated by Urban Water Parks," *Land Economics,* vol. 49 (February 1973), pp. 22–34.

6. B. A. Weisbrod, "Collective-Consumption Services of Individual-Consumption Goods," *Quarterly Journal of Economics,* vol. 78 (August 1964), pp. 471–477.

7. See Darling, "Measuring Benefits."

8. Because public funds are periodically set aside for establishing and expanding systems of urban recreation centers, cost-effectiveness measures (such as attendance per dollar) can be used to help evaluate decisions on the size, spacing, and location of recreation centers, so that recreation resources are used effectively in serving the needs of people. See for example, Donald M. McAllister, "Planning an Urban Recreation System: A Systematic Aproach," *Natural Resources Journal,* vol. 15 (July 1975) pp. 567–580.

9. Outdoor Recreation Resources Review Commission, *National Recreation Survey* (Washington, D.C.: Government Printing Office, 1962).

10. See W. S. Pattison and W. E. Phillips, "Economic Evaluation of Big Game Hunting: An Alberta Case Study," *Canadian Journal of Agricultural Economics,* vol. 19 (October 1971), pp. 72–85; R. E. Capel and R. K. Pandey, "Estimation of Benefits from Deer and Moose Hunting in Manitoba," *Canadian Journal of Agricultural Economics,* vol. 20 (July 1972), pp. 7–16; Judd Hammack and G. M. Brown, Jr., *Waterfowl and Wetlands: Toward Bioeconomic Analysis* (Baltimore, Md.: Johns Hopkins University Press, 1974).

11. John Krutilla, "Evaluation of an Aspect of Environmental Quality: Hell's Canyon Revisited," *Proceedings of the Social Statistics Section, American Statistical Society* (1971), pp. 198–206; or chapters 5 and 6 in John V. Krutilla and Anthony C. Fisher, *The Economics of Natural Environments* (Baltimore, Md.: Johns Hopkins University Press, 1975).

12. R. G. Ridker, *The Economic Costs of Air Pollution* (New York: Praeger, 1967).

13. A study which attempts to make the linkages and demonstrate the difficulties is J. B. Stevens, "Recreation Benefits from Water Pollution Control," *Water Resources Research,* vol. 2 (1966), pp. 167–182.

14. For example, see Leland S. Burns, Robert G. Healy, Donald M. McAllister, and B. Khing Tjioe, *Housing: Symbol and Shelter* (Los Angeles: International Housing Productivity Study, University of California, 1970); and Leland S. Burns and Leo Grebler, *The Housing of Nations* (London: Macmillan Press, 1977).

15. For a good collection of case studies including social impacts and social program evaluation, see *Benefit Cost and Public Policy Analysis,* An Aldine Annual (Chicago: Aldine, 1971–1974).

NOTES TO CHAPTER 9

1. Nathaniel Lichfield, "Evaluation Methodology of Urban and Regional Plans: A Review," *Regional Studies,* vol. 4 (August 1970), pp. 151–165.

2. Nathaniel Lichfield, "Cost Benefit Analysis in Town Planning: A Case Study of Cambridge," Cambridgeshire and Isle of Ely County Council, 1966, p. 20.

3. This is an arbitrary assumption that may not be accurate in many situations. I will avoid, here, getting into the issue of whether revenues would increase or decrease as a result of higher prices, because it would divert attention from the main purpose of this section.

4. Ibid.

5. Morris Hill, "A Goals-Achievement Matrix for Evaluating Alternative Plans," *Journal of the American Institute of Planners,* vol. 34 (January 1968), p. 24.

6. Ibid., p. 21.

7. Ibid.

8. Morris Hill, *Planning for Multiple Objectives,* monograph series, no. 5 (Philadelphia: Regional Science Research Institute, 1973).

9. Hill, "A Goals-Achievement Matrix for Evaluating Alternative Plans," p. 22.

10. Ibid., p. 24.

11. A good description of the study is in, Nathaniel Lichfield, Peter Kettle and Michael Whitbread, *Evaluation in the Planning Process,* (Oxford: Pergamon Press, 1975), pp. 189–225.

12. Lichfield, "Cost Benefit Analysis in Town Planning," p. 204.

13. Hill, *Planning for Multiple Objectives,* p. 217.

14. In more recent research Hill has utilized qualitative criteria. See Morris Hill and Rachelle Alterman, "Power Plant Site Evaluation: The Case of the Sharon Plant in Israel," *Journal of Environmental Management,* vol. 2 (April 1974), pp. 179–196.

15. M. Hill and M. Shechter, "Optimal Goal Achievement in the Development of Outdoor Recreation Facilities," in *Urban and Regional Planning,* edited by A. G. Wilson (London: Pion Press, 1971), pp. 110–120.

16. Hill and Shechter, "Optimal Goal Achievement," pp. 114–115.

17. Hill, "A Goals-Achievement Matrix for Evaluating Alternative Plans," p. 27.

18. Morris Hill, "A Method for the Evaluation of Transportation Plans," *Highway Research Record,* no. 180 (1967), p. 25.

19. Morris Hill, "A Goals-Achievement Matrix for Evaluating Alternative Plans," pp. 27–28.

20. Nathaniel Lichfield, Peter Kettle, and Michael Whitbread, *Evaluation in the Planning Process* (Oxford: Pergamon Press, 1975).

NOTES TO CHAPTER 10

1. M. Slesser (ed.), *Proceedings of the IFIAS Stockholm Workshops* (Stockholm, Sweden: International Federation of Institutes of Advanced Study, August, 1974).

2. Alternatively, some scientists believe that the limited ability of the earth's ecosystem to absorb thermal pollution is more limiting. In either case the conservation of energy reserves is important.

3. Howard T. Odum, *Energy, Power and Society* (New York: John Wiley, 1971), p. 34.

4. Ibid.

5. Ibid., p. 297.

6. Ibid., p. 296.

7. The conversion factors are from H. T. Odum (ed.), *Simulation of Macroenergetic Models of Environment, Power and Society* (Gainsville, Florida: Energy Center, University of Florida, 1974), p. 5, as cited in Martha W. Gilliland, "Energy Analysis and Public Policy," *Science,* vol. 189 (September 1975), p. 1053.

8. For criticisms see, for example, Gerald Leach, "Net Energy Analysis— Is It Any Use?," *Energy Policy,* vol. 3 (December 1975), pp. 332–344, and Michael Webb and David Pearce, "The Economics of Energy Analysis," *Energy Policy,* vol. 3 (December 1975), pp. 318–331.

9. All the assumptions or conventions upon which the estimates are based should be clearly stated in the analysis. For an overview on the issues of

conventions, see P. F. Chapman, "1, Energy Cost: A Review of Methods," *Energy Policy,* vol. 2 (June 1974), pp. 91–103. A uniform set of conventions was adopted by an international group, reported in M. Slesser, *Proceedings of the IFIAS Stockholm Workshops.*

NOTES TO CHAPTER 11

1. Several versions of the method are reviewed in Carl Steinitz, et al., *"A Comparative Study of Resource Analysis Methods,"* Department of Landscape Architecture, Harvard University, Cambridge, Mass., 1969.

2. The efforts of Christian and Hills are among the earliest. See for example, C. S. Christian, "The Concept of Land Units and Land Systems," *Proceedings of the Ninth Pacific Science Congress,* vol. 20 (1958), pp. 74–81, and G. Angus Hills, "The Ecological Basis for Land-Use Planning," research report no. 46, Ontario Department of Land and Forests, Toronto, 1961.

3. Ian L. McHarg, *Design with Nature* (Garden City, New York: Natural History Press, 1969).

4. Ibid., p. 5.

5. Ibid., p. 23.

6. Ibid., p. 5.

7. Ibid., p. 19.

8. Ibid., pp. 24–25.

9. Ibid., p. 29.

10. The following offer examples of the approach, all designed to determine recreation suitability: Richard C. Allison and Roger S. Leighton, "Evaluating Forest Campground Sites," Extension Folder 54, Cooperative Extension Service, University of New Hampshire, Durham, N.H.; John A. Dearinger, "Esthetic and Recreation Potential of Small Naturalistic Streams Near Urban Areas," Water Resources Institute, University of Kentucky, Lexington, Ky., 1968; Soil Conservation Service, "Guide to Making Appraisals of Potentials for Outdoor Recreation Developments," U.S. Department of Agriculture, Washington, D.C., 1966.

11. McHarg, *Design with Nature,* pp. 31–41.

12. Ibid., p. 41.

13. Examples of this approach are found in the work of C. S. Christian and G. Angus Hills, previously cited. The work of Philip Lewis, like that of McHarg, includes both approaches. See, for example, Philip H. Lewis,

"Regional Design for Human Impact," prepared for the U.S. Department of the Interior, National Park Service, Northeast Region, Madison, Wisc., 1967.

14. McHarg, *Design with Nature.*

15. Ibid., pp. 79–93.

16. Steinitz computerized several versions of LSA in his comparative study. See Carl Steinitz, "A Comparative Study of Resource Analysis Methods."

17. J. Lyle and M. von Wodtke, "An Information System for Environmental Planning," *Journal of American Institute of Planners,* vol. 40 (November 1974), pp. 394–413.

18. L. B. Leopold, *Quantitative Comparison of Some Aesthetic Factors Among Rivers,* U.S. Geological Survey, Circular 670 (Washington, D.C.: Government Printing Office, 1969).

19. Elwood L. Shafer, Jr., John F. Hamilton, Jr., and Elizabeth A. Schmidt, "Natural Landscape Preferences: A Predictive Model," *Journal of Leisure Research,* vol. 1 (Winter, 1969). pp. 1–19; and Elwood L. Shafer and Michael Tooby, "Landscape Preferences: An International Replication," *Journal of Leisure Research,* vol. 5 (Spring, 1973), pp. 60–65.

20. R. G. Hopkinson, "The Quantitative Assessment of Visual Intrusion," *Journal of the Royal Town Planning Institute,* vol. 57 (December 1971), pp. 445–449.

21. D. L. Linton, "The Assessment of Scenery as a Natural Resource," *Scottish Geographic Magazine,* vol. 84 (December 1968), pp. 219–238; G. McK. Wright, "Landscape Quality: A Method of Appraisal," *Royal Australian Planning Institute Journal,* vol. 11 (October 1973), pp. 122–130.

22. Erwin H. Zube, "Rating Everyday Rural Landscapes of the Northeastern U.S., *Landscape Architecture,* vol. 63 (July 1973), pp. 370–375; and Stephen E. Gauger and J. B. Wyckoff, "Aesthetic Preference for Water Resource Projects: An Application of Q Methodology," *Water Resource Bulletin,* vol 9 (June 1973), pp. 522–528.

23. K. D. Fines, "Landscape Evaluation: A Research Project in East Sussex," *Regional Studies,* vol. 2 (September 1968), pp. 41–55, and Zube, "Rating Everyday Rural Landscapes."

24. Zube, "Rating Everyday Rural Landscapes," p. 375.

25. Shafer et al., "Natural Landscape Preferences."

26. Shafer and Tooby, "Landscape Preferences."

27. Fines, "Landscape Evaluation."

28. Ibid., p. 43.

29. E. C. Penning-Rowsell and D. I. Hardy, "Landscape Evaluation and Planning Policy: A Comparative Survey in the Wye Valley Area of Outstanding Natural Beauty," *Regional Studies,* vol. 7 (June 1973), pp. 153–160.

30. I am not suggesting here that landscape aesthetics is totally subjective. No doubt there are dimensions affecting human response that can be objectively measured, but there are other dimensions that are fundamentally subjective.

NOTES TO CHAPTER 12

1. For a more complete description, see Norman C. Dalkey, et al., *Studies in the Quality of Life* (Lexington, Mass.: D. C. Heath, 1972).

2. Ibid.

3. A preliminary description of the method was reported in I. Whitman, et al., "Design of an Environmental Evaluation System," Battelle Laboratories, Columbus, Ohio, 1971. The complete description is found in Norbert Dee, et al., "Environmental Evaluation System for Water Resource Planning," Battelle Laboratories, Columbus, Ohio, 1972, pp. 1–188. A summary of the key features of the method is reported in Norbert Dee, et al, "An Environmental Evaluation System for Water Resources Planning," *Water Resources Research,* vol. 9 (June 1973), pp. 523–535.

4. Dee, et al., "An Environmental Evaluation System," 1973, p. 525.

5. Ibid., p. 526.

6. Ibid., p. 532.

7. The 1972 report seems to support the notion of flexibility in a brief comment on p. 101, but the 1973 summary article makes no mention of it.

8. The idea of obtaining citizen inputs for setting the value weights was discussed in the 1971 preliminary report and in the 1972 complete report. The 1973 summary article mentions only indirectly that the weights might be "established by society," but indicates that the weights were set by the research team without any recommendation that it might be done otherwise in the future.

9. Dee, et al., "An Environmental Evaluation System," 1973, p. 525.

10. However, GAM could be modified to do the same thing.

11. George L. Peterson, Robert S. Gemmell, and Joseph L. Schofer, "Assessment of Environmental Impacts: Multidisciplinary Judgments of Large-Scale Projects," *Ekistics,* vol. 37 (January 1974), pp. 23–30.

12. Ibid., p. 27.

13. Ibid., p. 25.

14. Walter Isard et al., *Ecologic-Economic Analysis for Regional Development* (New York: Free Press, 1972).

NOTES TO CHAPTER 13

1. Martin Wachs and Joseph L. Schofer, "Structuring a Participatory Decision Framework for Public Systems," paper presented at the Specialty Conference on Human Factors in Civil Engineering Planning at the State University of New York at Buffalo, June 18–20, 1975, sponsored by the American Society of Civil Engineers.

2. For more on the subject of achieving genuine participation, see Peter Marris and Martin Rein, *Dilemmas of Social Reform* (Middlesex, England: Penguin Books, 1972), especially pp. 336–364.

3. Edgar S. Cahn and Jean Camper Cahn, "Maximum Feasible Participation: A General Overview," in *Citizen Participation: Effecting Community Change,* edited by Edgar S. Cahn and Barry A. Passett (New York: Praeger Publishers, 1971), p. 10.

4. Based primarily on Philip Sanderson, "Citizen Participation in the Development of the Venice Community Plan of 1977," University of California, Los Angeles, Calif., 1977.

5. Ibid.

6. Based on George Turnbull, "Citizen Participation in the Del Mar Community Plan Revision Process," University of California, Los Angeles, Calif., 1977.

7. Based mainly on Francis H. Palmer, Jr., "The Role of Citizen Participation in Determining the Future of The Santa Monica Pier," University of California, Los Angeles, Calif., 1977.

8. Based mainly on Curtis Williams, "Citizen Participation in North Los Angeles County," University of California, Los Angeles, Calif., 1977.

9. Based mainly on Rob Scofield, "An Evaluation of the Public Participation in the LA/OMA Sludge Management Project," University of California, Los Angeles, Calif., 1977.

10. LA/OMA Project Staff, "Phase I Report," LA/OMA Sludge Management Project, Los Angeles, Calif., 1976.

11. Based mainly on Marjorie Martz and Carolyn Thomas, "The Public Participation Elements of the Southern California Association of Governments' AQMP and 208 Plans," University of California, Los Angeles, Calif., 1977.

12. Based mainly on Daniel M. Hamson, "The Yosemite National Park Planning Process: A Study in Citizen Participation," University of California, Los Angeles, Calif., 1977.

13. The procedure was designed by Pat Collum, with a few suggestions by the author, while she was completing her studies for a Masters degree in urban planning at UCLA. It is reported in Planning Environment International, "Preliminary Evaluation of Alternative Tactics and Strategies for the South Coast/Southeast Desert Air Quality Maintenance Plan," prepared for the California Air Resources Board, Los Angeles, Calif., 1976.

14. It is interesting that although CBA promotes the practice of ratings in public decision making, the economic theory on which it is based suggests that households reach *optimal* consumption decisions by comparing many unlike units *without ever resorting to ratings.*

NOTES TO CHAPTER 14

1. Although it is true in a relative sense that pollution impacts can be estimated more accurately than the consequent damage to people and nature, in an absolute sense our ability to estimate pollution impacts leaves a lot of room for improvement. See W. David Conn, "The Difficulty of Forecasting Ambient Air Quality—A Weak Link in Pollution Control," *Journal of the American Institute of Planners,* vol. 41 (September 1975), pp. 334–346.

2. The use of economic and energy indices in the same evaluation could cause double counting, because many energy impacts are also monetary impacts. The overlap is not necessarily undesirable, because the two measures reflect somewhat different concerns, but its existence should be made clear to reviewers so that they can avoid double counting in their minds.

3. Nathaniel Lichfield, Peter Kettle, and Michael Whitbread, *Evaluation in the Planning Process* (Oxford: Pergamon Press, 1975).

4. The difference, nevertheless, is great enough that it can pose personal conflicts for the experts on the evaluation team trained to follow scientific procedures and taught that anything less than this is unacceptable. Perhaps by making the difference explicit and acknowledging the practical importance of expert judgment and rule-of-thumb calculations to a successful in-design evaluation, the personal conflicts can be reduced. The distinction might also

help headoff an overreaction to the situation, resulting in the opposite view that top-of-the-head judgments alone are acceptable for post-design evaluations (for clearly they are not).

5. Another form of verbal summary is to identify the set of values that would support the alternative. A simplified example is, "If you favor the preservation of plant and animal species and the conservation of nonrenewable energy resources, you will prefer plan *A* to *B* and *C.*"

This form was devised by Al Herson in research he conducted under the author's supervision. See Albert Herson, "Land Based Sewage Sludge Management Alternatives for Los Angeles: Evaluation and Comparison," Masters thesis, University of California, Los Angeles, 1976; and Albert Herson, "Trade Off Analysis in Environmental Decisionmaking: An Alternative to Weighted Decision Models," *Journal of Environmental Systems,* vol. 7 (1977–78), pp. 35–44.

6. John Dewey and James H. Tufts, *Ethics* (New York: Henry Holt and Company, 1932).

7. Ibid., pp. 349–350.

8. Ibid., p. 351.

9. Ibid., p. 350.

INDEX

303
Index

Davis, R., cit., 291n.1
Dee, N., cit., 297nn.3, 4, 5, 6, 9
Delphi procedure, 217–219, 230, 254
Dewey, John, cit., 279, 280, 283n.4,
   300nn.6, 7, 8
Discounting (or treatment of time).
   See Cost-benefit analysis
Dollar democracy. (*See* Cost-benefit
   analysis)
Dubos, R., cit., 60

Eckstein, O., cit., 290n.12
Effectiveness, 81, 273
Emerson, Ralph Waldo, cit., 46,
   47, 48, 60
Ends
  ultimate, 16
  versus means, 14–16, 24, 73–74
  visible, or ends-in-view, 16, 18, 24
Energy Analysis
  as a comprehensive methodology,
   173–178
  as a tool for addressing energy
   impacts, 179–182
  calorific value of energy, 175
  energy conservation studies, 179–
   180
  energy development studies, 180
  energy theory of value, 172
  grand index, 172, 180–182
  importance of energy, 173
  indirect energy consequences, 174
  measuring economic impacts, 178
  measuring impacts in energy
   units, 174–178
  nonrenewable energy the key, 173
  "quality" of energy, 175
  rating measurement, 172
  three views of its role, 172
  uniform measurement, 174–
   175, 181–182
  value weights implied by, 179

Environmental evaluation system
  commensurate units, 220
  composite score, 219–224
  critique of, 224–227
  environmental quality scale, 222–
   224
  environmental parameters, 219–
   221
  expert judgment, role of, 219, 220
  impact categories, 219, 225
  intangibles, 219, 223, 224
  nonadditivity question, 224
  rating system, 219–224
  red flags, 224
  value function, 220, 222–223
  value weights, or "parameter
   importance units," 219, 221,
   223–224, 225–226
Environmental indicators, 270
Equality
  absolute, 30–33, 39, 261
  proportional, 30
Equity, treatment of in evaluations.
  See Cost-benefit analysis; *and
  other methodologies*|
Evaluation
  analysis vs. systhesis, 6–7, 67–
   68, 184
  as a branch of ethics, 279–281
  as a process, 75–77, 80–81, 262,
   272–278
  definition of, 3
  in-design, 6, 77, 80–81, 186,
   217, 272–276
  in the planning process, 5–6, 80
  more art than science, 278
  post-design, 6, 77, 80–81, 272–
   276
  some key issues in, 10–11
  synthesis
   formal approach to, 8–10, 69,
    184, 253–255, 277–278